Never Marry a Farmer

A NOVEL

PHYLLIS BOHONIS

www.3rdseason.ca

Never Marry a Farmer © 2019 Phyllis Bohonis

First 3rd Season Publication October 2019

This is a work of fiction. Any resemblance to actual persons, events, locales or organizations is purely coincidental. All rights reserved.

No part of this book may be reproduced or transmitted in any form or by any means, electronic or mechanical, including photocopying, recording, electronic transmission, or by any storage and retrieval system,
without written permission from the author.

Cover photo © 2019, KuzPhotography
Author's photo © 2014 Mick Bohonis
Cover Design © 2019 Crowe Creations

Interior design by Crowe Creations
Text set in Palatino Linotype; headings in AR JULIAN

3rd Season
ISBN: 978-1-9994378-2-4

To Margaret,

Enjoy a peek at life on the prairies

Phyllis Bohonis

To Okemakwe Indian, Antoine Desjarlais, Francoise Desjarlais, Louison Blondeau, Philomene Klyne, Rosa Young — my mother and her prairie ancestors whose whispers inspire me.

Also by Phyllis Bohonis

Romance
Tomorrow's Promise

Romantic Suspense
Fire in the Foothills
The Wilderness
The Track

73 Windsor Series
Helen Whittaker
Margaret McFarland
Coming soon in this series: Sarah Eisenboch

"As we approached the by-pass around Winnipeg, I suggested we stay at one of the hotels near Polo Park but Gran insisted we push on to Portage la Prairie. It didn't surprise me she wanted to spend the night in a setting from which she could watch the prairie twilight once again descend over her beloved wheat fields and glory in the unencumbered view of the rising sun in the morning."

Phyllis Bohonis, from her book of memories

ONE
1963

THE TALL GOOD-LOOKING GUY WAS making his way through the crowd gathered around the edges of the dance floor. *Is he looking for me?* His hazel eyes lingered momentarily when he spotted her. *He sure can dance.* It was with great reluctance she had let go of those strong arms when the disc jockey called for everyone to switch partners.

Maisie hadn't had time to go dancing for many years. She had no time for men or a social life either. Her mother's advice was a constant whisper in her ear, "Get an education, Maisie. Make your own way in this world. Don't become dependent on any man and above all — never, ever, marry a farmer."

She knew her time wasn't her own. Wouldn't be for months. So why was she here dancing the night away at this community centre in the middle of the prairies? She really shouldn't have accepted her friend's invitation.

"We've had the good time. Shall we try for the long time?"

Turn away, Maisie. Turn away now. You know you can't do this. Not now when you are so close to the finish line.

She felt his breath on her ear. The scent of his aftershave enclosed her. When she turned, his hazel eyes were just a few inches from hers. His wide, gorgeous mouth was even fewer inches from hers.

Why was she here in an eye-lock with this stranger? A good-looking stranger. With her luck he was probably a farmer.

Without answering, she accepted this stranger's extended hand and moved with him to the dance floor. What had he said his name was? Glen something. Oh yes, Glen Grayson. Alliterative. Maybe his parents liked to keep the initials simple. She just hoped his middle name wasn't Andrew or any A name. With initials like that, who could take him seriously?

"I told you my name before we were forced to switch partners. I didn't learn yours." He made it sound so dramatic. He smelled as wonderfully masculine as he looked. She really wanted to rest her head against his shoulder and bury her nose in his neck so she could breathe in his male fragrance.

"I'm Maisie Forbes."

The words to a morning television show, *Friendly Giant*, came to mind as she held her head back to answer. *Look up. Look way up.* Glen Grayson was not a giant — just tall and friendly. "Do you live here, Glen?"

"No. I have a farm near Estevan. I just decided on the spur of the moment to accept a friend's invitation to come up for the evening."

Damn. A farmer.

"That's my story also. Almost."

"Oh, you have a farm near Estevan too?"

"No. The accepting a friend's invitation on a whim part." She smiled at his humour.

"Maybe both of our friends should be toasted for arranging us to be in the same place at the same time."

How had his shoulder shifted so that her cheek was now resting against it? Had it been his move or hers?

"So when Miss Maisie Forbes isn't visiting with friends or attending community socials, what is she doing and where?"

"I'm working in an accounting office in Regina and studying hard to become one of them."

"And you decided to take a weekend off and visit your friend?"

"No. I take most weekends off to visit my mother. She isn't feeling well this weekend though and sent me on my way, so I decided to pay a long overdue visit to an old friend."

"Your mother lives in Centreville?"

"My mother lives in Weyburn."

"Good, that's even closer to Estevan."

"And that's a good thing because?"

"Did I tell you I have a farm near Estevan?"

Maisie couldn't help giggling. It had been a long time since she had flirted or been flirted with. *Even though he is a farmer*, she thought.

Working full time in Regina and studying to achieve her CGA accreditation left her with scarcely any leisure time. On most weekends, she travelled to Weyburn to help her mother with the heavy cleaning and to make sure there were groceries for the week. Her father had suffered a fatal accident on the family farm during her first year of university. The pain of having to give up her education was lessened slightly when she found a job as a bookkeeper with Whittier Whittier and McLean, an accounting firm, in whose employ she had remained for the last six years. With perseverance, she could write her final examination and become a full-fledged CGA within another year.

When she had arrived at her mother's the previous evening, it was to find the woman suffering from a cold. A bad one. Not wanting her daughter to catch it, she had sent Maisie on her way after only one night. On a whim, Maisie decided to act on a friend's invitation to "drop by anytime" and consequently was dragged along with Jessica and her husband to an old-fashioned country social. Jessica, a friend from the office, lived about forty-five minutes outside Regina and had repeatedly expressed disappointment at Maisie for continuing to travel through rather than stop in on her way to Weyburn.

Maisie had visions of sitting at a table with some of the locals listening to tales of town history when Jessica suggested staying overnight and attending the dance with her and Doug. The dance was part of "Community Days" an annual celebration of Centreville becoming whatever it was. A town, or was it a village? She hadn't hesitated as she always enjoyed socializing with people of all ages and backgrounds. Having a gorgeous male like Glen Grayson pay her special attention was a bonus.

And special attention was exactly what she was receiving. When he didn't have his arm around her on the dance floor, he was bringing fresh drinks out to the patio where they retreated after every set. She had caught Jessica winking at her a couple of times as they passed each other on the dance floor. He did it all. He waltzed like Fred Astaire and jived with a real bounce. His twist was better than Chubby Checkers'. When the band started playing "Roll Out the Barrel", she had to hang on for dear life. Kindly, it was followed by a slow waltz.

"So, if a fellow wanted to call a certain Maisie Forbes in Regina, Saskatchewan, how would he go about it?"

"I can be found most weekdays in the office of Whittier Whittier and McLean."

"Are personal calls allowed on company time?"

"We'll certainly find out because that's the only way you're going to reach me, Mr. Grayson."

"You don't have a home number?"

"It's unlisted."

"Hmm. I see." Some of the sparkle left his eyes. Maisie almost relented and went against her own rules of not giving out her number freely. Everyone important to her knew what it was. She was finding her accounting course increasingly difficult therefore needed to spend almost all her spare time working her way through assignments. She had promised herself that by 1964, just next year, she would have those initials behind her name. The hazel eyes were looking at her questioningly, but she held firm and told him she would be happy to accept his call at work, anytime.

Before he could continue the conversation, Jessica and Doug arrived on the patio, announcing that the car was leaving with or without its passenger. Maisie made the introductions and Glen explained he, too, had come with his friends in their vehicle and would be leaving with them shortly. He offered her his arm and walked with her to her friends' car. As he opened the back passenger door for her, he lightly brushed his lips against her ear. "Next time I'm in Regina, I *will* be calling you, Miss Maisie, and maybe we can have lunch or dinner."

A smile, a wink and he was gone.

TWO

DURING THE FOLLOWING WEEK, MAISIE phoned her mother every morning and every evening. She didn't like the sound of her mother's cough. At fifty-six, her mother should be strong and healthy. She certainly wasn't old enough for pneumonia to be a life-threatening concern, but the severe congestion was a worry. Madeline Forbes, Maisie's mother, was still what most people would consider a young woman, but the hard years of farm life had left her a bitter widow and Maisie worried that she had given up all thought of becoming a whole, productive, happy female again. Between Maisie's studies and anxiety about her mother, the week flew by and before she knew it, she was back on the highway to Weyburn for the weekend. The junior Mr. Whittier, her supervisor, had taken the afternoon off, enabling her to leave the office early.

Seven minutes after she left, the office receptionist took a call from a man with a deep, smooth voice. "May I speak with Maisie Forbes, please?"

Maisie plied her mother with soup all weekend and made sure they sat out in the sun often to breathe in the warm, fresh air. A neighbour had picked up a prescription for antibiotics for Madeline during the week, so by the time Sunday rolled around, Maisie had been happy to see considerable improvement in her mother's condition. She prepared a few things for her mother to eat during the coming week. The woman was so thin, her clothes were hanging off her.

She avoided talking about the dance the previous weekend, knowing her mother would have endless questions if she knew Maisie had met an interesting man. Everything would be perfect if Glen were not a farmer with hundreds of acres of wheat as well as a few head of beef cattle and several horses. Maisie did not want to get into a discussion with her mother about the plight of being a farmer's wife.

Her dad had been a good father and a loving husband, but her mother had just never adjusted to rural life. Of course she had been forced to suffer through tough times — the worst times, really, for farmers. They hadn't always had water and many crops had failed. No conveniences like a vacuum cleaner. Even the wringer washer had needed repairs so many times, her mother often had used a scrub board to get the laundry done. Hydro was not reliable, so water often had to be heated and meals prepared on the old cook stove kept for emergencies, which meant many hours in a hot kitchen, feeding and cleaning up after the seasonal farm hands. Many times, her mother was too tired to enjoy simple pleasures like listening to the radio or, in later years, watching television in the evening. Many times, she barely pulled herself upstairs to bed at the end of the long, hot summer days.

Maisie felt that if her father had ever offered to sell the farm and move into Weyburn, her mother would have kissed his feet daily. She always knew, though, that as much as her mother hated the farm, her father loved it. She often wondered why her mother had married her father in the first place, but when her father was killed by a combine, while helping a neighbour several years earlier, Maisie came to realize the deep love her parents had felt for each other. Madeline told Maisie that the farm had killed her spirit many years before and now it had killed the only man she had ever loved. Maisie's mother accepted the first decent offer received for the farm and moved into town before those fields could do any more damage. Maisie's older brother, Jeremy, had completed university the year before their father's death. He had no desire for farming but did love animals. About the time his father died, he had just set up a veterinary practice in Swift Current. He and his wife, Jeanne, now lived in a modest home on the outskirts of that town. He visited his mother regularly and helped keep her home in good repair. It was only Maisie's education that had been affected by their father's death. Her mother had no pension and the sale of the farm realized barely enough for her to live on. Even though the money had been invested wisely, being widowed at a relatively young age, she would have to make it stretch to support her for many more years. It was as if widowhood had laid another mantle on her shoulders that was to be borne with meek endurance: the price she had paid for giving her love to a farmer. She had tried babysitting two children in her neighbourhood, but found she just didn't have the stamina to keep two pre-schoolers entertained for eight hours each day. When the young mother moved to another part of town, Madeline had decided to tighten the budget a little more and live on her small investments.

She was determined that Maisie deserved more than she herself had ever had and encouraged her at every opportunity to become self-sufficient. She almost drove her daughter crazy with her constant natter about building up her bank account before she gave her heart away to any man, and practically made her take an oath she would never marry a farmer.

"But Mom. I can't help who I fall in love with."

"Well, child, love doesn't help when the well runs dry. And love doesn't bring on the rain clouds when your crops are turning to dust. Love doesn't even help when your grocery bill is so high at the co-op store you wonder if you'll ever get out from under it. Only cold, hard cash can help. When the time comes, make darn sure that the love of your life lives in the city and that you have nice appliances and that he takes you out to a restaurant once in a while and that you go away on a holiday, even if it's just for a weekend, once a year.

"Otherwise when you go to bed at night so tired that your bones ache and your muscles cramp and the house is so hot you can hardly breathe, you forget that you love that man climbing into the bed beside you. It's only when he's given his life to the soil and the animals in the field and God calls him home that you remember he was a good man. A man who simply forgot that even our Creator took a day off. I loved your father with my whole heart, Maisie, but God help me, if I had it to do over, I would run away before I could lose my heart to him again."

Maisie blew a sigh of relief when she left her mother's house late on Sunday afternoon without having to give an accounting of her previous weekend's activities and the country dance.

She always enjoyed the drive back and forth, especially in the late summer when the fields were golden with wheat and she was able to arrive home before sunset. The prairies had always been her home. Her mother was right in that family vacations had not been a part of their life, so she had never seen the majestic Rocky Mountains one Province to the west. She had seen them in pictures, of course, and had learned about them in school, but when she looked across the vastness of the prairies, where there was nothing to block the horizon, she could not imagine living among mountains rising thousands of feet high, mountains that cast shadows over everything and even limited the hours of sunshine in a day. Someday she would go for a visit but for now, she enjoyed the panorama around her and the unobstructed sunshine. Even the state of North Dakota, less than a couple hour's drive south, seemed foreign to her. A different country. A way of life that had never entered into hers. She drove on with radio blaring and windows wide open letting the fresh prairie breeze cool her. Her prairie. Her home.

She usually picked something up at the Chinese food place down the street from her apartment, to eat while she watched the Regina

Sunday evening news. An office friend, the receptionist, called shortly after she got home informing her that a man named Glen Grayson had called minutes after she left the office. When she had asked about a message, he said he had just wanted to meet up with Miss Forbes in Weyburn for brunch on Sunday. He had left his home number for her to call.

It would be rude not to explain why I didn't return his call earlier in the weekend, wouldn't it? However, her mother's voice was whispering to her, "He's a farmer. Don't get involved." Maybe her mother was right. She really should nip it in the bud. What were the chances she would ever run into him again?

She opened the bag containing her supper and turned the television on. Her glance wandered to the telephone, but she shook her head. After watching the weather forecast for the next day, Maisie emptied her laundry hamper and went to the laundry room. The temperatures were supposed to cool somewhat tomorrow so she decided she'd wear a suit to the office. After the scorching temperatures of the last ten days, she welcomed the opportunity to wear something a little more professional. She loved dressing up and her wardrobe showed it. She watched the sales and managed to keep herself well-dressed while keeping within a budget.

She transferred the laundry to the dryer and ran the vacuum around her small one-bedroom apartment. She had been lucky to find a rental unit in a residential neighbourhood close enough to her office to walk to work. The saving in gas helped with her stretched-to-the-limit budget. Her space was tiny, but the rent included utilities and free laundry facilities located just across the hall.

She was drawn once more to the telephone and the Estevan phone number the receptionist had given her.

"What the hell. It's really only good manners." She dialled the number.

Eight rings later, she was about to disconnect when she heard a deep, "Glen here."

"Hi, Glen. It's Maisie Forbes. I just got home and learned about your invitation."

"So that means you're already back in Regina."

"Yes, I am. I arrived about an hour ago."

"Well, I'm relieved that you called. I thought you were ignoring my invitation."

"Sorry about that. I left the office earlier than usual on Friday and, as a rule, nobody calls me at my mother's. I enjoy my weekends off and leave my work behind when visiting her."

"Smart woman. I should have called earlier in the week but I didn't want to appear over-zealous. You know, it's hard for a guy to know just how long he should wait. Is there a rule of thumb on that I wonder?"

She could almost hear the grin in his voice. "If there is, I haven't come across it."

After a slight pause, "Would you have accepted?"

"Probably not … With thanks."

"Oh."

"If you remember, my mother was very ill the weekend before I met you. I wanted to spend as much time as I could with her this weekend. She is on the mend and we had a lot of work and things to catch up on this time."

"Can I extend an invitation for next weekend then?"

"Glen, I would really like to wait and see what this week brings. If I can give you an answer closer to the weekend, I would appreciate it."

"Fair enough. So what did you and your mother do all weekend?"

They chatted for almost half an hour before saying their goodbyes. After they hung up Maisie was relieved he hadn't asked for her home number again even though she knew he did not like having to call her office to speak with her.

On Wednesday afternoon, Mr. Whittier Jr. informed Maisie that she would have to put on hold anything she was currently working on. They were to catch a supper-time train to Saskatoon to attend a client's emergency shareholders' meeting the next morning. The financial crisis might find them working through the weekend. Maisie barely had time to rearrange her appointments for the remainder of the week, go home to pack her bags, and call her mother to explain why she wouldn't be going to Weyburn on the weekend. They would have driven, but Mrs. Whittier needed their car for the weekend and Mr. Whittier Jr. wasn't about to travel in Maisie's aging car. The train had barely left the station when the office receptionist again fielded a call from Glen Grayson.

THREE

THE FINANCIAL CRISIS DID INDEED take the balance of the week, the weekend, and meetings all of the following Monday to resolve. Maisie was very appreciative of the knowledge gained through this exercise. Her accounting course was very demanding and first-hand experience concerning an audit and corporate machinations was the best teacher. Exhausted as she was by the time she dropped her briefcase inside her own entry, she knew the hard work in the past week had been worth it.

The first thing she did was kick off her pumps and change into a pair of jeans and a T-shirt. A quick look around her apartment reminded her that she had left in a hurry. She could almost hear her plants crying, "water me, water me". When they were well-soaked and smiling once again and her mail had been rifled through, Maisie found the makings for a sandwich and settled on the sofa with several days of newspapers that her neighbour down the hall had collected for her. Through a telephone call to her mother over the weekend, she had learned, to her delight, that the woman's chest was clear and that she was actually feeling stronger than she had in a long time. It was much later in the evening when she received a telephone call from the office receptionist telling her that Mr. Grayson had called on Wednesday. The young lady said she had informed him that Maisie would be out of town with Mr. Whittier through the weekend. Maisie cringed, hoping that Glen and any other persons who might have called in her absence hadn't misinterpreted the message. Mrs. Whittier might also take exception to the inference of her husband spending a weekend with the single, female, junior accountant in the office.

After checking her watch, she decided it was too late to call Glen this evening. From first-hand experience, she knew that farmers start working their farms before daybreak and did not appreciate late-night phone calls. She couldn't help the faint pangs of guilt at not having called him before she left on her business trip. After all, this was the second time his invitation had been ignored. "Maybe, it's an omen and we really aren't meant to pursue a friendship." Giving voice to her thought made her ponder that possibility. She decided to let it slide and if he called her again, then she would worry about it.

Another scorching week went by uneventfully and by Friday morning, when rain clouds moved in on the western horizon, everyone looked heavenward and breathed a collective sigh of gratitude. The sky had turned a dark charcoal by late afternoon and when thunder started rolling before Maisie reached home, she decided the morning might bring better driving weather. Her mother was surprisingly understanding and insisted she not rush out too early if the rain hadn't eased somewhat. A neighbour was willing to take her mother for groceries. When the morning skies were even heavier than the evening before, a phone call from her mother reassuring her that she was not in dire straits, that her friend was indeed available as a chauffeur, Maisie welcomed the opportunity for a quiet weekend at home.

It was late the following week before it hit her that she had not received another call from Glen Grayson and remembered her thoughts that perhaps a relationship of any kind, friendship or otherwise, was not in the cards. By the time she was driving down the highway on Friday evening toward Weyburn, her resolve to ignore him was niggling at her conscience. He had, after all, issued two invitations and both had been declined or postponed and a third phone call had been ignored completely. Should she call and at least offer an explanation or an apology? She had to admit that she missed his phone calls. She missed him. A decision to call from her mother's finally allowed her to enjoy the balance of her drive.

"But, honey, he's a farmer! Have you not listened to anything I've told you?"

"Mom, I'm not going to marry him. I only want to phone and apologize for not returning his calls."

"Why? You live in two separate cities. You have a great career going for you and in a few months you will have initials behind your name that will open many doors for you. Why would you want to waste your time worrying about a friendship with a farmer?"

"My father was a farmer."

"Yes, dear, and I loved him deeply. It's because I loved him that I lived the hardship of farm life and became an old woman before my time. I want more for you — an easier life and modern conveniences, a nice home and a man that isn't so worn out from working from dawn to dusk that he can't take you out to dinner or a movie once in a while. You wouldn't be able to go away for a weekend, even, because there are always animals to tend and farm hands to be fed. Oh, Maisie. Stop this before it begins. Please." Her pleading was genuine and Maisie knew it came from her mother's heart.

"Mom, he's a very pleasant, nice man and I was rude to him. I just want to let him know that I'm a pleasant, nice person, too, and that if he does want a companion for dinner anytime he's in Regina, I would be happy for the invitation. I am too busy with my accounting course to have a relationship with anyone. After I graduate, I hope those doors of which you speak so often will open and I will be too busy establishing a career to have time for anyone for a few years. When I'm ready to settle down, it will have to be with someone who is willing to let me have a career outside the home. I won't have time for milking cows or cooking huge meals for farm hands. However, I do hope I will have some male friends to take me to dinner now and then, or to a Roughriders game once in a blue moon. I don't intend to be a recluse and never enjoy a man's company."

"Honey, I'm sure he's as nice as you say he is. All the more reason not to hurt him. You wouldn't want to start something you can't finish."

"Why don't I invite him to come here tomorrow for lunch and you can meet him and see that there are no sparks flying between us? He doesn't know many people in Regina and I'm sure he has business there from time to time. All he's looking for is a friend to call."

Madeline reluctantly agreed to meet her daughter's friend and expressed her hope that her daughter was not getting in over her head with someone who could only bring her heartache. However, when Maisie dialled Glen's number, she wound up giving her invitation and her mother's phone number to a housekeeper with a request that he call when convenient. Maisie hoped he wouldn't call while they were out. The telephone remained quiet during the balance of the day and when it finally rang around ten that evening, Maisie was surprised at the delight she felt when she heard Glen's voice.

"I was surprised at the invitation."

"I'm sure you must have been. Glen, when you called the last time, I had just left town with my boss. It was an urgent matter and I only had an hour to pack and get to the train station. The problem was a rather complicated one and we were kept in Saskatoon longer than we had anticipated."

"And you came home and found your phone was not in working order, I gather."

"I deserve that. I'm sorry. Not only do I not have a good reason, I don't even have a lame excuse for not calling sooner."

She was met with total silence. "Glen?"

"At least you're honest."

"Are you free tomorrow?"

"I could be. What time is lunch?"

"At lunch time."

She was relieved to hear him chuckle. When she heard the sound of her mother pouring bath water, she lifted her feet onto the hassock and stretched out. His voice had a way of wrapping itself seductively around her, and she could picture his hazel eyes staring into her own dark brown ones. There was no way she was ready to terminate this conversation yet.

"Tell me what you've been doing with yourself since I last saw you."

"I'm afraid summers don't allow me much time for anything other than farming."

Maisie frowned, remembering her mother's words.

"However, I have been in Regina a couple of times on business. Both times I reluctantly had dinner alone. I have an elusive friend there who keeps disappearing on me."

"Maybe the third time will be the charm."

"I'll settle for lunch with her and her mother in the meantime. Why don't you let me take you ladies out to eat? I know where we can enjoy a luncheon buffet that offers just about anything your heart desires. Then maybe we could go to the sulky races in the afternoon."

"That sounds like fun. I haven't been to a horse race in years. If I remember correctly, my mother used to be quite an expert when it came to picking winners."

"How have you been filling your time when not working?"

"I think I may have told you that I am taking an accounting course, so between that and working full time, I don't have much leisure time. I'm afraid I lead a rather boring existence."

"No man in your life?"

"If I did, I wouldn't be inviting you for lunch."

She could almost hear the smile in his voice. "I may have to come to Regina for another business meeting sooner than I expected."

"I'll give you my home phone number. It would appear we are not having much success with you leaving messages at my office."

She heard the bathroom door open and then her mother's bedroom door close just as Maisie finished giving Glen her number. "I better go now. I promised my mother a pedicure before she goes to bed."

"Maisie?"

"Yes?"

"Sweet dreams." His whispered words tickled her ear.

"Good night, Glen."

"I may not see sparks flying but there are definitely stars in those eyes, Maisie Kendall Forbes."

Startled that her mother was standing in the doorway, she quickly placed the receiver back on its base and met her eyes with a smile.

"Glen accepts our invitation with the exception that he would like to take us out for a lunch buffet and then to the horse races."

Maisie noticed the momentary gleam in her mother's eyes. Remembering that her mother enjoyed the single horse race their family managed to attend annually, Maisie wondered how long it had been since the woman had been to one.

"You seem quite taken with your young man."

"He's not my young man, but yes, I do like him and so will you."

"Maisie, no matter how charming he is, he's still a farmer."

"Arrggh! You have a one-track mind, Mother." When she saw her mother's stubborn chin come up, she continued, "Yes, he's a farmer. A handsome, charming farmer who wants to take us out to a restaurant and to have some fun. He's not asking us to come and milk his cows or help him with his crops. You said a man should be willing to take me out for fun once in a while. Well here it is. A chance to have some fun. I need a change from working and studying."

Madeline seemed subdued and reflective as Maisie gave her a pedicure. Just when the silence was reaching the oppressive stage, the older woman looked toward her closet and asked her daughter to help her pick out something to wear the next day.

"It's been a while since I've been to a horse race and since we'll be eating out first, I'm not sure what to wear."

Maisie smiled and opened the closet. Her mother had always been a conservative, almost dowdy, dresser and now, looking at mostly empty hangers, Maisie realized how limited her mother's wardrobe was. She chastised her for not keeping up with the current styles. "Mom, you're only fifty-six years old. Your closet contains such outdated dresses and hardly any pants. We're going shopping next weekend to buy you a few things that don't make you look like an old woman. You know you are still young enough to attract a man of your own again. A non-farmer of course."

After searching through her mother's hangers and drawers, Maisie finally pulled together a pair of slacks and a crocheted cotton top, a classic style that would never be outdated. Maisie added a light sweater of her own that blended nicely with the colour of the slacks. After finding a pair of open sandals, she was satisfied that her mother would look, if not chic, at least a woman of the '60s.

Glen arrived late morning in a shiny black pick-up that appeared to have just been driven through a car wash. Much to Maisie's relief, her mother was polite and civil while they enjoyed a cup of coffee prior to leaving for the restaurant. Before going out the door, Madeline just happened to remember a noisy pipe in the basement that perhaps Mr. Grayson wouldn't mind looking at. Twenty minutes later and with only one small grease stain on his shirt sleeve, Glen walked them out to the truck. He winked at an embarrassed Maisie as he slid behind the wheel and sidled in next to her.

Before being seated at the restaurant they perused the offers on the buffet table and true to Glen's promise, the array of food would satisfy the palette of the most discriminating diner.

"Who's looking after your farm while you take this time off, Mr. Grayson?" Madeline's question had just the right amount of innocent interest.

"I have farmhands who take turns tending to the animals on the weekends, and please call me Glen."

"Who feeds them?"

"The animals?"

"No, the farmhands."

"I have a housekeeper who prepares enough food on Friday to take care of us for the weekend. If that doesn't work, then one of them will usually head into town for a pizza or something."

"I see. Is she a live-in housekeeper?"

"Anna lives nearby and comes in three days a week."

"Who feeds your farm hands when she's not there?"

"Mom, I don't think Glen lets his men starve. It's his day off, why don't we talk about something else?"

Glen laid his hand on hers. "That's okay. I'm sure your mother remembers what it was like a generation ago when women got up at the crack of dawn to make bread and prepare vegetables for soup and stew to feed a large midday meal to the farmhands. Now with the assistance of freezers and the advent of supermarkets, preparing meals is not the chore it used to be." He smiled at Madeline. "I hardly grow any vegetables myself. I buy them from the farmers who do. Maisie's right though. My men are well-fed and we all get days off when we want or need them. Labour laws have changed to include farming and ranching. No one is overworked, including my housekeeper."

"I'm sorry to ask so many questions. After having spent all my married life on a farm, I'm just curious how things work now. It was such a hard life for women in my time, one I wouldn't wish on anyone."

"Especially your daughter."

"Especially my daughter."

"Mom, that's enough. Glen, I'm sorry. I had no—"

She was cut off from finishing her sentence. "I can understand your mother's concern. My own mother died of a heart attack while working beside my dad. The hay had to be brought in before it rotted in the fields that year. It had been a particularly wet fall. They couldn't afford to hire any more than the usual help, so Mom took up the slack. The hay couldn't wait, and she knew how to drive the tractor. Unfortunately, she had a valve problem that no one was aware of and she died before an ambulance could reach her. My dad never forgave himself for allowing her to work the fields like a man."

"I'm sorry to hear that, Mr. Grayson … Glen. In my case, it was my husband who died in the fields. I sold the farm as quickly as I could and swore I would not allow another member of my family to suffer the life of a farmer. Or a farmer's wife." She stood. "I'm glad my children both chose to get an education. My son is a veterinarian and he and his wife live in a nice house in Swift Current. Maisie will be an accountant in Regina and will not have to worry about the weather or the hard work on a farm." She excused herself and turned to leave the table. "I'll wait outside for you two to finish your dessert."

Maisie was about to go after her, but Glen caught her arm. "Let her go. I appreciate that she was candid with me and let me know exactly how she feels. At least I know it's my career choice and not me personally that she finds repugnant."

"I am so sorry. This is very embarrassing." She looked at him through tearful eyes. "It seems I apologize a lot to you."

"Tell me. Is it because of your mother's prejudices against farmers or farms in general that has kept you from seeing me until now?"

"Glen, I'm seeing you now in spite of my mother's prejudices."

"Will this be a problem for us in future?"

After a slight hesitation, she shook her head. "No."

"Will it be a problem for your mother?"

"Yes. I'm afraid so."

"I see." He placed his napkin beside his unfinished dessert. He looked at Maisie for several seconds before moving his chair back from the table. "I guess we better not keep her waiting. Let's take her to the races."

FOUR

TIME PASSED AND MAISIE'S RELATIONSHIP with her mother could best be described as tenuous. She had let Madeline know she had overstepped her bounds, but Maisie was sure her mother would do it again given the opportunity. Madeline said she had found Glen Grayson a charming, pleasant and well-mannered man, but unfortunately for Maisie, he was a dedicated farmer. The weekend visits from Maisie had disintegrated to every two weeks and Madeline expressed her concern one day on the phone that they might dwindle to once a month over the winter.

"I hope I won't be spending Christmas alone." When no response was forthcoming from Maisie, she continued, "Hopefully, God is more understanding and forgiving than you are, Maisie Kendall Forbes."

It was a Wednesday afternoon in late September when Maisie received a call from the reception desk telling her she had a visitor. When she approached the waiting room, she was startled to see Glen leaning against the reception counter.

"Glen? What are you here for?"

He turned, smiling with something akin to teasing in his eyes. "You."

"Come into my office." She turned without smiling and preceded him down a narrow hallway, broken by several doors on either side. At the entrance to her office, she stepped through the door and turned to wave him in.

Hers was the smallest office in their building. It was brightened by a large window with an excellent view of the roof on the building next door. If she stood very close to it and looked down, she could see the alley below. She had always been tempted to paint the glass blue with white clouds. The only saving grace was that it was close to the washroom and across from the small kitchen where a percolator usually held fresh-brewed coffee. She didn't have to walk far for either type of break.

Glen looked around the small, neat office and commented, "I guess I don't really know you at all. The real you, that is."

On the walls were several pictures: one of her mother carrying a small child, beside her stood a tall, slender man. Hanging onto the man's hand was a boy of about five.

He pointed to the boy. "Your father and brother?"

She nodded.

There was another of Maisie taken at her high school graduation. What seemed to catch his eye, however, was the array of trophies and ribbons on top of an old metal filing cabinet.

"Those are the former me."

"Obviously, you were a tennis player of high regard? Mixed in with those trophies, I see a couple for swimming as well. You must have been quite an athlete. Do you still participate in either sport?"

"No. That's how I got into university. I competed during high school and won a small scholarship which helped with the tuition fees for the first year. After my father died, however, I had to give all of it up to support myself and help my mother."

He looked around the small room and the stack of files on her desk.

"It appears you've done well for yourself since then. You mentioned you would get your accounting designation in the very near future."

"It's been a long battle, but I'm almost there."

Glen reached for one of her hands and drew her close. "I really don't know why I'm here, Maisie. I know I shouldn't have come."

"Then what prompted your visit, Glen?" She didn't remove her hand from his.

"Aw, Maisie, you are all I can think about. I tried staying away. I know that your mother would rather I drop right off the face of the earth, but I couldn't go another day without seeing you."

Maisie looked at the hand that held hers. She stared at it for several moments. She knew she should ask him to leave. She said nothing, however. She just kept staring at her hand in his. She could feel calluses on his palm. A sign of hard work. Farm work. Slowly, she placed her other hand over the one holding hers and brought it to her cheek closing her eyes. She leaned into him as she brushed his hand across her lips. She kissed the line of calluses. "I was afraid I would never see you again."

He wrapped his other arm around her waist and drew her closer. Leaning forward, he seemed hesitant to bring his lips to hers. Was he suddenly shy? Was he afraid she might ask him to leave if he tried to kiss her?

She lowered her eyes to his lips then closed the distance. Maisie was certain he felt the same sparks she did when he applied pressure to her back and fit her body against his. Her arms found their way around his neck and her fingers tangled his hair wishing this kiss would never end. When it finally did, she buried her face in his neck and kissed his jaw line, then her lips found their way to his again.

The phone on her desk rang twice before she reached back to answer it.

"I'm sorry, Maisie, but Joan Cameron is on the line. She can't keep her appointment in the morning but wants to know if there's any chance she can see you this afternoon."

"Is she my first appointment tomorrow?"

"Yes."

"Do I have an opening this afternoon?"

"Your four-thirty cancelled so you could see her then. It's your last one of the day, by the way."

"Set it up and put a line through that morning appointment."

"Done."

Maisie hadn't taken her eyes from Glen's. "Are you in Regina for the evening?"

"I could be. I had no intentions of coming here until I found myself driving into your parking lot after my business was finished. I didn't know if you would even see me."

"I have two more appointments. If you have nothing more to do, I'll give you the key to my apartment and maybe you won't mind making yourself comfortable there while I finish the afternoon here."

She fished in her purse and found a set of keys from which she extracted the largest. She handed it to Glen. "I can't believe you still wanted to see me after ... after ..." She struggled to find a voice for the rest of her thought.

"... after your mother made clear her feelings for me?"

Maisie just nodded.

"I guess I had to overcome the coward in me and find out if those were your feelings as well."

FIVE

MAISIE LOOKED AT HER WATCH as Joan Cameron rambled on. She had divorced her husband six months earlier and received an extremely generous settlement. The only problem she was facing at the moment was the fact that she had become a chronic shop-a-holic. Her ex-husband was a successful car dealer in Regina with a healthy bank account. There were many who felt he still had the proverbial first dollar he ever earned. Joan had made do with the basic necessities while their three children were growing up. She was often forced to swallow her pride and shop at the Goodwill Store for her own clothes. The divorce papers were barely signed when she went on a shopping rampage that threatened to bankrupt her unless it was curbed. A friend had suggested she see Maisie about getting her financial affairs in order, then perhaps an investment firm to help her keep whatever money she had left.

Maisie had her doubts that Joan would follow through on the suggestions given to her but when she finally closed the door on the retreating divorcee, she decided Joan's problems would not be her problems this evening. Tonight was meant for her and Glen. Tonight, she was going to make up for the time wasted in misunderstandings. Tonight, that tall cowboy waiting at her apartment was going to receive all her attention. Maybe they could go out for a late dinner — a very late dinner.

She felt like she was inches above the ground on her walk home. After taking the few steps from the stairway to her apartment door, Maisie paused and breathed deeply. The aroma emanating from the other side made her salivate. She stood for a few minutes anticipating the possibilities awaiting her. Finally, her hand went to the doorknob and she sniffed dreamily as she stepped inside.

Glen was busy at the small stove, tea towel tucked into the front of his pants apron style. "I hope you like spareribs and beans."

"I love anything I don't have to prepare myself. You didn't have to cook. We could have gone next door for a pizza or a steak. Not that I'm complaining, mind you."

"Why go out? I much prefer having you all to myself for the whole evening. I figured even if you received a last-minute call from a client needing you immediately in Timbuktu, you would have to come home to pack and I'd be here with a hot meal waiting."

"You must have gone to the grocery store to get all the ingredients for this sensational-smelling food."

"The cupboards were pretty bare. Don't you eat?"

"Between working and studying, I don't have a lot of time for cooking. I usually just make a salad or open a can of soup." She leaned over his shoulder and lifted a lid. "I thought it took all day to cook beans. How did you make this so fast?"

"I cheated. I used canned kidney beans and added a few ingredients." Glen gave her a spoonful from the pot to taste.

"Mmm. I'll change into my jeans and then I'll set the table."

Strangely, after not seeing each other for so long, they ate mostly in silence just like an old married couple. Maisie was enjoying her meal too much to talk and Glen was obviously enjoying watching her eat. When she finally put her napkin down, she looked across the table and saw the amusement in his eyes.

"Okay, so I have a healthy appetite. Is that against the law?"

"I don't know how a salad or a bowl of soup is normally enough for you. Of course, you didn't mention that you probably chop a side of beef into it." He ducked as her napkin flew across the table at him.

"I'll ignore that remark and just to be polite, I'll put the coffee pot on." She bent over him as she stood and placed a kiss on his cheek. "Thank you for cooking dinner. It was delicious."

When the kitchen was tidy and the coffee poured, Maisie asked, "You're not driving back tonight, are you?"

"I don't know. Am I?" The hazel eyes darkened as he waited for the answer.

Maisie looked from his eyes to his mouth and back to his eyes again. "No. But I do have an assignment that I have to finish for mailing tomorrow. Then I'm all yours."

Glen kissed her softly on the lips. "I'll take my coffee into the living room while you do your work. I think there's a special on television tonight about the aerospace program. If the noise doesn't bother you, that is."

"Not at all. I'll try to be quick."

"Being accurate is more important. I can entertain myself."

An hour later, Maisie sealed the envelope containing her assignment and joined Glen in the living room. "I'm sorry to have taken so long but now I can relax and enjoy the rest of the evening."

He opened an arm inviting her to slide in beside him on the sofa. "I'm so glad you didn't boot me out of your office. I'll take whatever time you have available and be glad of it."

When she snuggled in under his arm, he outlined her lips with his thumb. Her body came alive at the gently sensuous touch. She had a hard time looking at him. "Do you have a bag to bring in? I only have one toothbrush and any clean underwear I can lend you only comes in pink."

"I have everything I need in my truck. I wasn't sure if my cooking was going to be enough to warrant an invitation to stay. I'll go down now and bring it up."

Outside, Glen breathed deeply with relief. He wanted to shout with happiness. Maisie was interested. An invitation to stay the night was more than he had hoped for, almost. He had his knapsack out of his truck and was racing back upstairs in record time. He was determined to prove her mother wrong. Farm life was not like it had been even a decade ago, but he knew he had set himself an onerous task in making both women see this. Maybe if Maisie visited his farm and saw all the modern equipment and the comfortable house, she would be convinced. The only problem was that he had to convince his future mother-in-law too. Future mother-in-law. Was that such a wild dream?

Maisie wondered if she was doing the right thing. Glen Grayson was one sweet-looking man. If farmers were off limits, they shouldn't be allowed to be so handsome. Or sexy. Or charming. This long tall cowboy was all of that. Was it too late to change her mind? Maybe she could pretend she intended for him to sleep on the sofa.

Glen stepped through the front door and dropped his knapsack on the floor. "I'll just have time to cook you breakfast in the morning before I hit the road. I have an appointment at the bank tomorrow afternoon in Estevan. Are you going to Weyburn this weekend?"

"I haven't been going as often. My mother has been doing great on her own, so I've used the extra time to work ahead on my course. I should be able to write my exam before Christmas." Maisie had turned the television off and was in the process of doing the same with the living room lamps. "I don't have bacon or eggs for you to cook for breakfast. You may have to settle for toast and leftover beans."

"I took stock of what you had before I went to the grocery store. You now have both bacon and eggs."

"A little sure of yourself?"

"Let's say, more hopeful than sure."

A muscular arm circled her shoulders. She hesitated momentarily, then picked up his bag and motioned him toward the bedroom. His presence filled the room. The bed had never looked so small nor had the oxygen felt so scarce. Maisie slipped into the bathroom to shower and brush her teeth. Why was she so nervous? *Because the most gorgeous man in the world is in your bedroom waiting for you, silly.* Her thoughts were racing a mile a minute. Would he have protection? She was not in the habit of inviting men to her bedroom, so she had never felt the need for birth control. In fact, her sexual experience was very limited. *Limited? Yeah, right! Make that non-existent since university. How did I get myself into this situation?*

She heard the headboard bump against the wall and knew he would be waiting for her. She slid into her short nightie and bathrobe hanging behind the bathroom door. With a deep breath she moved with determination, opened the bathroom door and with relief, stepped into a darkened bedroom. *Thank goodness for that. The man is considerate.*

His consideration was followed by tenderness. His lovemaking was slow, gentle and oh so thorough. Before long she was matching his caresses, moving from tender to passionate with every brush of his lips, every caress of his hands, every soft word whispered in her ear. He held her close for a long time after, murmuring her name several times before rolling onto his back.

A car revved its engine in the distance. A neighbour was calling his barking dog inside. A car horn sounded way in the distance. All sounds of normal everyday living. All sounds she had never noticed before. All her senses were heightened. His hand found hers. His lips brushed her skin. As she stared at the ceiling, feeling every sensation, she thought how nice it would be to experience this every night.

"Maisie, are you on birth control?" He turned to her.

"Uh, no."

"Well, I hate to bring it up now, but we did not use protection."

She lay still thinking of the consequences, while trying to count dates and days. "I think it might be okay, but I can't know for sure."

"I guess it's a little late to worry about it now. I am so sorry. I should have stopped at the drug store near the supermarket." He brushed a strand of hair from her cheek and tucked it behind her ear.

"Neither one of us was thinking with our brains."

"You're not angry with me?"

"It's my fault, too. I had thought of it earlier but then … I got distracted."

"By what?"

"By your, uh, nakedness."

"You didn't seem distracted." He moved closer again.

"I was trying to remain … calm."

He grinned. "Calm."

"Yes, calm. As in not nervous."

"Why were you nervous?"

"Well, you have, um, let's say, a well-muscled body …"

"And well-muscled bodies make you nervous."

She rolled toward him. "Not anymore." She laughed as she nipped at his shoulder.

With a smile, he pulled her to him. "In that case, Miss Maisie, I'm afraid you may have to take a nap at your desk tomorrow to make up for your lack of sleep tonight."

She murmured, "You may have to pull over to the side of the road to catch a few winks yourself."

"And here I thought you were shy."

"After the incredible way you just made love to me, I don't have a shy bone left in my body."

"Well, I'm still naked and there may be a bone or two of yours, shy or not, that hasn't felt my touch."

"My mother should have warned me to never even *dance* with a farmer."

SIX

WHEN THE ALARM SOUNDED, MAISIE was tempted to shut it off and pull the covers over her head. The smell of frying bacon kept her from doing so. She made a quick detour to the bathroom on her way to the kitchen.

"Good morning, sunshine." Glen was flipping pancakes in ... Was that a new frying pan?

"How can you be so wide awake?"

"I'm a better man than you are."

"I'm having a quick shower. Alone," she added as she saw the grin taking shape on his handsome face.

"Darlin', as much as I would love to join you, I know there's no time. We both have our jobs to get to. Besides, I can't remember who said, 'Always leave 'em wanting more'." He ducked as she threw her slipper at him.

They went downstairs together. Glen solicited a promise from Maisie that she would try, in the very near future, to spend a weekend at his farm. A long kiss, a warm hug and each went in a different direction.

The weather on the weekend kept everyone at home. An early winter storm blew in and traffic stopped. Maisie took advantage of the time to study and work ahead. She had sent for previous exams from the CGA program and spent every waking hour writing and re-writing them. If that wasn't enough, she knew that as the final months in every calendar year drew near, the accounting business would boom. From early November through the end of the taxation period in April, the hours at desks were long and meals often overlooked.

Glen called several times each week, many times not able to get through. When Maisie did pick up she often had to cut the conversation short. She had called him when her period arrived right on schedule, relieving them both of that anxiety so early in their relationship. Around the third week in November, he left a message at the office that he had business in Regina on Thursday and would look forward to sharing whatever time she could spare.

Missing him terribly and feeling somewhat guilty, Maisie called him back and asked him to spend the night either Wednesday or Thursday, whichever was more convenient for him. Wednesday, she received a call mid-morning, that an emergency had come up on the farm and he would not be arriving either day. After much thought and deliberation, Maisie decided to swallow the bullet and take a run down to Estevan on the weekend. Friday, she left the office early, threw her books in the car and headed south. She took Highway 33 to 47 and bypassed Weyburn altogether.

Her mother was aware that she was spending the weekend at Glen's farm and had expressed her feeling in no uncertain terms about it. Maisie didn't feel a need to stop in and listen firsthand to more of her mother's recriminations about her foolishness — or her morals.

It had been dark for a couple of hours when she saw Glen's name on a mailbox at the end of a driveway. Feeling somewhat foolish for not calling with a warning about her arrival, she took a deep breath and turned into the drive.

When she neared the house, the front lights came on but when no welcoming committee opened the door, she guessed the lights were on a motion sensor and hoped *someone* was home. She glanced around and saw a large, well-cared-for, two-storey brick home. The front entry was under the roof of a wide front porch complete with a swing at one end. At least, the frame of the swing was there. The cushions must have been stored for the winter. A good-sized barn stood a little distance to the back and the customary tall silos beyond that. Several other outbuildings with varying heights of doors lined a lane way that went beyond them and out beyond the area the lights encompassed. The house was surrounded by fields lightly dusted with snow. Warm yellow light was visible through several of the main floor windows.

A ring of the doorbell brought on loud barking from somewhere inside. Soon, a shadow was visible on the other side of the curtained window on the door. Maisie could hear Glen telling the dog to sit and stay while he slid the bolt and opened the door.

"Do you have a bowl of soup for a weary traveler?" She hugged herself against the cold.

"What the —? Maisie, darlin', come on in."

She was grabbed, pulled inside and hugged in quick order. The dog started barking again. When she crouched down to rough up his golden coat, he almost knocked her over in an attempt to cover her face with wet kisses. "My goodness, I was worried I wouldn't get a warm reception."

Glen looked beyond her to the car in the driveway. "Are you alone? You drove down by yourself? You came to stay?"

She laughed. "I'm quite capable. I've been making most of the journey for several years. My Chevy is still in pretty good condition even though it's eight years old. I know how to change a tire and I have a blanket, candles and a thermos of hot chocolate on the front seat."

"I'm sorry. I didn't mean you're incompetent. I'm just so surprised to see you. You should have called me. I would have watched for you or picked you up at your mother's." He hugged her again before holding her at arm's-length and looking her up and down. "My God, I can't believe you are here. It's been, what? A year since I saw you? I was concerned distance definitely wasn't making your heart grow fonder. I guess I was worrying needlessly."

Maisie pulled him to her and wrapped her arms around his back. "Don't exaggerate. I've been busy, but I'm a long way from dead. I thought you would know how much I miss you." She leaned into him.

"So it's my body you're after, Miss Maisie Forbes."

"That too. Right now, I'm seriously after a bowl of soup." She kissed his cheek and stepped away. There was a hallway that led toward the back of the house. "I know there has to be a kitchen in this big house somewhere."

He laughed as he smoothed her hair. "I guess I impressed you with my cooking. Okay, let's feed you and see where that takes us. You can get acquainted with Parker while I get your things from the car and see if I can rustle up something more than soup."

After a plate of left-over macaroni casserole, a glass of red wine and a bowl of rice pudding, Maisie was quite content sitting on the sofa in front of a huge fireplace, Parker lying quietly at her feet. He had been named Nosy Parker as a pup due to his insatiable curiosity and nose for trouble, but now that he was a little more mature, just plain Parker seemed appropriate.

"If the stack of books is any indication, I would guess that your time will be divided between studying and me."

"It's coming down to crunch time, Glen. Sorry, but I had to make the decision to study alone all weekend, or study during most of it and spend *a little* time with you. I opted for the latter. I thought a little time with you was better than no time at all."

Glen sank into the sofa beside her, stretching his long legs out to rest on a hassock. He leaned closer. One arm went around her shoulders and pulled her to him. "You thought right. I'll content myself with looking at you slaving away on the kitchen table and know that the harder you study, the quicker it will be behind you. Actually, I admire your determination and self-discipline." He kissed her temple and said softly, "I'll try not to distract you too much. It means a lot to me that you drove all the way down here just so we could be together."

The next morning, Maisie awoke to the sound of Parker's non-stop barking outside the bedroom door. She was alone in the bed and appeared to be alone in the house except for the dog. "What is it, doggie? Do you want outside?" When the tempo of the barking picked up considerably, she jumped out of bed and grabbed her robe. The floor was warm, so she went downstairs barefoot and was almost knocked off her feet by the dog racing her to the door.

After letting him out the back, she noticed a note on the kitchen table.

"Sorry you slept through breakfast, but I figured you needed the rest. Bread is in the fridge, toaster on the counter and cheese, peanut butter and jam are all set out for you. If it's before nine when you get up, the coffee should still be potable, otherwise you'll have to make fresh. I'll be back before noon. A farmer's day starts at daybreak, but I can take recreation breaks anytime. Wink. Wink. Do not, I repeat, do not shower till I get there. Love and hugs. Guess who?"

My first love letter from him. She clutched it her chest. Her body was still sore from the long, shared shower last night. What a man. What a lover. She was pretty sure most men weren't that thorough in their lovemaking. His hands certainly had a magic of their own.

Still in her bathrobe, she made toast, tested the coffee and found it palatable. The Saturday morning newspaper was on the counter, so she settled herself at the kitchen table, feeling quite at home.

A half hour later, the back door opened and a gust of cold air blew in. "Well, if that's not a picture a man can treasure, I don't know what is."

"I haven't even washed my face or put a brush to my hair so it can't be that great."

"Any day I come in to see you sitting at my kitchen table, eating breakfast in your bathrobe, is a treasure, darlin'." He hung his jacket inside the door and removed his boots. "Did you have enough to eat?"

"Yes, I did."

"You found the newspaper, I see."

"Yes. I read it while I ate and now I was about to go upstairs and dress."

"Want some company?" He grinned as he motioned her toward the stairs.

Later, they were still in the bedroom when Parker started barking noisily at the back door. "That damn dog has been spoiled. Always wanting inside when he should be staying outside."

"It must be below zero out there."

"Far from it and it's warm in the barn but he won't shut up till I let him in." Glen looked at her lying on the bed. "Don't go away. I'll be right back."

After several minutes grew to ten and then fifteen, Maisie got up and started down the hall. The dog had come up the stairs and gone back down again so she knew Glen had already let him in. What could be keeping him? When she reached the top of the stairs, she could hear voices in the kitchen. There was Glen's deep tone then another man's raspy voice with an urgent sound to it. She went back into the bedroom and waited a little longer then, chilled, Maisie slipped into her underwear, jeans and a pullover sweater. She slid her feet into a pair of moccasin slippers and started downstairs.

Halfway down, she stopped. The other man's voice was getting louder. "I thought I could count on you, Glen Grayson. Your father would have supported me. Us farmers stick together."

"Sorry, Duncan, but I think he would have felt the same way I do. We have to fight these big corporations. If we sell out to them, what will become of everything we've ever fought for? Our farms are our heritages. Mine has been in our family for three generations. What would I do for a living? What will you do? Farming is all I know. All I want. You'll have to look for your support elsewhere. Quite frankly, I hope you don't find it."

Maisie heard a few choice expletives from the other man and then the door slammed. She wasn't sure whether to go down to Glen or wait for him to come up. When there was no further sound from the kitchen, she continued down to the main floor. Glen was sitting at the kitchen table staring at the floor, hands clasped, elbows on his knees.

"Glen? Is something wrong?"

He didn't answer for a few seconds; then smiled as he looked at her. "Oh, the same old, same old. Another huge industrial farming corporation has given me and a neighbouring farmer an offer he feels he can't refuse. The only problem is the offer includes my farm as well as his or none at all. I'm not interested, and that upset Duncan, my neighbour. He thinks it's an opportunity too good to pass up. His assumption is that they're going to phase us out. That our farms won't be worth anything down the road. His feeling is to grab at the opportunity while we can or we may lose everything."

"I've read that these corporations are becoming a real problem."

"Yes and no. They might some day, but for now, I have no intention of selling out so it doesn't concern me." He stood and reached for the coffee pot. "Would you like some fresh coffee, Maisie?"

She knew the subject was closed so accepted the offer of coffee. It seemed that the recreation break was over as well.

"Do you mind if I take it in the dining room? I should get down to my studying or I'll be up half the night doing it."

"Of course, sweetheart. I'll take the night and give you the day." He kissed the top of her head. "I'll get some of my chores done. I have a tractor that needs a little mechanical work before I can put a blade on it for snow plowing. Why don't you work in the den? My sister-in-law does some of my bookkeeping and she's even got an adding machine in there."

"That would be great. Can I get anything ready for supper?"

"I have a smoked ham in the basement I'll bring up. Will you have time to do some potatoes to eat with it?"

"I'm sure I can squeeze that into my schedule." She kissed him warmly before taking her coffee cup into the dining room.

"What time are you planning on leaving tomorrow?"

"I would like to be home before dark if possible."

"Why don't we plan on going out for Sunday brunch then, before you go? In fact, I can follow you up to Weyburn and we could take your mother out if you want. She seemed to enjoy that place we went to last summer."

"I don't think that's a good idea, Glen."

"Why not?"

"She has not changed her opinion of my dating a farmer."

"I see. Does she know you are here this weekend?"

"Yes."

When nothing more was forthcoming from her, he frowned and went out the door.

SEVEN

MAISIE ARRIVED HOME IN REGINA by late afternoon on Sunday. The atmosphere had been a little cooler after she had mentioned her mother's continued reluctance to accept Glen. Their lovemaking had not lost any passion but there was a slight tension in the air outside of the bedroom.

Glen continued to phone and in mid-December, he made a trip up to Regina. He was disappointed that Maisie had been too busy to decorate her place for Christmas. Obviously, the holiday was important to him. He brought a tree in for her and set it securely in a stand. She had wanted an artificial one, but he wouldn't hear of it. She managed to scrounge a few decorations and she had to admit that the place had a more festive air to it. He had even gone out and bought a crèche to place under the tree. "That's what it's all about, isn't it?" He seemed pleased with himself.

Maisie had learned that her final exam would not take place until late February and wondered at the reason for the scheduling of it during the busiest time of year for accountants. However, she was determined to be up to the task.

Maisie had accepted her mother's invitation to spend Christmas in Weyburn with her. She wondered whether she might be allowed to invite Glen for dinner or at least for Christmas Eve. When Maisie approached her mother about it, her mother agreed to have him for Christmas dinner.

"I'm pleasantly surprised, Mom. Thank you."

"I haven't changed my mind about anything. I just don't want any bad feelings spoiling the Christmas holidays."

Madeline Forbes was no dummy and Maisie figured that her mother was hoping that once she had her accounting designation, she would not be content counting cattle on a farm. Maisie knew her mother was not weakening on the Glen issue, just biding time and trying to keep Maisie close.

On Christmas Eve, the two women went to the service at the Knox Presbyterian Church and came back to enjoy mulled apple cider and a light late-night lunch. Among the gifts from her mother was an engraved silver case for business cards. She read her name, followed by the initials, CGA

"Are you not a little premature, Mom? What if I don't pass the exam?"

"You'll pass."

Maisie smiled and ran her fingers over the engraving. "I don't know who will be happier to see those initials behind my name, you or me. We've both wanted it for a long time."

"Your father would be so proud to know that his little girl didn't lose out on her education after all. That's all he wanted. To see both you and your brother with university educations. He knew neither of you were interested in farming, so he wanted for you to have whatever career you chose. I have to give him that."

"Thanks, Mom. I know your life with Dad was not always easy, but I also know that you loved each other deeply. I hope to enjoy that kind of love someday."

"When you start your career, many doors will open for you. You will find someone with whom you have lots in common so will want to share everything. I'll have real peace of mind knowing that you won't have to sacrifice like I did to make sure your children are educated, too."

Maisie wanted to remind her mother that she had sacrificed nothing; that the sacrifices and hard work had been done totally by Maisie, herself. However, she didn't want to spoil her mother's good mood, especially with Glen coming for dinner the next day.

When Glen's truck could be heard in the driveway about mid-afternoon, Maisie noticed a stiffening of her mother's spine and offered up a silent prayer that the afternoon and evening would go smoothly.

It appeared that all were enjoying the spirit of Christmas and sharing peace on earth, goodwill toward men. Madeline thanked Glen graciously when she opened the gift box containing a rhinestone pin and even laughed at several of his jokes.

The table was formally set with the china that had belonged to Madeline's mother. It wasn't bone china but a pretty good facsimile. Maisie proudly displayed the silver flatware she had inherited from her paternal grandmother. She had brought it down from Regina just for their Christmas dinner. Glen had brought a bottle of white wine and some sherry for an after-dinner drink. Madeline asked Glen to say grace before the platters and bowls of food were passed around the table. Maisie could take no credit for the savoury meal as cooking was not one of her skills, nor did she derive any pleasure from it. Madeline, however, was an excellent cook and the cuisine lacked nothing.

When Glen finally placed his fork and knife across his plate, he exclaimed, "I've never tasted richer stuffing and gravy in my life, Mrs. Forbes. Everything was perfect. I'm certainly grateful for the invitation to share this meal with you ladies."

"You still have room for pumpkin pie, I hope." Maisie stood to clear the table of the main course remnants. "I thought we might enjoy a glass of your nice sherry first."

Glen patted his belly. "I can probably handle a slice of pie a little later, Maisie. For now, a glass of sherry sounds great."

With a controlled tone to her voice, Madeline suggested that Maisie perk some coffee while in the kitchen.

After her daughter had left the room, she turned to Glen with a purpose in her eye. "Maisie received her notice for her accounting examination. It's scheduled for the end of February. Did she tell you?"

"Yes. I have confidence she'll pass it without too much effort. Her determination and study habits certainly have earned her excellent marks in her regular tests."

"Still, it won't be easy. I understand there are many who are required to write it several times before achieving a passing grade."

"Are you afraid Maisie might be one of them?"

"I'm not afraid of anything, Mr. Grayson, except that you might be a distraction from her required study time." Madeline had reverted to calling him by his last name rather than the friendlier first name.

"I don't believe Maisie's marks have deteriorated a single point since she and I have been seeing each other. Your daughter's self-discipline cannot be thwarted by anything I might suggest or request. She has tunnel vision where her accounting course is concerned."

"I'm glad to hear that." Madeline used her forefinger to pointedly tap the table. "Becoming an accountant has been the *only* thing Maisie has wanted since she was a teenager. I would hate to have her lose sight of that goal when she is so close to the finish line."

"Believe me when I say that I sincerely hope she achieves her goal. I support her wholeheartedly."

"Even if it means the end of the relationship between you?"

"Why would it do that?"

"Because she intends to start her own accounting business in Regina when she's fully accredited. That doesn't sound to me like she's going to be doing any cooking, cleaning or working on a farm in Estevan. She will be staying in Regina just as her father and I intended.

Have I made myself clear? She *will* be staying in Regina." She glared into the startled eyes across from her.

Maisie carried a tray through the door on which sat two small glasses, the bottle of sherry Glen had brought, and a steaming cup of coffee. "I wasn't sure if you were ready for your pie, Mom."

"No, thank you, dear. I'll take my coffee with me to the living room if you'll excuse me."

Two sets of eyes watched as Madeline flashed a smile at Glen and without hesitation carried her cup to the other room. Maisie lifted her eyebrows at Glen, but he shook his head in an attempt to assure her that nothing had driven her mother from the table.

After they drank their sherry, Maisie took Glen's hand in hers. "The moon is almost full and the wind has died. I thought we might take a little walk around the neighbourhood to see the Christmas decorations. We can have our coffee and pie when we return."

"Sounds good. I could use some exercise." He patted his midsection. "You and your mother are wonderful cooks."

They walked for close to an hour gazing through living room windows at colourful trees and up at the snow-covered roofs with Santa-clad chimneys. The wood burning in so many fireplaces created a blanket of sweet-scented smoke over the neighbourhood. To Maisie, everything blended into her vision of a Christmas card. When they walked up the sidewalk at her mother's house, Glen hesitated at the bottom of the front steps.

"Maisie, I think I'll pass on the coffee and dessert. It's time I hit the highway."

Astonished, Maisie turned wide eyes to him. "It's a clear night, nice and bright and safe for driving. I didn't think you would leave so early."

He looked down at his feet then slid his hands behind her elbows. "I had an early morning. The animals don't know it's Christmas and somehow they'll expect to be fed at the same time tomorrow morning." He nudged her a little closer and kissed the tip of her nose. "I had a grand time. Thank you for sharing your Christmas with me ... And thank your mother for me."

Maisie's arms went around his neck as she stepped up to the first stair. With her eyes almost on the same level as his, she tilted her head and kissed him lightly. "I thought we might still have a couple of hours together."

"Next time, maybe. Good night, Maisie." He returned her light kiss, then with a moan, wrapped her tightly in his arms and kissed her with a passion that left her breathless.

When he eased her arms from around his neck and suddenly pushed her away from him, she tried to catch his arm. He was too quick and was inside his truck before she could reach him. With a honk of the horn and a blink of the lights, he and his truck were on the street and heading east before she could even catch her breath.

Unseen by Maisie, from her upstairs bedroom window, Madeline watched the scene playing out below. A smile played across her face.

EIGHT
1964

TEN DAYS AND SEVERAL UNANSWERED phone calls later, Maisie knew that Glen was avoiding her. She had absolutely no inkling what the problem was. Between extended office hours and time required for completing her course, she could not spare a weekend for a drive to the farm. Weekend? At this time of year, they were non-existent.

What was wrong with him? He had certainly taken off at breakneck speed after their Christmas dinner. Her mother denied there were any angry words between her and Glen and she certainly hadn't heard raised voices. But something had gone wrong. She needed to find out what. Her mother had suggested that maybe her young man was having second thoughts. Having no success with verbal attempts with him, Maisie decided to write him a letter.

When no reply was forthcoming in the next two weeks, she had no alternative but to accept that he was not going to respond. The pressures of work and school did not allow her any time for self-pity or crystal ball gazing. Winter had settled in and she knew people were staying off the highways unless it was absolutely necessary. She didn't have winter tires on her car, so she even cut back on trips to her mother's. The winter winds blowing across the prairie highways could polish them to a high sheen of ice on which her little car wouldn't stand a chance. She knew Glen had regular business in Regina and a truck with tires that could match the Saskatchewan winter. He must have been in town at least once if not more since Christmas. He hadn't called her. She had no alternative but to put Glen Grayson on a back burner — for now.

January and February passed so quickly, Maisie was sitting in the University of Regina with her accounting exam face down on her desk before she even had time to be nervous. The proctor was watching the second hand rotate to the top of the white-faced clock on the wall.

Finally, "You may turn your examination booklets over and proceed now."

A month later, Maisie received the manila envelope in the mail that she had been anticipating and dreading. As long as it hadn't arrived, she was not a failure by her estimation. She sat at her kitchen table and stared at it for half an hour before picking up the scissors and cutting it open.

Closing one eye helped as she opened the folded pages. "I passed," she whispered to herself. "I passed!" The tears came, then the laughter. "I passed! I passed! Oh, my God, I passed!"

She reached for her ringing phone. "I passed," she shouted into the phone not thinking who might be on the other end. "I passed."

"I knew you would, dear." Her mother laughed as her own tears started.

"It's all behind me, Mom. All those lessons and the endless studying. It's all behind me."

"Congratulations, darling. I never doubted for one minute that you would succeed. Shall I phone Jeremy and tell him, or will you?"

"I'll call him and extend an invitation to my graduation exercise at the same time. I'll be so excited to tell Mr. Whittier tomorrow morning. He's asked several times if I had received my results yet."

"Maybe he'll give you a promotion and a raise now that you have your designation."

"We'll see. I'll be surprised if he does. The firm seems to be overloaded at the top end and more in need of junior help."

"Then you can open your own office — like you've always dreamed of doing."

"I'll take one step at a time, Mom. I have to build some clientele of my own before I can make any decision. I'll hang up now and call Jeremy and Jeanne with my news."

Her hand was still on the phone and the temptation to dial Glen's number was almost impossible to ignore. He had never responded to any of her phone calls nor had he answered her letter. Knowing she was being a coward, she called her brother instead to share her news with him and his wife. "At least I know *he'll* be happy for me," she told the plant on the windowsill.

At the end of April, Maisie, along with thirty-three other graduates from across Saskatchewan, traipsed up on stage in the auditorium of the University of Regina. Later, her mother, brother and sister-in-law took her out for a dinner of steak and lobster, her favourite. It all seemed a little empty. She felt Glen's absence at their table.

As suspected, Mr. Brian Whittier, while proud of her achievement and feeling somewhat responsible for her success because of the tutelage she'd received from him, was sorry that he could not offer her a senior position in the firm. Maisie agreed to stay on with a modest increase in salary and a bonus promised for any new clients she brought to the firm. In the meantime, she made up her mind to look around for any other possible opportunities.

Glen saw the list of graduates with their pictures filling a whole page of the Regina newspaper. He was undecided whether to send a congratulatory card, or just to continue the silence on his part.

"What do you say I should do, Parker?"

His dog sat at his feet and tilted his head when he heard his own name. One ear and one eyebrow perked up. He tilted his head to one side, but continued to sit in stony silence, staring at his master.

"You're right. Silence it is. I don't trust my own resolve when it comes to Maisie. No point in opening up a can of worms."

He went to the barn and saddled Thunder, his prize-winning roan, and took his frustration out on the fields behind his farm. The fields were ready for planting and soon another summer would be upon him. Thirty-four years old and still single. He had never given any thought to his aging process but now he suddenly felt like life was passing him by. Should he give Maisie another opportunity to refuse his farm and his lifestyle? Could he bear the rejection if she did? But what if she accepted him? Would she come to regret it later? She had a promising career ahead of her. Did he have a right to ask her to forgo it? Could she build a suitable practice to work from a home office on the farm? Too many questions. Too many opportunities for a negative response. "Hell, sooner or later I'm going to have to realize she's not mine, Thunder. Her mother is right. She belongs in the city. Better I give her up now and get on with my life."

The horse whinnied in response.

The following week, Glen was in his bank in Estevan, when he noticed a new teller behind the counter. A tall blonde, wearing a matching set of blue sweaters, smiled at him as he filled out his deposit slip. He went to the first available teller, the one next to the attractive girl giving him the eye.

When he turned to leave, she motioned him to her station. "Glen Grayson, don't you recognize me?"

He took a closer look. She seemed familiar. "You look like a Thompson. Are you one of Timmy's little sisters?"

"Well, not so little anymore. I'm almost as tall as my brother, much to my mother's chagrin. I'm the youngest one. Shelley."

"Well, I'll be damned. You *are* all grown up. How old are you now, about nineteen? Twenty?"

"Why, Mr. Grayson, didn't your momma teach you never to ask a lady her age?"

"To be honest, Shelley, I wouldn't know whether to invite you to dinner or for a ride on the merry-go-round in the park."

"Why not both?" She winked. "And I accept. You can pick me up at six o'clock Saturday evening and we'll figure it out. I promise I'll leave my Barbie dolls and skipping rope at home."

Mid Saturday morning a few weekends later, Parker started barking at the sound of a car door closing outside Glen's farmhouse. "Who's there, Parker, one of those pesky magazine salesmen again?"

When he opened the front door, he felt like he'd been sucker-punched in the gut.

"Hello, stranger."

NINE

"MAISIE." HE FINGER-COMBED HIS HAIR as his thoughts played tennis in his brain.

"I can't even say I was in the neighbourhood this time, Glen." She smiled shyly at him. "I made a special trip down just to see you."

"Maisie." He shuffled his bare feet a few times before stepping out and closing the door behind him.

"Um, did I come at a bad time? You have a cow about to drop? Someone's waiting for you in the shower?"

Her attempt at humour only seemed to make him more ill at ease. His only reaction was to turn and look at the door he had just closed.

"Oh, my. You do have someone inside. Someone you'd rather I didn't meet."

Before he could answer, the door was opened by an attractive young blonde. All three of them seemed surprised by the encounter.

"Glen, you didn't say you were expecting company." The attractive woman appeared to sense some tension and backed up looking uncomfortable. "I'm sorry, sugar. I'll go back inside."

"No, there's no problem. I'm not company. I was just asking directions." Maisie looked from the girl to Glen and back again trying to look and sound nonchalant. "I was to meet a client at a farm near here and I took a wrong turn." Maisie backed down the steps. "Thank you, mister. Sorry to bother you."

She couldn't get back to her car quick enough, humiliated and embarrassed by her assumption that Glen would be sitting at home pining away for her. She stepped on the gas so hard dust billowed in her rearview mirror. She hadn't even given him a chance to respond. It didn't register until she was back on the main road that he hadn't appeared about to give an explanation anyway.

She was driving way too fast but didn't care. The hurt and the need to put distance between her and Glen Grayson were making her careless. She hadn't anticipated a round trip this day nor had she wanted one. She had hoped to be welcomed with open arms and spending the weekend in bed making up for the lost winter. The tears started. After driving ten miles or so at breakneck speed, she pulled to the side of the road and shut the engine off. She pounded the steering wheel and let all her fury and frustration loose. It took a while before she was calm enough and the tears had subsided sufficiently for her to start the car and get it back on the pavement again. She hiccupped her last sob as she got to full speed. The *legal* maximum speed.

Maybe I'll stop in and see Mom. Tell her I decided to come at the last minute. After a quick look at the distraught reflection in the mirror she decided that wasn't such a good idea. *She'll see right through me. She's a mother after all.*

TEN
1966

MAISIE HUNG UP THE PHONE and looked around her large, well-furnished office. She straightened the painting of a panoramic Saskatchewan sunset which had been done in oil by the mother of a colleague at Whittier Whittier and McLean and which now graced the wall behind her desk. It had been a departing gift from the management and staff. She had picked up the warm tones from it in the furniture and wall décor around the room. The rust, gold and charcoal brown area rug in the centre of the office offered an invitation to sit in one of the armchairs, and the two matching sofas placed strategically around a coffee table were to encourage conversation with her clients.

After achieving her designation as a Certified General Accountant she had remained at the offices of Whittier Whittier and McLean.

Brian Whittier, her immediate superior and senior partner in the firm, had come through on his promise of an increase in salary and that, along with the bonuses she received for new clients, allowed her a reasonably good income. She only wished female employees were recognized with the same pay scale as the male accountants. She worked equally as hard and brought her fair share of clients into the firm, but she knew the males considered her only a shade above a secretary or bookkeeper. The company-acquired clients she was given to handle were the smaller businesses, and the least complicated of the corporations, as though a female brain couldn't deal with complex accounting as well as male brains could. Six months earlier, after another male accountant was hired and placed above her in the pay scale, she decided to follow her dream and open her own office. She had been like a dog with a bone in her pursuit of rural businesses, farms in particular, in her roster of clients. Even though Regina was a provincial capital it was not a metropolis by any stretch of the imagination. However, it was still big enough and busy enough to give her the diversity of clients that her hard-earned education was meant to facilitate.

As she looked out the window at the busy street and the landscape of the buildings around her, her gaze wandered once again to the art on her wall and she relaxed in confirmation that she had made the right decision. She had the best of the two worlds Regina had to offer, the clients from rural Saskatchewan and the commercial and government clients from within the city. One of her former co-workers had told her that Whittier Whittier and McLean were not happy as increasing numbers of clients followed her when she branched out on her own. She had opened her office a few miles from where her former employer's offices were. She hadn't wanted to appear in competition with them. If clients followed her, they had to travel across town to do so. And a fair number had.

Her business had been open less than two months and already her billed fees were more than covering her rent and utilities plus the salary of her part-time bookkeeper, Ruby Sawchuk. She felt positive about her future. It was time now to hire a receptionist. The phone call she had just completed was to set up an interview with a young lady who had graduated with a clerical certificate from the community college and was looking for a full-time office job. Her lack of experience would have to be considered in discussing her pay scale, but she had sounded professional enough on the phone.

By 2 o'clock that afternoon, terms had been agreed upon and Ellen Webster was hired and ready to start work the next morning. Maisie's first full-time employee. Ruby would be working in the office the next day and available to help with Ellen's training. It had been a productive day. A proposal Maisie had presented to a prairie-wide trucking firm had been accepted with the result that a new client was added to their files. She had a smile on her face as she turned the lights out and locked the door. A new employee and a new client.

"Maisie, are you sure you can afford a full-time receptionist? You have to be careful." Her mother sounded worried about every dollar she spent.

"Mom, I'm an accountant. I advise businesspeople every day on what they can and can't afford. I think I'm qualified to figure out my own office budget."

She would have been surprised and somewhat disappointed if she hadn't received an argument from her mother. "Besides, a pretty good-sized account came on board today and I have several other requests from prospective clients that I just haven't had time to consider yet. I don't want to lose new business and if I don't have more work for Ruby soon, she's liable to go elsewhere. I've been putting off offering her more hours. I can only stretch myself so far so now is the time to hire someone to take over the reception and secretarial duties. Then I can concentrate on new accounting clients for Ruby and me."

"I guess you know best, dear. I know you're busy. It's been a while since you've been able to come for a visit."

Maisie cut her mother off before she could start into her usual poor-neglected-me tirade.

"Why don't you come to Regina, Mom? You could stay for a week or so and maybe get some shopping in. We could go to hear the symphony one evening and maybe catch a movie."

"Oh, I don't know, dear. What would I do with myself while you're at work all day? I don't know my way around the big city. And all that noise. How would I ever sleep?"

"Well, maybe it's time you learned your way around. Regina is not Toronto or Montreal. It's easy to get around by bus and you can get your hair done, maybe shop for some patterns. You're always talking about how much you miss your sewing. You could meet me for lunch a couple of times. And I'd love for you to see my office."

"But you only have one bedroom in your apartment. You know I must have a comfortable bed for my bad back. I can't expect you to sleep on the sofa for a whole week when you need your rest for work."

Maisie rolled her eyes listening to her mother go on about her bad back. She sounded like an eighty-year-old every time she mentioned her lumbago. "Oh, for heaven's sake, Mom, it's not like I'm sleeping on a sofa. Really. It's a hide-a-bed and I'm perfectly comfortable on it. Jeremy has slept on it a couple of times when he's come to the city and says it's comfy. If it's good enough for him, I'm sure it will be good enough for me. Come. It will be fun."

"Well..."

"I won't take no for an answer. I'm going to get you a bus ticket and you are coming. No argument."

"But what will I bring to wear? I don't have proper city clothes."

Maisie had to bite her tongue. "That's the whole idea. Bring the clothes you normally wear to go to the doctor's or to church. You just need a couple of outfits. It will be a good opportunity to update your wardrobe. We'll buy a few things and you can buy material and patterns for a few more."

She bought a Greyhound ticket for her mother for three days later and dropped it in the mail. She didn't want to give the woman too much time to ponder all the reasons why she shouldn't come to Regina.

The next morning Ellen Webster and Ruby Sawchuk arrived at the same time. The nineteen-year-old Ellen showed obvious delight at the sight of a brand-new turquoise-blue Underwood typewriter sitting on her desk and the latest intercom system connecting her desk with her boss's. "This office is equipped better than the classroom at the college."

Maisie had had to do some fast shopping at the local office supply store the afternoon before. She knew she couldn't expect a new receptionist to use the old typewriter with the sticking keys, so she was delighted when she found this latest model newly arrived at the store. The telephone company had installed the intercom system just two weeks before.

Ruby was pleasant to the young girl and showed her how to make coffee in the electric percolator and how much water to put in each plant in Maisie's office. This room along the west side of the building had several windows covered with venetian blinds that Maisie usually kept completely open to give the sun full access to her office. Many plants soaked up that western sunshine and thrived on the window ledges. The reception and bookkeeping area took the space across the whole front of the building. Ellen's desk sat near the door with an area for Ruby's desk behind, next to the expanse of windows that ran across the southern wall. It was a large room with a small kitchenette and storage room and a double-door closet facing the waiting room where staff and clients could hang their coats. A washroom down the hall was shared with a dental office, the only other tenant on this second floor of the three-story building. An elevator was available for any handicapped visitors. Maisie knew the space was more than they needed but she had rented the office with an eye for the future. She had visions of her company becoming at least a three-accountant firm.

"Are there any special rules I should know about? Any dos and don'ts that Miss Forbes will expect?"

Ruby went through the routine with her. "Miss Forbes likes her privacy. She keeps her personal life separate from this office. We are her employees, not her friends, no matter how friendly she may be. Keep your personal phone calls to a minimum or while on your break if possible. There is only one telephone line into the office right now and it's not fair for a client to hear a busy signal because you or I are on a personal call. There is no smoking allowed, even by clients. You will see no ashtrays about." She pointed to a sign indicating this on the wall in the reception area. "Always let her know when someone is waiting and their identity. In the morning when you first come in, check her appointment book and pull the files of all the morning clients and place the first two on the corner of her desk. Then as the day progresses, replace each one. When alone, she likes to work with her office door partly open but always remember to close it after you have brought a client to her."

Just then, Maisie breezed into the office with some doughnuts and good mornings were exchanged. Ellen quickly opened the appointment book, found the files of the first two clients of the day and placed them on Maisie's desk. Ruby winked at the younger woman and gave her a thumbs-up.

"Thanks for being here to introduce Ellen to the morning routine." Maisie motioned Ruby to follow her into her office.

"That's okay. I remember how nervous I was my first day at my first job. Good God, that's almost twenty-five years ago. Where the hell have the years gone?"

"You don't look old enough to have started working twenty-five years ago." Maisie knew Ruby was in her mid-forties but in spite of the woman's not hiding the few strands of grey in her hair, she was full of energy and kept herself fit and trim. She was always dressed professionally, and her make-up was exquisite.

"Some days I feel like I've been working for thirty or forty years but for the most part, I believe it's the *busyness* of work and being out in the public that keeps me feeling like a twenty-year-old. At this time of year, I have no time to think about gravity starting to tug at my body parts."

Maisie chuckled, then the two women went over the files for which Ruby would make the initial entries before turning them over to Maisie for completion.

About an hour later, Ellen's voice came over the intercom to tell her a woman was in the waiting room. The visitor's name was Mrs. Grayson and she wanted to talk to Miss Forbes about the company doing the taxes for the farm which she and her husband owned.

ELEVEN

NO, IT CAN'T POSSIBLY BE ... Dear God, don't let it be ...

Maisie wracked her brain trying to remember if Glen had ever mentioned having relatives with a farm in the Regina area. If he did, surely he would have mentioned visiting them on his trips to the city. She glanced at herself in the mirror above the credenza. She looked okay. She ran her fingers through her unruly curls. *Nothing I can do without notice. Suck it up and go meet the woman. Graciously.*

"Mrs. Grayson, please come in and sit here." Maisie pointed to one of the chairs on the other side of her desk. She sometimes invited clients to sit on one of the sofas but not sure if this woman might be *the* Mrs. Grayson, she decided to keep a desk between them.

When the woman sat opposite her, she recognized the young blonde from Glen's front porch. *Dear God, why are you doing this to me?*

She forced one of her best smiles and shook the woman's offered hand.

"I'm sorry to come unannounced like this, Miss Forbes, but I had an early doctor's appointment and decided to take a chance that you would have an opening. It's a bit of a drive from Estevan so I'm trying to kill two birds with one stone."

Estevan. Maisie now had to determine if this visit was a personal one or if this young woman had told the truth to her receptionist about possibly hiring her accounting service.

"Have we met, Mrs. Grayson?" This seemed like an innocent enough question. She wondered if the woman knew of her involvement with Glen or if the couple had discussed using Maisie's accounting firm and if so, why? Should she mention that she knew this woman's husband?

"Oh, please call me Shelley. No, we've never met but I understand that you and my husband know each other."

Well, at least I don't have to lie or pretend about that.

"My receptionist mentioned that you were interested in learning about my accounting service for your farm. Isn't Estevan a long way to come for bookkeeping?"

"I do the bookkeeping for the farm. It's only the year-end financial statements and tax filing that we require your expertise for."

"Why me? There are accounting firms closer to you, probably right in Estevan." Something didn't feel right about this.

"We've used an Estevan firm in the past, but they haven't proven to be reliable. We've missed out on a number of tax breaks that have cost us considerable amounts. Glen decided it was time to look for a new firm and started asking around. My family owns a farm in the area, and I used to work for a bank in Estevan, so I'm familiar with some of the larger farmers there and in the Weyburn area, and in discussing our search for an accountant, your name came up several times. You appear to have gained quite a positive reputation in the south Saskatchewan farming community, Miss Forbes."

Maisie managed a smile. "Please call me Maisie. Does your husband know you are here this morning?"

"No. I thought we could go through what you would need from Glen and me, whether you even have time to complete our year-end and also what your fees would be. When I go home, I'll bring all the information for him and we'll discuss the practicability of using your firm. As I said about killing two birds with one stone, I'm here now so why waste another trip? I was surprised but quite happy to see your window sign when I was sitting in the doctor's office across the street. I figured if I could see you now, it would save a future trip."

Maisie felt her jaw tighten and her teeth on the verge of grinding. What was she to do? Tell this woman she was too busy, all the while continuing to advertise for new clients? What would Glen's reaction be to the news his wife had been discussing their business with his old girlfriend? His *wife*. She didn't even know he was married for heaven's sake! She wanted to think of the girl as a child bride. Her first impression of her on his front porch that day had been one of a girl barely out of high school, but on closer scrutiny she didn't appear to be that many years younger than Maisie. Her first impression of her as a bimbo went out the window, too. The girl was obviously intelligent enough to do the farm bookkeeping and discuss finances with other farmers. *Well, Glen Grayson, maybe I'll drop this decision in your lap.*

"Do you have any paperwork with you, Mrs., excuse me … Shelley?"

"No, I don't but if you tell me what you need to know I can probably give you most of the figures from memory."

They discussed the farm revenue and expenses for another forty-five minutes and Maisie was impressed by the financial success of the farm. She quoted her rate per hour and the retainer fee she would require. Shelley asked Maisie if the secretary could type it out for her to take with her. When she left, Maisie had a new respect for this gorgeous young woman whom Glen had chosen as his wife. Her beauty wasn't her only asset. Shelley had come from a long line of farmers herself, knew the ins and outs of running a farm, and loved the life. Glen had chosen well.

She didn't have to wait long for a response. Three days later, Ellen buzzed to inform her that Mr. Glen Grayson called for an appointment so she had put his name in the appointment book for 11 o'clock the following day. Maisie was to pick her mother up at the Greyhound bus depot at 3 o'clock the same day. Again, it was as if the gods were playing a cruel joke on her. She shook her head. *Wonder how she'd feel if I suggested Glen pick her up on his way through Weyburn and save a bus fare. Wonder how he'd feel.* The thought of them riding in a car together for an hour and a half made her laugh out loud. So loud that her intercom buzzed immediately. "Miss Forbes? Did you call me?"

"No, Ellen. I just noticed something funny outside my window."

TWELVE

"GLEN, HOW NICE TO SEE you again."

"Good morning, Maisie."

He stretched his long frame at an angle as he settled on the sofa. She took a chair across from him. He lifted one foot to rest on the other knee as he accepted the mug of coffee that Ellen brought in for him.

He still made Maisie's heart flutter which made her angry.

"You have a charming wife. I neglected to ask Shelley how long you've been married."

"Two years."

"She seems well-versed in the farming sector and concerned about your previous, or maybe I should say current, accountant's diligence in securing all the tax credits to which you're entitled."

"Yes, she's the perfect wife, especially for a farmer."

He hadn't taken his eyes from Maisie's. It was somewhat unnerving for her but she was determined to present a cool façade.

"Do you have children?"

"I'm surprised she didn't tell you. We're expecting our first in about six months."

"Congratulations. I'm sure you must be delighted."

"Let's cut the crap and get right to the chase, Maisie. I think you're just as surprised and uncomfortable by the position Shelley has put us in as I am."

Startled, Maisie sat upright. "There's no need to be rude, Glen. I wasn't aware we were caught up in 'crap'."

She stood and moved to her desk. She picked up the file folder that Ellen had placed on it when Glen had arrived. "Let me see. I believe you have a copy of the quotation I gave your wife for my services. If you don't like the terms, you are under no obligation to my firm. If you have questions, please ask away. I'll try not to give you any crap."

He took a drink of coffee then placed the mug on the coffee table and stood. Again, he stared directly at Maisie as he moved toward her. Her instinct was to move behind the desk thus placing a barrier between the two of them — symbolic or not. However, she stood her ground and extended the file to him. "In case you haven't read it."

"I've read it. I like it. And I accept it." He stopped a few feet in front of her, ignoring the offered file.

"You do?" She was having a hard time hiding the anxiety. Taking Glen and his wife on as clients was not a good idea. Not a good idea at all. She had hoped he would refuse outright and that would be the end of it. She should have known better. If that had been his intention, he would have done so by telephone or in writing.

"I do."

"Glen, I …"

He took the file from her hand and moved to place it on the desk behind her. This brought him uncomfortably close.

"You … what?" When she didn't answer right away, he continued. "My wife was here. If I had known she was coming I probably would have discouraged it. However, she was impressed with you, the ways you suggested we might save some money, and she liked your fee. She feels you're the right person to handle our affairs. Your excellent portfolio didn't leave me much room for argument. So here I am, accepting your proposal."

With a sigh, Maisie walked around the desk toward the door. "I'll have Ellen type up a formal agreement. You can send me the retainer cheque with the required paperwork for my assistant to start work on your year-end."

"I have a box in my truck with everything you told Shelley you would need. I have a cheque in my pocket for the retainer."

She could see the corner of his mouth twitch and a slight gleam in his eye. "Is there anything else you need to seal the deal?"

"No." She wanted to say yes, a kiss would be nice. "That should be everything. Ellen can type the necessary papers while you retrieve your records from your truck."

"I was hoping that Ellen might type the papers while we celebrated our new alliance over lunch."

"I, I…"

"That sounds like an 'aye, aye' to me. Shall we eat at the restaurant on the corner?"

She hesitated, but only for a moment. She knew if her firm was going to be handling his financial affairs then she would have to get over any qualms she had about personal contact with her new client. "I'll check my appointment schedule."

Ellen informed her she was free until a 1:30 appointment and then her mother would be arriving at 3 o'clock.

They sat in a booth at the restaurant run by a Ukrainian family who offered daily specials reminiscent of their homeland. The lunch special happened to be one of Maisie's favourites: borscht. Glen ordered the same with a side of perogies. It felt so comfortable to be sitting opposite this tall handsome man from her past that it almost made her *un*comfortable. The conversation flowed easily as they caught up on the intervening years.

"Shelley's pregnancy isn't without complications. She has been experiencing bleeding and a little cramping. She even had to give up curling which is her main wintertime activity. Our family doctor fears that she may miscarry and recommended that she see a gynecologist here in Regina. That's why she was in town last week. Apparently, his office is right across the street from yours. She saw your sign and remembered your name from a number of recommendations that some of your clients had given her. I was surprised to learn that you specialized in accounting for the farming industry given your antipathy toward farmers."

"You forget, it's not me who has the dislike of farmers. It's my mother. I, on the other hand, found that farming is strong and profitable in Saskatchewan, extremely so in southern Saskatchewan. I learned this while employed at Whittier Whittier and McLean. Consequently, I pushed to be given any new farm clients that came to the firm. The other accountants were more interested in corporate and government contracts, so I had the field pretty much to myself. It's been my experience that most farmers are excellent clients. They tend to have similar accounting needs, they don't question the fee structure, they are grateful for any extra time given to answer their questions and they pay on time. Corporations come and go, and they tend to expect a discount for early payment, otherwise they take ninety days. Contracts with the provincial and municipal governments move around with whichever party is in power. Farming is here to stay. Why would I not want to do business with the industry?"

"Why indeed? I have always felt that farming is the field to be in — no pun intended. I am proud to be a part of it. It's too bad it took you this long to find out how well we may have complemented each other in our chosen fiel— professions." He smiled, reached for her hand resting on the table, and enclosed his own around it.

When she looked up at him, his smile was more wistful than smug.

She broke the silent stare. "Hindsight, as they say. We are not all blessed with it. However, you have achieved everything a farmer could want. A productive farm, a beautiful wife who can knowledgeably — and more important, lovingly — share all the aspects of farming with you. You have a new son or daughter on the way to carry on the farm tradition. You have it all, Glen. It may not have had the same storybook ending had it been me in the picture."

"And you? Have you achieved all that your heart desires?"

"I am well on my way. My success as an accountant has allowed me to venture out on my own. My ability as an entrepreneur has yet to be proven but I'm happy with what I've achieved so far."

"Is there a man in your life?"

"I'm working on that." She pulled her hand from his and looked at her watch. It was shortly after 1 o'clock. "My next client will here in less than a half hour and I still have to go over his file. It was nice seeing you, Glen. I will let you know when I have your tax figures together. We can go over them before they are filed. I'll pick up this tab in appreciation for the work you have given me."

"I'll go with you to your office and give your secretary that cheque and get a receipt for Shelley."

He was leaving the reception desk as her next client arrived. Maisie shook Glen's hand and asked him to give her regards to his wife and expressed her hope that the pregnancy would go without any further problems.

THIRTEEN

MADELINE FORBES'S BUS ARRIVED ALMOST thirty minutes late. It was a good thing Maisie hadn't scheduled any further appointments for the afternoon.

Her new apartment was not far off Victoria and handy to a lot of amenities. She could find just about anything she needed within walking distance. The drive to work was only minutes, so even though it wasn't fancy, it suited her just fine. A slight improvement over the first apartment she rented when she had made her move to the city, it was comfortable and the rent was reasonable. It was only one bedroom but quite roomy. She was gradually furnishing it in her own style as her business grew and allowed her the means. Soon she hoped to buy her own house, but for now, she was comfy enough renting without the upkeep of home ownership.

Maisie watched as her mother unpacked her suitcase and hung

her things in the bedroom closet. She took note of Madeline's dated wardrobe and vowed that her mother was going to leave Regina with at least three new inter-changeable outfits.

"Do you want to stretch your legs a bit by walking to the corner grocer with me? I thought we'd eat in tonight and maybe catch an early movie."

"That sounds marvellous, dear. I don't want to keep you from any work you might have, though."

"I have a clean slate until mid-morning tomorrow then I'll be tied up in the office until late afternoon. Let's check the paper and see what's playing at the movies."

They decided on a James Stewart/Maureen O'Hara movie which was light and entertaining. Maisie wanted her mother to have happy memories of her time in Regina. If she could keep Madeline in an elevated state of mind, perhaps she would be willing to come back and gradually come out of the near-reclusive lifestyle she had fallen into. Her mother was far too young to sit at home crocheting, knitting and reading day after day, night after night, with only the odd bingo game thrown in from time to time.

The next morning, they both had appointments for haircuts at a salon not far from Maisie's office. The older woman was delighted with her image reflected in the mirror. Maisie talked her into staying to have a manicure after she left for the office and her first appointment.

A half hour later Maisie could hear her mother's voice in the outer office. As soon as her client left, she stepped out and found her mother enjoying a muffin and coffee with the two office assistants. Ellen was about to apologize for sitting and chatting rather than working but Maisie caught her mid-sentence and thanked her for entertaining her mother until she was free. The women had been talking about sewing and Ruby Sawchuk, who had a break between clients, volunteered to walk with Mrs. Forbes to a fabric store which was located two blocks over.

Maisie went into her office and opened the box that Glen had left the day before. She started sorting and recognized the scent of his aftershave. It was all she could do to stop herself from burying her nose in the papers. She did notice a trace of a more feminine fragrance, too, but tried not to dwell on it. The papers were well organized. Everything was labelled just as she had requested. Some of it was photocopied but most were originals such as the bank statements, the tax bills and the copies of loan agreements and the purchase of a 1965 Chevrolet sedan.

She had asked for the previous year's financial statements and tax filing. It was all there. Mr. Glen Grayson was making a more-than-decent living for himself. She noticed he had fewer hired hands than some farms which meant he was more hands-on than some. She also noticed that Shelley drew a small salary from the business, which was not uncommon for farm wives. In Shelley's case, it was charged to bookkeeping and it appeared she had indeed filed a personal income tax return showing the income she earned. Maisie had just finished sorting and preparing the papers for Ruby to enter into their ledgers, when her bookkeeper returned.

"Did she find anything she liked?"

"Yes, we picked out patterns for a skirt and a nice long-sleeved blouse. Then we found some beautiful material. She told me she brought her dressmaking scissors with her in case she found a pattern she liked."

"Where is she now?"

"On a bus to your place and she's excited to get there and start cutting the patterns out."

"Thanks so much, Ruby. You be sure to book those hours on your time sheet. I don't expect you to entertain my mother on your own time."

"What are you talking about? I enjoyed it and we've made arrangements for her to ride in with you tomorrow morning."

"Tomorrow? Aren't you off tomorrow?"

"Yes. We're going to take the bus over to the new mall on the other side of town. Is that okay?"

"Okay? Of course, it's okay. Is it something you really want to do?"

"Your mother isn't all that much older than me. We have a lot in common and we're going to spend the day doing stuff I've been wanting to do but never had anyone to do it with. So, hell yes. It's something I really want to do."

"Then go have fun." Ruby was almost out the door when Maisie remembered the box from the Grayson farm. "I have the new client's work ready for you to start working on. I'm hoping we can have it finished by the end of next week so we can get it approved and ready for filing before the end of April."

"I'm off tomorrow, but my work is pretty well caught up so I won't have a problem getting my part of this done early next week."

"Good enough. Their farm is near Estevan so they won't be breathing down our necks while we're working on it, but I do want to give them ample time to go over it in case any adjustments are necessary before we file their taxes."

"Estevan? Wow. You'll be pulling clients from Alberta soon."

"It seems a couple of the Weyburn farmers we've been working with are more than satisfied and spreading the word."

Maisie went back into her office and continued with the file of the new trucking client while Ellen prepared advertising posters for an upcoming seminar.

That evening Maisie helped her mother cut and pin a pattern onto the fabric for her skirt and blouse. The next morning, Madeline and Ruby greeted each other like old friends and were off to catch a bus to the mall without even taking time for a cup of coffee.

Maisie started training Ellen on the fundamentals of basic bookkeeping. She had proven to be a quick learner and if she could master some of the rudimentary, and more tedious prep work, it would free up some of Ruby's time and hers for the more intricate work. The end of April and close of tax season was fast approaching and they still had taxes for several clients to complete. As usual, there were latecomers who waited until the last minute with the expectation it would all be completed on time.

Quite late in the afternoon, Ellen gave her the message that Madeline and Ruby would be grabbing a bite to eat before taking the bus and she was not to wait for her mother. Maisie almost broke out whistling. She couldn't have been happier. The thought of Ruby and her mother getting along and maybe forming a friendship hadn't even entered Maisie's mind. If anyone could break Madeline out of her shell and help her forget her aches and pains, it would be Ruby.

FOURTEEN

THE FOLLOWING WEEK FLEW BY. Mother and daughter spent a few evenings at concerts. They even took in a Regina Pats playoff hockey game. Their other evenings were spent sewing Madeline's new outfits and going to a few restaurants that Maisie had been wanting to try. Ruby had taken her new friend on a couple of shopping expeditions, forcing Madeline to buy another suitcase to hold all her purchases.

"I love your new shoes, Mom. I want to get a pair of those T-straps for myself. Once the tax season is finished, I'll take a day or two off to do a little shopping."

Maisie was smiling as her mother modeled her new purchases. Having doubted the wisdom of inviting her mother for an extended visit, she was now happy she had. Ruby was already making plans for a weekend visit to Weyburn in late May. Madeline had a fresh smile on her face these days instead of her perpetual downer look. Maybe there was hope for them to have a loving, laughing, mother and daughter relationship yet. For as long as Maisie could remember, her mother had always seemed to be full of spite and hard to please. Nothing made her happy, and if it did, Maisie was certain it wouldn't last.

The next morning, Maisie put her mother's bags in her car and dropped the older woman at the beauty salon to have her manicure freshened and her hair styled once more before catching the bus for home. She had three clients coming in for final approval of their financial statements and to sign their tax forms for remittance. When she arrived in her office and saw the names on her appointment sheet, she had a moment of panic at the sight of Glen Grayson being the last one listed.

My mother and her not-so-favourite farmer will be arriving and probably sharing the waiting room at the same time. That will probably dampen her happy send off. I knew I should have mentioned that he was a client of mine now. Please, God, let his wife be with him.

She shook her head and reminded herself that she was a mature, successful businesswoman now and did not need her mother's permission or approval of clients. *Yeah, right!*

Luck was on her side; her second client didn't need all his allotted time and Glen arrived early. He was barely seated inside her office and the door closed behind him when she heard Ellen greeting her mother in the outer room. They would still encounter each other when he left but at least it would save the uncomfortable situation of sitting in the same waiting area for what could have seemed like an eternity.

"Shelley didn't come with you?"

"No. She wasn't feeling well this morning. That's why I came early in the hope you might be able to take me a little sooner than scheduled."

"I'm sorry to hear that. I hope she doesn't suffer from ill health throughout her pregnancy."

"Our doctor is considering complete bed rest for her for the next four to six weeks. I think the trip up here a couple of weeks ago took a toll on her."

"You weren't with her when she came? I hope she didn't drive by herself."

"No, her mother drove her. In fact, her mother has been staying at the house helping with the housework and meals."

"Okay, let's make this brief so that you aren't kept away any longer than necessary. I should have asked if her signature was required on any of the paperwork."

"No. I value her input and help and consider her my partner in the operation of the farm, but it's not on paper. I've maintained ownership and I'm the single shareholder of the corporation."

Maisie tried not to show her surprise. This was the sixties after all, and women were recognized more and more as full partners in their husbands' businesses. Maybe Glen was more old-fashioned than she had believed, maintaining his right to be the head of the family holdings.

As if he read her thoughts, "It's been written in the Grayson wills for several generations that the corporate ownership be maintained by the male heirs until or unless such time that there are none. My great-grandfather was insistent that it remain a Grayson land right."

"I see." Maisie could not help the slight rise in her eyebrows.

"You don't approve?"

She looked at him and again noticed the slight upturn on one side of his mouth and the almost unnoticeable gleam in his eyes. This male succession of ownership certainly didn't fit his personality and it surprised her that he continued it. Hmm. Did Shelley know this before she married him? Maybe it didn't matter to her.

"It's not up to me to approve or disapprove. That's between you and your wife. My only concern in the matter is that all necessary signatures appear on the dotted line. If that means only yours, then so be it. Now let's go over some of these figures."

It took a half hour for her to point out the slight changes she had made concerning certain assets and the re-delegation of some expenses and the reasons behind them. She had drawn his attention to some depreciation that had not been taken previously and also the capital loss on the sale of a piece of equipment the year before that should be captured in the current year. When she was finished, Glen leaned back on the sofa, picked up the papers and shook his head.

"Now, I see why you came so highly recommended. I'm glad that Shelley took the initiative to set up an appointment with you and insisted that I follow through."

"She had to insist?"

He set the papers back on the table in front of them and lifted one foot to rest on the other knee. "I think I told you that I was hesitant at first when she told me she had spoken to you. Having taken the fork in the road that I did a few years ago, I was reluctant to go back and travel down that other one."

Maisie took a deep breath. "I was … surprised, to put it mildly, when she appeared in my office the way she did. I was uncomfortable and wondered if she knew about our past. However, when she said she was aware that you and I knew each other, I relaxed somewhat and felt that you were okay with the possibility of me taking care of your financial matters. Had I known there would be any hesitation on your part, I would have ended the conversation with your wife before it even began. I had wrongly assumed that my name had come up as a possible contender for your business."

"Your name was on a short list of recommended accountants that we had collected in our pursuit of a new firm to help with our taxes. Since Shelley is an excellent bookkeeper, I bowed to her expertise in researching the candidates. I didn't know, nor did she, that her search would bring her to your office that day. It was quite by accident that she saw your sign in your window and decided to take the opportunity to talk to you. She was impressed with you and your proposal and suggested we follow through on it."

"Even though she's aware we were once lovers?"

"Even though she's aware we once *knew each other*."

"I see." Maisie crossed her arms and thought for a moment. "She didn't recognize me from the day I foolishly arrived in your driveway?"

"Not at all. She also doesn't know that had she not been there that day, there's a good possibility she would not be my wife now."

Maisie did a double take at that statement. "Glen, I … I don't want to even go there. Shelley is your wife and we've both moved on. You are awaiting your first child, hopefully a son, to carry on the tradition of the Grayson Family Farm." She couldn't help the sarcasm in the last part of her diatribe. "Now if you'll sign the papers, I will get them filed in both the provincial and federal offices before the deadline."

Glen continued to look at her for a few seconds before signing where she had indicated. She slid a copy for him into a manila envelope and sealed the others in pre-addressed and stamped envelopes for mailing to the governments, and one for her own files.

"Ellen will prepare my final invoice and send it to you in the mail. I do want to thank you and Shelley for choosing my firm as your accountants this year. I hope we can look forward to your business again next year."

She started toward the door and had it halfway open when she offered him her hand. He chose to lean over and kiss her on the cheek and say, "I will definitely look forward to our continued relationship."

She heard a chair scrape and saw her mother stand.

"Mr. Grayson? I wasn't aware that you had a continuing relationship with my daughter." Her face was almost purple.

"Mom, I …"

"Mrs. Forbes, it's nice to see you again. Maisie was kind enough to do the tax work necessary for our farm and has agreed to do so again next year."

"*Our* farm?"

"Yes, my wife actually was the one who hired Maisie as our tax accountant."

"Your wife?"

Maisie had collected herself and responded. "Yes, Mother. Glen has been married for several years and they are expecting their first child in the early fall. I'm pleased that they've chosen my firm to represent their farm in any financial affairs."

Madeline looked from one to the other. "My congratulations on your marriage and your expected child. I'm sorry I jumped to the conclusion the *relationship* was something other than business."

Glen's smile deepened and he shook Madeline's reluctant hand as he backed toward the door, wishing both ladies a great day and gave Ellen a salute and a thanks on his way out.

Madeline didn't look totally convinced, but she obviously knew better than to carry the conversation any further in front of Maisie's employee.

"Shall we be off then? There's a nice little restaurant between here and the bus depot that I've been dying to try." Maisie smiled and took her mother by the arm. "I'll be back in a couple of hours, Ellen. Just put the gone for lunch sign on the door when you take your break."

Lunch went better than Maisie had anticipated. The conversation was light as she admired her mother's hair and they talked about Ruby's anticipated visit to Weyburn. Madeline said she was hoping there might be a rodeo while her new friend would be in town. Glen Grayson was not even mentioned until her mother was about to step onto the bus.

"I hope there will be no need to consult with Mr. Grayson before tax time next year. Or if there is, perhaps you and his wife can handle it. Goodbye, dear. I had a really great time and I know it was difficult for you during your busiest time of the year." She had her foot on the first step before she whispered, "I love you." She kissed her daughter and continued inside.

Maisie was stunned by these parting remarks. Surely, her mother didn't think there was anything going on with Glen. He was married and had moved on. Maisie wished he had shaken her hand rather than kissed her on the cheek. She could see how that must have looked to her mother. She watched the bus pull out, waved, and tried to remember the last time her mother had said she loved her.

FIFTEEN

THE SPRING CAME AND WENT. The summer was an endless one of thirty-degree temperatures and little rain. Maisie's business continued to grow and so did her staff. Ruby was now working full time. Ellen had been promoted to secretary while continuing with her bookkeeping training. These changes produced a need for a new receptionist. They were now actively taking on small business clients, with a new fee schedule that included a rate for bookkeeping. The building industry was booming and Maisie managed to get her share of the new construction companies opening shop all over town. Two small workspaces had been divided from the large reception area by frosted acrylic walls to give Ruby, and soon Ellen, a measure of privacy and quiet. Ellen had followed Ruby's example of dressing professionally and always putting the office first. She didn't watch the clock and stayed after hours often. The age difference between the two women was such that they didn't associate with each other after hours and this enabled them to be friendly without becoming too involved in each other's personal matters. Maisie couldn't be happier with her staff and the way her office was humming along.

Madeline had returned to Regina once in late July for another visit and ended up staying for two weeks. Three new clients had kept Maisie working longer hours which worked out fine for her mother as it gave her an opportunity to make new curtains and slip covers for Maisie's apartment. Then when Ellen took a few days off to attend a family wedding in Vancouver, Ruby and Maisie had to split reception duties and Maisie had to type her own correspondence. By Friday, after Ellen's two-day absence, they were barely coping so Madeline brought in lunch.

Maisie was tied up in her office with a client and Ruby was speaking with another, so when the phone rang as Madeline was laying the salad on the reception desk, she picked up the phone and greeted the caller with the name of the firm. She carefully took down the name and number of the person wishing to speak with Maisie and promised a call back as soon as Miss Forbes was free. Ruby's client left just in time for the bookkeeper to catch the tail end of Madeline's telephone conversation.

"You handled that very well. Maybe Maisie should look at hiring you as our new receptionist." She said it jokingly, but it seemed to make sense, especially when Madeline had to process a couple more calls over the next hour.

Later in the afternoon when Madeline had left and Maisie finally had time to grab some salad from the fridge to eat, Ruby approached her with the idea.

"Are you nuts? That's all I need is my mother here screening my calls and talking sewing patterns with whomever will listen."

"I don't think you're giving your mother a fair assessment. She handled several calls in a calm, professional manner. She did so without being asked to or getting flustered, Maisie. She saw it needed to be done and she did it."

"I'm sorry, I didn't intend to sound demeaning to my mother. Of course, she was able to take a couple of messages but there is more to the job than just answering the phone. She has no business training and nothing in common with any of our clients. How would she interact with them in the waiting room? You know there are delays sometimes of a half hour or more. There is typing to be done, mail to be sorted, endless filing and other odd jobs to do. Sometimes the receptionist has to run errands out of the office and my mother doesn't drive." She shook her head. "I don't think we want to open that can of worms."

"Look, Ellen isn't going to be back in Regina until Tuesday evening. Why don't you let your mother come in and answer the phones during the day on Monday and Tuesday? It will give her something to do and it definitely will help us out. You don't have to even discuss with Madeline the possibility of staying on permanently, just try her out. Get a feel for her. If I'm wrong, those two days will show us that. You can thank her and let her go back to Weyburn and she won't even know she was on trial. You can post an ad for a receptionist and no one will be hurt. Think about it over the weekend, will ya? Hmm?"

Maisie said nothing as she chewed her food and Ruby fielded another phone call.

"Okay, I'll think about it." When Ruby smiled, Maisie added, "No promises. I'll just think about it."

Madeline came to work with Maisie on Monday morning and manned the phone calls. She looked quite professional in one of her latest outfits. Ruby showed her the filing system they used and gave her several folders to put away. They had only a few clients' appointments on those days, but Madeline managed to find common ground for conversation in all instances, mostly resorting to the latest television news. Maisie gave her receipts to sort and total on the adding machine. It took longer than it should have because Madeline had to one-finger her way around the numbered keys, but she handled it well.

At the close of day on Tuesday, all three women celebrated

Madeline's initiation into the working class at a restaurant down the street. When supper was drawing to a close, Ruby motioned Maisie toward the washroom.

"Are you not going to invite Madeline to come on board as receptionist in the office?"

"No — ." Before she could continue the door opened and someone came in. Maisie caught the disappointment in Ruby's eyes before they rejoined Madeline at their table.

Maisie explained to her on Wednesday morning in the privacy of her office, that she was more than pleased with her mother's work but felt it would be too much to uproot her mother from her home and expect her to make a new home in a city she was not all that familiar with.

"Besides, I'm afraid I'd have no life of my own. Nor would she. It's better she maintain her independence. Mom would anticipate our sharing an apartment and I would be spending twenty-four hours a day, seven days a week with her. We're getting along well now and she's confident enough to come up and visit whenever she wants. She's becoming interested in what's going on around her and not afraid to try new things, like joining a bowling league. It's not a given anymore that I'll travel to Weyburn every weekend I have free. She's getting physically stronger. I can't remember the last time I heard her complain about feeling weak or bone-achy. Or that her lumbago was bothering her.

"The business is doing well and I'm reaching a point where I'd really like to get a life of my own. I'm not involved in anything that isn't business related and it would be nice to find a man I can enjoy some evenings with."

Ruby's face lit up. "I was hoping you hadn't forgotten there's a whole part of life that you're neglecting. I didn't think about Madeline becoming your sole companion. I thought her being here and involved in your business might free up some of your time to get a social life. I always felt bad when your weekends were taken up travelling to go help your mother when you should be curling, or dancing, or going to movies where you might meet a nice man." Ruby grasped Maisie's hand. "I shouldn't have interfered. I guess I'm just that much closer to your mom's age that I find her fun to be with. I forget that she's your mother and you don't need her involved in every minute of your day … and night. Forgive me." She started toward the door then stopped. "Oh, by the way, that client of yours, Glen Grayson, called just as I got in this morning, looking for you."

"Oh. Does he have a question about his farm business? Am I to call him?"

"No. He just said to tell you that his wife gave birth a month early. He said you would be happy to know that mother and son are both doing well and that the Grayson Family Farm tradition is in fine health as well."

SIXTEEN
1969

TAX SEASON. LIKE CHRISTMAS SEASON is to merchants, tax season is to accountants. About seventy per cent of their entire annual income is amassed between December 31 of one year and April 30 of the following year. Maisie thought she had prepared herself for it by taking a two-week vacation in Florida during the latter part of November. She had done so in the fall of 1967 also. It was only mid-March, but she was already counting the weeks until May. The first day of May was akin to the start of a vacation.

Her business had remained steady. Ruby had decided it wasn't too late for her, at her matronly age of forty-seven years, to enrol in the Certified General Accountants program. Maisie was ecstatic and was happy to sponsor Ruby's training. Ruby passed the first level with ease but was finding the second level more taxing. Maisie tried to involve her in their clients' tax requirements as much as possible.

"I'm going to give you the Grayson Farm file to work with. They have a good clean bookkeeping system so it shouldn't be a problem for you. Mrs. Grayson, Shelley, is meticulous with her posting and balancing so there hasn't been too much that needed adjusting at year end in the past. You worked on it the first year they came to our firm. Remember?"

"When do you usually get their file?"

"I'm expecting it any day now. They've been pretty good at giving us about four to six weeks to work on it. Glen usually hand delivers their box of goodies. We've received their permission letters to contact their bank for the confirmations and loan statements already, so it's just a matter of receiving their files."

"Didn't I see something in the news recently about their farm being on the leading edge of a new process for the seeding or harvesting of wheat? I believe they're one of a select few prairie farms using the process. It was on the local news. A shorter blurb was even on CBC News."

"I didn't see it. I wonder if they received a government grant. We'll have to make a note and remember to ask Glen about it."

"How is Ellen doing with our new restaurant chain? She was having difficulty understanding the franchise system, and how royalties are accounted for."

"She's learning. One good thing is she's not afraid to ask questions. I can't believe how much she's enjoying bookkeeping. She doesn't miss secretarial work at all. I think she's got a future in accounting, Maisie. I wouldn't be surprised if she doesn't move in the same direction as you and me."

"Good. I wish I could say the same thing about Tess. She is struggling. As a secretary her skills are adequate, but as a receptionist, she's lacking in personality big time." Tess was the office clerk who had replaced Ellen.

"She is quiet. I don't hear her chatting to the clients at all. A simple greeting, 'Take a seat,' and that's it for conversation. I still think your mom does a great job when she's here."

Every now and again, Ruby would remind Maisie that the clients commented kindly about Madeline when she filled in on Tess's increasingly frequent days off. It was worth thinking about, Maisie supposed, but it would be at a cost to Maisie's personal life which, at the present time, was non-existent. She had tried to make time for social activities, but time after time she found herself cancelling meetings and events. The romance department wasn't much better; the men she met were either shallow and self-centred or too eager to become bed mates. Every time she joined a social or athletic group of some kind, work took over and she ran out of excuses for last-minute cancellations. She had pretty well come to terms with a work/home existence and she didn't need her mother reminding her she should marry and think about starting a family like her brother. Too many times she had to listen to the same old litany about how her sister-in-law, Jeanne, was able to manage a career and a healthy home life for Jeremy and their son. If she can do it so should Maisie be able to, *yada yada yada*. When in the office, her mother tended to look at every male client as a candidate as husband for her single, long-in-the-tooth daughter.

Maisie gave Ellen a client's bank statements to reconcile then checked her schedule for the day. Around mid-morning she heard someone calling her name in the outer office.

"Hello? Is anyone here? Maisie? Yoo-hoo."

It was Shelley Grayson. Glen's wife. "Is your receptionist on her break?"

"Oh. Sorry. Maybe she's in the washroom."

The phone rang and when Tess didn't reappear, Maisie excused herself to answer it. The caller was looking for information and preferred to get the answers now rather than have to call back. Shelley seemed irritated at being left standing, and plopped huffily into a chair. When the call was completed, Maisie went to Ellen's desk and asked her to take over reception until Tess came back.

"I'm very sorry, Shelley. Come into my office. Would you like some coffee?"

"No, I'm in a hurry. I just came to drop our work off since I had to be in the city anyway."

She had come in empty-handed and Maisie was going to question where the box was when she noticed the sling holding Shelley's left arm. "Did you have an accident?"

"I, uh … yes.

"Oh, no. What happened?"

"I fell."

"Were you alone?"

"I … No. Yes. It's okay, no great harm done." She looked around the office.

Was she embarrassed? It was apparent she didn't like Maisie questioning her.

"Do you mind sending someone down for the box? I can't carry it. As you can see."

"Of course, you can't. I'll go down with you and get it myself. Is there anything you want to talk about while you're here? Any questions?"

"Talk about? No." She seemed confused. "Oh, you mean about the book work. No. It's pretty straight forward just like previous years. If you have any questions you can call me … or Glen. Can we go and get it now? Like I said, I'm in a hurry."

"Certainly. Let me get my jacket. Are you in the parking lot?"

"I'm on the street out front."

Sure enough, she was in a no parking zone and blocking traffic. They retrieved the box from the back of the station wagon and Shelley bid her a quick goodbye before taking off down the street. Maisie was left standing on the sidewalk holding the heavy box and wondering what in the world had just happened.

"Was that Mrs. Grayson I heard a few minutes ago?" Ruby came out of her office and took the box from Maisie.

"Yes."

"I was hoping to go through her work while she was still here in case I had to ask her anything."

"She was in a hurry."

"She must have been. Her husband certainly is more sociable than she is. He at least takes time to have a coffee, a muffin and some conversation before he leaves."

"Maybe you can start on their work tomorrow. Once you have it sorted, if you have any questions, give them to me and I'll call them. Shelley seemed perturbed that she was kept waiting while I took a telephone call. I can't say as I blame her. I hate it when I'm in a place of business and the staff pays more attention to the phone than they do the customer in front of them. Speaking of which, where is Tess?"

"I don't know. Her purse is gone and there's no sign of her."

"I'll speak to her when she decides to grace us with an appearance."

About ten minutes later, Maisie heard Tess back at her desk and went out to confront her, but a client came in before she had a chance to speak to the young woman.

The day progressed with everyone working on backlogs on their individual desks. Around 4 o'clock, Tess buzzed Maisie that Mr. Grayson was on the phone.

"Hello, Glen. Your beautiful wife was here this morning with your bookkeeping files."

"So she *was* there. About what time did she leave?"

"She wasn't here more than a few minutes. I believe it was around ten or ten-thirty."

"Did she say where she was going from there?"

"No. Sorry. She only said she was in a hurry. She wasn't her usual talkative self. Is there a problem?"

"I'm not sure. I expected her back by early afternoon. It's not like her to be late. Billy has to be picked up from his babysitter's and I'm not available this afternoon. However, that's not your concern." Maisie could picture him running his fingers through his hair as he did when in the middle of something. "At least I know she got there okay. I'll call the babysitter and ask her to hang onto our boy for a little while longer. Maybe Shelley's going straight there. Nice talking to you, Maisie. Call if you need anything more for the year end."

He disconnected the call.

Strange. I hope there isn't a problem. Shelley certainly wasn't herself this morning.

The next day, she found a pretext to call. She was concerned about Shelley's frame of mind and the fact she had a bad arm with which to drive a long distance. Ruby informed her they were missing items they would need, so Maisie used that as an excuse to call their home. She was relieved when Shelley answered.

"Good morning, Shelley. It's Maisie Forbes calling." She decided not to tell the woman about Glen's call the afternoon before. "I hope you had a pleasant drive home yesterday. I couldn't help thinking about your driving your big car all that way with a lame arm."

"I wouldn't say it was a pleasant drive, but I made it. Is there something you need?"

Maisie again was astounded by the woman's abruptness. "It's not urgent, but we are missing two statements concerning the line of credit from the bank. We need them to determine what portion of the payments involved are interest charges. If you can mail those to us, it will help to expedite the completion of your books."

"I'll look for them. I don't understand why they're not in the box. I keep everything together. Is that everything?"

"Yes, I believe so for now."

"You believe so? As in you don't know for sure? Maybe I'll wait a day or two in case you find something else is missing. Postage is expensive and it's best if I can send it all at once. If I don't hear from you by the end of the week, I'll go ahead and post them."

"Thank you, Shel—" She heard the hum of a dead line.

"And a pleasant day to you, too." She frowned as she placed the phone on the receiver.

SEVENTEEN

TWO DAYS LATER, GLEN WAS waiting in the outer office when Maisie returned from lunch.

"Glen. Did we have an appointment?"

"No. I have the papers you needed and since I was in the neighbourhood ..." He smiled sheepishly.

"In the neighbourhood, eh? Okay. Come into my office."

She instructed Tess to hold her calls and closed the door behind Glen.

"What's going on, Glen?"

"What makes you think there's something going on?"

"Two days ago, your wife was in here unannounced and in a hurry. It was a long drive for someone with an injured arm, by the way. She was abrupt when I called to tell her about the papers we needed. In the meantime, you called to question her whereabouts and now today you show up unannounced with the papers she was going to drop in the mail. We are not a mere twenty-minute drive from your farm, Glen. So, I will ask again. What is going on?"

He rested one leg over his knee as was his habit and ran the fingers of both hands through his hair. He motioned for her to sit opposite him.

"Do you want coffee?"

"No. I want you to sit down. I don't really know why I came here."

"If you don't, then who does?"

He hesitated then leaned forward, elbows on knees. "Did Shelley tell you what happened to her arm?"

"She told me she fell."

"That's the story she's sticking to." He shook his head then stood and paced the room.

"Is there another version?"

"I don't know. Doc Mooney says it looks more like someone twisted it. The bruising and the way the bone is broken isn't consistent with a fall."

"I see. Why would she lie?"

"That's what the doctor asked me."

She looked up quickly. "Stand still, for heaven's sake. Better yet, sit back down."

After he had settled on the sofa again, she buzzed Tess and asked her to bring in two cups of coffee. Surprisingly, the girl was at her desk and brought them in quickly while avoiding eye contact with Glen, then left.

"Are you saying the doctor thinks you did that to her?"

"He didn't come right out and say it, but yes, I think he does."

"If Shelley didn't fall, who do you think would hurt her and why wouldn't she tell you?"

"I don't know. Look. All I know is that she was out a couple of weeks ago and called me from the hospital to tell me she had been with friends, had fallen and broken her arm, and could I come and get her?"

"And you don't believe her?"

"I did until the other day when she showed up here. She had told me that the doc wanted her to see a specialist in Regina to make sure the bone was set properly and that she'd bring our books up for you. I didn't even know she had come that particular day until the babysitter called and said she had left Billy with her. I had to meet a guy in Indian Head that day, so I had left around seven o'clock and got home around two. After the babysitter called, I phoned the doctor's office to get the number of the doctor in Regina, but Doc's receptionist was surprised and said he never issued a referral. When she wasn't home by four o'clock, I called you to see if she had even gone up to Regina. She finally got home with Billy, having gone straight to the sitter's and was surprised and seemed upset that I had beat her home. When I told her the doctor didn't know anything about a referral she got all hyper and started screaming about me not trusting her and that it was all done through the hospital. I've never seen her get so hysterical, so I let it go. She's hardly spoken to me since, except to tell me you needed some papers and she was going to put them in the mail. I told her I needed to come to Regina so I'd deliver them."

He stopped and stared at the floor. "I don't believe her, but I don't have any good reason not to, except she's been tense lately and won't talk about it."

"I don't know what to say, Glen. I don't know Shelley well, only from her few office visits. She's always been pleasant and friendly. Until this last time. She seemed, as you say, tense and in a hurry. I went outside with her and after I got the box from the car, she took off so quickly I barely had time to jump out of the way. She definitely was not herself. Do you think she might have some health issues she doesn't want you to know about? Maybe she did see a doctor here but not about her arm. Or maybe it was and there's a problem developing that she's concerned about."

"She didn't say where she was going from here?"

"No, only that she was in a hurry."

"It's tops a two-hour drive. If she left your place around ten thirty, even with an appointment soon after, she should have been home by three o'clock. I don't know what to make of it. I wish she'd talk to me about what's bothering her." He stood again and walked to the window. "I especially wish she'd tell me what really happened to her arm."

Tess buzzed to tell Maisie her scheduled client was waiting for her.

"Glen, you must know her friends. Can you not ask one of them if they know what happened?"

"Not without Shelley finding out I was questioning them." He moved closer to where she was standing and placed his hands on her shoulders. "I don't want to upset her any more than she already is. She is a good wife and mother, Maisie. I hate to see her in the state she's in. She's never been secretive or dishonest with me. This is something new. Thanks for listening." He kissed her forehead and turned to go. "I really do have an appointment this afternoon. Any chance you're free for an early dinner later?"

She took a deep breath and released it. "I'm not sure that's a good idea, Glen. Not while there are unanswered questions in your relationship with your wife."

He hesitated as if to argue but nodded and said, "You're probably right."

She worked her way through meetings with two more clients before settling in to actually working on some accounts. The other women finished their work and locked up as they left. Maisie continued to work until well past 9 o'clock then closed the last ledger and went home in time to watch the evening news. That night she broke into tears and sobbed herself to sleep. She hadn't felt the loneliness of her existence until Glen had left her office after her refusal of his dinner invitation. An invitation she would have given almost anything to accept. God help her, she still loved the man.

Ruby soon had the Grayson file completed to the extent she was qualified to work on it. She discussed a couple of items with Maisie before an appointment was scheduled for the following week. Since Maisie was going to her mother's for the weekend anyway, Glen agreed to meet her in Weyburn to discuss their file and sign the papers..

EIGHTEEN

MAISIE LEFT THE OFFICE EARLY on Friday. She was meeting Glen at 5 o'clock in Weyburn for an early dinner before an overnight at her mother's. It was a warm mid-April day with the promise of a great weekend. Much better weather than the weekend before in which she had celebrated Easter by working. She shouldn't be taking any personal time this weekend either but Ruby and Ellen seemed to have a good handle on the current files. It looked promising that everything would be finished in good time for their clients' tax filings. Tess was not proving to be much help at tax time. While she was an excellent typist, she was not good with figures. Her attendance at work had improved somewhat. She was a smoker and left the office often to go downstairs for a cigarette. Ruby had mentioned that the girl tended to hang around Maisie's door when she had clients in her office. Almost as if the girl were eavesdropping. Maisie said she'd keep an eye on it.

She now locked the drawers in her desk just in case the girl was snooping. There was nothing she could do about customer files because Tess needed access to them.

It was a bad time to be going to her mother's, but she couldn't help it. She was staying only one night to help her mother move furniture and prepare her place for painters coming in. It had been arranged and was being paid for by the landlord, so Madeline didn't have too much say in the timing. Her mother had lived in the same small bungalow since moving to Weyburn. It had two tiny bedrooms, an adequate kitchen, a dining room and a comfortable living room. It was small but all her mother needed. Although how she could be content to spend day and night in that place without any social life was beyond Maisie.

She and her mother had become much closer since her mother had at least overcome her fear of travelling. Not only had Madeline made several trips to Regina the last few years, she had even gone to a concert with Ruby in Winnipeg — the first time her mother had traveled outside of Saskatchewan. They had travelled by train and she had enjoyed eating in the dining car. Soon, she may even be ready to get on a plane and go to Florida with Maisie.

First, though, she wanted her mother to see the grandeur of the Rocky Mountains. Maisie had only experienced the magnificence of them the year previously. An end-of-tax-season treat to herself last May. She had wanted her mother to come with her, but the woman was afraid the mountain air might not be good for her. In response, Maisie had bought her mother a copy of the classic novel *Heidi* before leaving on the train.

She had aimed to have the Grayson file completed before Easter, but they had been delayed by the wait for all the necessary paperwork. As she drove, she remembered Glen's visit to her office and hoped that everything was reconciled between him and his wife. The strange chain of events had left her feeling uneasy and Glen's invitation for a quick supper that night he was in Regina hadn't sat right with her. She had longed to go, had even been sorry she'd refused, but in the end, she knew she had been right to do so. That man still stirred emotions in her that she wasn't sure she could fend off if push came to shove.

Shove. That word made her remember Shelley's injured arm. Had the doctor been right? Had someone deliberately hurt her? Who? Glen? No, not possible. Not soft-spoken, gentle Glen. She believed that in spite of his friendliness to her, he really loved and respected his wife. If not him, then who? Of course, the doctor could be wrong and her injury *might* have been the result of a fall.

She approached Weyburn and slowed for the turn onto Government Road then onto Railway Street. She was early but Glen, she knew from experience, was always early, too. Sure enough, as she turned into the parking lot of the restaurant, she spotted his pickup parked near the door. It wasn't even 5 o'clock yet but that was fine, her mother would be pleased if she arrived early. Madeline still worried about her daughter on the highway after dark. Old habits die hard.

Glen stood as she approached the booth he was seated in. After the customary hug and kiss on the cheek they sat, and each ordered a beer. Glen sank into the comfort of the faux leather bench and their shoes scuffed together under the narrow table. Silly, but it sent a sensation through Maisie of bare toes entangled under a sheet. Their drinks arrived and Maisie ordered a plate of liver and onions, which caused a raised eyebrow from Glen. He ordered the meatloaf special.

"Liver and onions?"

Maisie unwrapped her knife and fork from the napkin. "I love liver but never think to buy it in the grocery store. It's what I guess you'd call a comfort food from my childhood years, so I order it whenever I see it on a menu."

"I would never associate liver with anyone's childhood except as something to shudder about."

"Really. A farmer with cattle who doesn't like liver!"

"I don't mind it once in a while but it's not something I would order from a menu."

During their meal, the conversation ran the gamut of the weather, hockey play-offs, the politics of Prime Minister Pierre Elliot Trudeau and finally arrived at the financial analysis of the Grayson farm. Glen glanced at his watch.

"I have the tax forms in my briefcase for you to sign. We can go over the financial statements before you do so. You can get the box with your files and ledgers from my car when we go out."

Glen was perusing the financial statements and finally the bottom line on the tax remittance. "We're managing to hold our own against the big boys."

"Yes, you are. I would say your family farm is quite healthy, Glen. You can be proud of yourself."

"Thanks. I hope we can maintain the health of the farm until my son grows into it."

"Yes, of course, the Grayson Family Farm. I don't think you have anything to worry about. Your farm looks like it will be self-sustainable for many years to come."

"I've been lucky. There have been a few lean years, but diversification has helped see us through."

"How's your son doing?"

"He's a strong healthy young boy. After getting off to a slow start, he's certainly made up for it and can hold his own with other youngsters his age. He'll be three years old in September."

"My, it doesn't seem that long ago that Shelley arrived that first time in my office. She was early into her pregnancy, but I guess it has been three years. I'm happy you have continued to use our firm for your accounting needs."

He glanced at his watch again.

"That was a difficult year for her. She had to stay in bed many days when she wished she could have been up and enjoying the nice summer. I keep thinking it would be nice for Billy to have a brother or sister, but I hate the thought of putting Shelley through another nine months of bed rest. I guess I should be happy with the healthy son that I have."

The waitress brought them coffee and he played with his spoon appearing to be deep in thought.

Finally, he looked across at her. "You've not married, Maisie. How come?"

His question caught her unawares. "I guess I've been too busy getting my business off the ground to even think about it."

"Ah, yes. Your career. Your mother had told me that you were intent on having a career at all cost."

"Pardon me? Where did that come from?"

"Sorry. I just remember that Christmas dinner I shared with you and your mother. She made it quite clear that nothing — nothing with a capital N — was to stop you in your pursuit of a career and independence. I can't remember her exact words but there seemed to be a veiled warning or ultimatum in them. It made me feel like a selfish bastard for wanting a portion of you for myself. You probably don't remember, but we went for a walk along the streets in her neighbourhood. We looked in all the living room windows and admired their decorations. That's when I realized that you and I were seeing different things. You were taking delight in the Christmas decorations, while I was looking at the happiness of the families inside those living rooms. That's when I realized our views of life were different. Your future lay in the growth of a career while mine lay in the growth of a family. If we continued on, one of us wasn't going to fulfill our dreams. I couldn't be responsible for you not reaching your goals. Not after the reaming out I was subjected to by your mother. I panicked and drove home that night. I had to think, and I did so for weeks. I decided that no good could come of our continuing to see each other. It would only lead to one of us resenting the other and neither of us being happy."

"I never knew my mother had threatened you. I knew she wasn't happy about you being a farmer, but I never once told her you were a threat to my career."

"I think she was just protecting your interests the only way she knew how." He looked at her with a strange expression. "Maybe *she* was the smart one. I think it worked out for the best. You've got a successful career and I've got a family. Everybody's happy."

Maisie didn't know how to respond. Was he happy? Was she? Her mother *never* seemed happy. Maisie somehow felt Glen wasn't completely happy. His wife seemed unsettled somehow. Maybe it was a temporary bubble in the Grayson family that all couples go through once in a while? But talking about his son had put a smile on Glen's face and a proud gleam in his eye.

"I guess happiness comes in different forms for different people." She didn't realize how much time had elapsed until he looked at his watch again. She looked at hers. It was almost 7 o'clock. "I guess we'd better get going. Our families will be wondering what's keeping us."

She moved to slide out of the booth when Glen put his hand on hers. "I haven't stopped caring you know. I wonder about you often … About what might have been." His smile was forced. "I'm glad I get to see you once a year."

He picked up the bill and strode to the cash register.

"You didn't have to buy supper. You are my client. I am the one who should be thanking you for your business." She opened the trunk of her car, which she had parked right next to his truck.

He lifted the box out and put it on the passenger seat in the cab of his vehicle. "I didn't buy supper as a thank you. I bought supper because I wanted to spend a couple of hours with you away from the office."

"Glen, don't even—"

"Don't stop this, Maisie. We both know we'll never be a couple. I'm married and I do happen to love my wife. I would never hurt her. I would never cheat on her. She knows where I am and who I am with. She even reminded me to pay for the supper because you saved us a trip to Regina. So the fact that I'm married shouldn't keep me from enjoying a couple of hours with you once a year. I'm not asking for, nor even suggesting, a relationship — of any kind. Just two hours in your company away from your office and my farm."

"I'm not sure that's a good idea."

"It's a very good idea. It lets me feel like the kid who goes to the circus once a year and pretends he's the guy on the flying trapeze. He knows it will never be him, but he enjoys the sensation if only for the moment. That's all I'm asking. To fly on the trapeze once a year. Don't you have fantasies, Maisie? Don't you ever wish for something even though you know there isn't a chance in hell you'll ever have it?"

He lifted her chin and kissed her firmly on the mouth. "Till the circus comes back to town, Miss Forbes."

NINETEEN

MAISIE REMAINED IN THE PARKING lot long after Glen had driven off. She was jealous. Jealous that he was going home to a beautiful wife and child, both of whom he loved and who loved him and she ... well, she was going to her mother's to help her move furniture. *Had* her mother been the smart one? *Had* everyone got what they'd wanted? She had her successful career and he had a wife and family. Everyone was happy he said. If she were so damn happy, why was she sitting here in a parking lot with tears in her eyes? Why was her heart aching beyond any pain she could have imagined a few years ago? Probably her mother was the happiest of all. She had a daughter who had *not* married a farmer. She had a daughter who *had* made a successful career for herself. She slapped the steering wheel. *Mom, if you knew how unhappy your happiness has made me, would you still be happy?* She knew the answer. Too late, she knew the answer. She turned the key in the ignition then turned her lights on.

"There you are, Maisie. I was starting to worry. I knew you left the office early to meet a client, but I thought you'd be here before dark."

"I told you not to worry about me for supper, Mom. I assumed you would take for granted it would be early evening before I got here."

"So have you eaten, dear?"

"Yes, I did." She hesitated then added. "As a matter of fact, I ate with my client at a restaurant just off the highway here in Weyburn."

"Your client is from Weyburn? You could have met with him or her right here. You didn't have to put out money for a meal."

"He's not from here and he paid for the supper. My client is Glen Grayson. Ruby finished his books a few days ago. I told him I was coming to Weyburn this weekend and I could save him a trip up to Regina. We decided to meet at that family restaurant over on Railway Street."

She set her overnight bag on the hallway floor and splashed some water on her face in the bathroom. Her mother motioned to some snacks on the table in the living room. "If you had supper, you may not want any of these until later."

"Right. Maybe later. I just want to put my feet up and relax for a little bit. It's been a long week and I want to unwind if I can."

She wasn't about to tell her mother that Glen had kissed her and how it had set off an inner turmoil. Damn him anyway! How could he do that and then drive home to his wife and son. She then wondered if that's what bothered her the most. Not that he had taken a liberty he shouldn't have, but that he had someone to go home to while she had only her mother — who detested the man.

She became angry with herself again but this time blaming him for ruining her evening with her mother. She certainly wasn't unwinding. In fact, she was doing the opposite, becoming more and more wound up just thinking about that kiss and, damn him, wishing for another.

"Is something the matter, dear? You seem unsettled. Can I make you a cup of tea?"

"A cup of tea would be nice, Mom. Thanks." She had to settle down. No point in setting off her mother's radar. "Why don't we play a few games of gin rummy?"

At 10 o'clock, the evening news from Regina came on. Thirty minutes into the broadcast, after the national news was finished, the local newscast was interrupted with a breaking story. An accident on Hwy 39 near Estevan resulted in at least one fatality and at least one other person was seriously injured. Police were on the scene and further details were not immediately available.

"Oh, my. That's terrible. People travel at such speeds now. I think this is the third fatality on that stretch of highway since last fall." Her mother was visibly upset by the news. "You can see why I worry about you on the highway. Especially after dark. It's not that I don't trust your driving, dear, but you just don't know about the other drivers on the road."

They had given the time of the accident, so she knew it had still been light out or at least not past dusk but she wasn't going to contradict her mother. The woman was visibly upset.

"Do you understand now why I'm not eager to get a driver's license? I don't need a car for getting about in town and you won't catch me out on the highway. I would be a nervous wreck before I even got anywhere near Regina."

"Mom, it's just good to know how to drive in case of an emergency."

"Emergency? What kind of emergency? Heavens. We have an ambulance service. And I cannot think of any situation that would force me to drive a vehicle."

"What if you and I were on the highway together and I took sick? We might be miles away from the nearest phone to call an ambulance. You would have to drive us to a phone or hospital."

"That's rather far-fetched but I suppose it could happen. I'll keep it in mind. In the meantime, I can't help feeling sorry for the families involved in this accident. How will I ever fall asleep not knowing what happened?"

"Turn on the radio on your bedside table. They may have more details before you fall asleep. Tune it to the Estevan station rather than Regina." Maisie stretched. "I'm quite tired, Mom. I think I'll turn in now. We have a lot of work to do tomorrow. While we've got things moved away from the walls, I'll clean your windows and wipe down the baseboards for you."

"I can do that myself. No point in you overdoing it when you have a busy week ahead of you. I just need your help to move everything to the middle of the rooms."

"What will you do when the painters are finished? You can't just leave it until I can come back again in a few weeks."

"The Barton boy up the street will come. I told him I would pay him and a friend of his twenty dollars to move it all back. I just can't afford to pay him twice."

Maisie knew it was useless to say she would have given her mother the money for the boy to come twice. Either the woman would think she didn't want to come, or her feelings would be hurt that she had to rely on her daughter for financial help. Better to let it go and not say anything at all.

When she got comfortable in the guest bed, her thoughts strayed to what Glen had said about her mother's conversation with him that Christmas right here in this house. Had her mother really threatened him? Maybe not threatened but made him feel selfish and undeserving of Maisie's love. She remembered the feeling of something not being quite right when she'd come back into the dining room and her mother's leaving so abruptly. Why had he not told her then instead of ignoring her calls and letters? It had been the following spring that she'd gone to his home and encountered Shelley for the first time. How differently their lives might have been if only he had taken her calls or answered her letters instead of ignoring her. And now that kiss tonight. She could still feel his lips against hers. She had just drifted off to sleep when she heard her mother's phone ringing.

Her mother was shouting and almost bouncing off the floor. "What do you mean you have to talk to Maisie? You can't just call her here in the middle of the night. You are a married man. Or have you forgotten that, Mr. Grayson? I'm hanging up this phone. You can call back in the morning with your supposed emergency."

She placed the phone back on the stand with force.

"Mom, what's going on? I gather that was Glen on the phone?"

"Yes. He claims he has to talk to you. He said it's an emergency. Does the man take me for a fool? He has a wife to discuss his emergencies with. You are his accountant not his doctor or lawyer. Nor, thank God, his wife."

"You should have let speak to—" The phone rang again. Maisie beat her mother to it. "It must be an emergency for him to risk your wrath by calling again. Hello?"

"Maisie, I'm at the hospital. Shelley is dead and my son may not make it."

"What? Oh, no. Oh, no. Were they involved in that accident that's on the news?"

"News? I don't know. I just know that my son might die and my wife already has. The police are questioning me. They wanted to know my whereabouts tonight. Apparently, the accident is suspicious."

Maisie fell into the chair by the phone. "My God, Glen. What are you saying? Do they think you're somehow responsible? What do you mean, it's suspicious?"

"I don't know the details. I've been sitting in the surgical waiting room. All I can think about is Billy. He can't die, Maisie. He just can't." His voice broke and she could hear him sobbing.

"Is it the hospital in Estevan? Do you want me to come there?"

"No. No. There's nothing you can do. It's just that I think the police may come to your mother's house. Just a minute." She heard him muffle the phone, but she caught a male voice in the background. Then … "I have to go. The police tell me I can't talk to anyone. I have to …" The line went dead.

Maisie did the same foolish thing that everyone does, clicking the button on the phone base. "Glen? Glen?"

"What's going on? Was it his family in that accident? Why is he calling you?"

"Yes, Mother. His wife is dead and his son may follow."

"What's this about the police?"

"Apparently, the accident may not have been an accident. He said there was something suspicious about it and the police are questioning his whereabouts during that time frame."

"Humph. I suppose it was while he was enjoying supper with you, Maisie?"

Startled by her mother's tone of voice, she looked quickly at the woman. "You make it sound like we were having a tryst while his family was being murdered."

Madeline started to speak but Maisie put her hand up. "Don't. Please don't. This is not the time, Mother." She went into the bedroom and put on her housecoat. "Glen said the police may come to confirm that he was here in Weyburn at the time of the accident."

"With you."

"Yes. With me. I'll make coffee because I won't be sleeping any more tonight."

"I'm sorry, Maisie. I don't want to be hurtful. It just seems that nothing good happens when you are with that man. I'll make the coffee. You go put some clothes on in case the police come."

The police did arrive within the hour and Maisie was able to give them the exact timing of their dinner together. She verified that it was a business meeting and she was able to show them her copy of the papers he'd signed. They thanked her and left. She inquired about news of his son, Billy, but they were unwilling — to tell her anything.

Her mother turned the kitchen radio on to see if there were any updates. The reports were mostly repeats of the original news with no names released pending notification of next of kin.

About 6 o'clock in the morning, there was a knock on the back door. It was the woman who lived next door. "I saw your lights on and figured you were up. I noticed the police here earlier and wondered if there was anything wrong. You weren't broken into or anything, were you?"

Madeline assured her neighbour there was no reason for alarm. She explained that the police had come with news of a death concerning one of Maisie's clients. She thanked her neighbour for her concern and told her to go back to bed. Madeline explained to Maisie that this neighbour was a snoopy old woman who didn't sleep well and probably heard everything that went on in the neighbourhood.

"That was nice of her to ask though, Mom. A lot of people just want to be left alone and can't be bothered worrying about their neighbours."

"What are you going to do, Maisie?"

"I honestly don't know, Mom. I don't know whether to stay here in case I'm needed or go back to Regina and wait for further word. I hope, once they realize Glen is not responsible for the accident, that they'll let him stay with his son at the hospital. It must be agony for him to know his son is fighting for his life all alone. Above all, I pray that his son survives. I don't know what Glen will do if that little boy dies. He's his pride and joy."

"Isn't there any other family member that can sit with the boy?"

"I don't know. Glen mentioned once that Shelley's mother came to help with the housework during her pregnancy."

She looked around the living room. "Why don't we just get started on moving this stuff. We'll leave it arranged so that you can get around it and watch TV and sleep in your bed tonight. I don't know how you're going to do that with the smell of paint in here."

"They assured me the paint they use doesn't smell as strong as some brands and that it won't be a problem at all. I believe them because my friend, Charlotte, had these same guys do her place and she was able to cook her supper that night and slept like a baby."

"Promise me that if you start coughing or wheezing, you'll open the windows wide and go to Charlotte's place. If you leave it to air out overnight, it should be fine by tomorrow. In fact, why don't you come back to Regina with me?"

"No, I can't do that. I have to be here for the painters and I'll be fine."

"Okay, Mom. What time do you expect them?"

"They promised to be here by eleven o'clock this morning."

"As soon as they arrive, we'll go out to the mall for lunch, see a matinee movie and do some shopping. By then, they should at least have your kitchen and living room finished. I'll head for home about five o'clock. I only hope we know more about Glen's son before I leave."

Madeline told her daughter she was glad she was going back to Regina and not to Estevan.

"You don't know that child, Maisie. You haven't even seen him. Or have you?"

"Shelley has brought him to Regina a couple of times and Glen is always showing us pictures of him. He looks like a sweet little boy. Glen will have a hard time dealing with it if that child doesn't survive."

"What about his wife's death? That won't bother him?"

"Of course, it will. They loved each other a great deal, but the death of a child I would imagine must be almost impossible to live with."

"He'll get through it. I don't know why it's your problem."

"It's not my problem but I do feel sorry for Glen. That poor man."

Her mother picked up their coffee cups and suggested that Maisie try to get a couple hours of sleep since she'd be driving home later in the day.

TWENTY

MAISIE ARRIVED HOME ON SATURDAY just as the sun was setting. She had heard nothing more from Glen but the news reports on the radio said that the child seriously injured in the highway accident was in critical condition with undetermined injuries. The cause of the accident was still under investigation and there were many unanswered questions regarding the scene. No comments were released from the police other than saying the husband of the woman killed had been questioned and released.

She was relieved that they hadn't held him in custody. He would want to be with his son at the hospital. Should she call him? What was suspicious about the accident and why would they look at Glen being involved? Why had they gone so far as to question her at her mother's? She was dying to talk to Glen and maybe get some answers but best she keep her distance for the time being. If he wanted to talk to her, he knew how to reach her. The poor man. She couldn't imagine what he must be going through. Her thoughts turned to prayers as she tried to picture the little boy lying in the hospital bed with who knows what kind of injuries. She had seen lots of pictures of him. Glen had a wallet full of them. Billy was smiling in all of them, beaming with the innocent happiness of a toddler. She prayed that Glen would see his son take over the farm one day.

Sunday, she worked all day in the office. Ruby came by in the afternoon to finish a file so she could start working on Monday on one of the several still being left daily at their reception desk.

"Any more word from Estevan? Have you spoken with Glen?" Maisie had called Ruby as soon as she arrived home on Saturday to tell her it was Glen's family involved in the horrific accident.

"No." She paused and laid her pencil on the open ledger on her desk. "Ruby, I'm sure you've heard on the news that Glen was taken in for questioning shortly after it happened. I don't know what they found that would make them think he had anything to do with it, but they even came to my mother's in the middle of the night to question me about the timing of our supper meeting on Friday evening."

"What? Why?" Ruby looked dumbfounded. Her eyebrow rose. "My God, don't tell me they think you and Glen are romantically involved! That's ridiculous."

"I don't know what they think. All I know is that he wasn't allowed to speak to me and I'm afraid to call him. I guess they're afraid of collusion even though my mother confirmed what time I arrived at her house. All they had to do was check with the restaurant."

"Why would the police ... Do you think the Graysons might have been suffering marital problems? I can't picture a better family man than Glen. My goodness, he talked constantly about his wife, his son and his farm. It seemed he was literally living his dream."

"Yes." Maisie tried not to show the discomfort she felt at Ruby's words. "He was living his dream."

"As for you, I pray all the time for you to find time for some romance. Maybe there's a nice man like Glen Grayson out there just fantasizing about a woman like you. But you live, eat and think this business of yours. When would you possibly have had time to have an affair with a man who lives at least a hundred and twenty-five miles away? That's almost a five-hour return drive."

"I guess our dinner on Friday evening could have raised a few eyebrows. Even my mother questioned my motive for meeting him at a restaurant in Weyburn instead of at her house."

"Madeline? Why would she do that? It's more professional to have a business meeting in a restaurant than in your mother's kitchen. She doesn't even know him, does she?"

"They've met."

"Even so. Why would anyone, including the police, jump to that kind of conclusion?"

Maisie could feel the warmth creeping up her neck. The flush might soon be noticeable. She had to change the direction of their conversation quickly. It was a surprise to find out that her mother had never told Ruby about her involvement with Glen years ago. Then again, maybe Madeline wouldn't have wanted to answer any questions about why her daughter and Glen hadn't pursued it.

She stood with her mug of coffee and went to the window. "The thought crossed my mind that with the death of Shelley, Glen has not only lost his wife, but he's lost his bookkeeper. I'm sure that hasn't even loomed on his radar yet. But sooner or later, we're going to have to deal with this. It's still early, but in another month or so, we may be called upon to help with the problem."

"How can we do his bookkeeping on a regular basis by long distance?"

"I'll try to figure out a few angles, but we'll wait until the dust settles. If things don't go well with his son, he may not even want to continue with the farm."

"That would be so sad. The farm is his life. I don't think that will happen. Do you know the extent of his son's injuries?"

"Only that they're life threatening. Whatever that means. I don't know if head injuries are involved or internal organs or broken bones. I'm wishing he would call. But of course he has more on his mind than his accountant."

"That's true."

Maisie sat down and picked up her pencil once again. Ruby poured a cup of coffee on the way to her own office.

On the late evening news, she learned that Billy had come out of a coma and was able to talk but was still in very serious condition due to severe lower body injuries. They were keeping him sedated to help with the pain. A newsman reported that apparently the accident had occurred at a junction of two roads and indications were that a vehicle must have forced Mrs. Grayson's station wagon off the road and into the lone tree on the side of the highway. She had been travelling at a high rate of speed and was unable to stop. The impact had thrown her through the windshield as she had not fastened her seatbelt. The young boy had been pinned by the dashboard into a toddler seat in the front of the vehicle. He had also suffered facial injuries from the broken windshield glass. There were no witnesses, but a skid mark indicated another vehicle may have caused the accident, and then fled.

The blinding sun had been low on the horizon casting everything in shadows. A woman in the first car on the scene did see a vehicle but it was too far in the distance to know what kind.

So it happened shortly before Glen and I left the restaurant. The sun had just set when we left around 7:15 p.m.

She was relieved that outside of some cuts to his face, Billy had not suffered brain injury. Broken bones could be fixed, but a damaged brain was another thing altogether. She wondered where Shelley had been going that she was travelling too fast to stop.

On Monday morning, everyone was busy working on various files. There were two weeks remaining to clean up all the income tax work for their clients. Maisie instructed her staff not to accept any new work no matter how much the potential client begged. If they insisted, they were to understand there would be no guarantee that the work would be finished by April 30. Maisie was giving guidance to Ellen on a matter when Tess told her there was a long-distance phone call for her from Mr. Grayson.

Silence fell in the office. The staff was aware of the accident and that Mr. Grayson was the client to whom Miss Forbes had been delivering the financial statements.

"I'm sorry, Miss Forbes, I know I should have taken a message when you're busy, but I thought, well …"

Maisie was already walking toward her desk. "That's okay, Tess. I'll take the call in here." She closed the door behind her.

"Glen?"

"Maisie. I don't know what I'm going to do."

"Don't worry about your business, Glen. We've done the tax filing and there's nothing more for you to do now but take care of your personal affairs."

"I'm not talking about my farm. I, I'm …"

"I am so sorry about Shelley. It must be such a blow to you."

"Thank you. But it's not Shelley. It's Billy."

She could hear Glen sobbing at the other end of the line.

"Oh, no, Glen. Did he …? Is he …?" She couldn't form the word.

"He's not dead. Not completely. Only half of him is." He broke into full blown sobs.

TWENTY-ONE
1970

MAISIE DROVE WITH ELLEN IN late March to Estevan. Between the two of them, they were going to make sure all the book work and necessary papers were included in the box coming to the office for the year-end financial statements and tax filing.

It had been a hectic, depressing year for everyone connected to the Grayson Family Farm. Shelley Grayson had been laid to rest amid confusion over the way she had died and whether it had been accidental or deliberate. The police file was not closed on the case. Glen had not been charged with any wrongdoing other than having supper with an old girlfriend at the time of his wife's death. The driver that caused the accident had never been found. Their son had suffered a crushed spine and was paralyzed from the hips down. He would be confined to a wheelchair for the rest of his life.

Glen had been beside himself with grief, more so for his son's disability than his wife's death, even though everyone knew he had been a devoted husband and cared deeply for his wife. After he had arrived one early autumn afternoon at Maisie's office, with one too many beers under his belt, he confessed to her that no matter how hard he tried, he couldn't help but blame his wife for her own death and their son's injuries.

"Why didn't she buckle herself in and why didn't she have Billy secured in the back seat? She insisted on us buying that new station wagon exactly for that purpose. She wanted a big safe car that had seat belts. She was adamant about it."

"Maybe she was in a hurry. Maybe she wasn't feeling well and just wanted to get home. Maybe Billy wasn't feeling good and she wanted him sitting up front with her." Maisie handed Glen a cup of black coffee. "There are so many possibilities, you'll drive yourself crazy trying to figure it out."

She gave him a dark look. "At least she wasn't driving drunk like you just did."

It obviously startled him to hear her tone of voice. "I didn't drink before I got to Regina."

"Accidents happen in the city, too. You could have hit a pedestrian. Glen, you have to think of your son. Who will drive him around if you were to get pulled over and lose your license for driving while under the influence of alcohol? Or what if you caused injury to another person's child?"

He immediately paled, obviously upset by her questions. He took several long gulps of coffee. "You're right. You are absolutely right!"

"Glen, it's natural to want to blame someone for what happened to Billy, but don't blame Shelley. She was the ultimate victim and she's not here to defend herself. You and she had a good marriage. I hate to see you turning your heart against her. She was an excellent mother and I'm guessing an excellent wife as well. Keep the good memories alive and throw the destructive ones in the garbage.

"You are not by nature a man who feeds hate. I've seen you turn the other cheek a few times. Don't judge when you don't know what was in her heart. Or on her mind. She seemed to be struggling with something that last week so give her a break. She would never intentionally be careless with her son. Deep in your heart you know that. Something was on her mind. We'll never know, but please give her the benefit of the doubt."

He stared at her for a long time. Had she overstepped her bounds? She didn't care. She did not want to see Glen turn into a rancorous, hateful person.

"You are right again. I do want someone to blame. I *need* someone to blame. I'll place my hopes on them catching that hit and run driver so I can tell him to his face what he's done to my family. He's ultimately the one to blame."

He started to cry. "My poor little boy. He doesn't deserve the hand he's been dealt."

"Then help him play it." She placed a hand on Glen's arm. "He needs you. He needs your strength. And he needs you sober!"

"Thank you." He placed a hand over hers. "Thank you."

They went on to discuss the farm bookkeeping. His sister-in-law had always taken care of it before he married Shelley but since then, his brother, who had never been interested in the farm, had moved to another part of Saskatchewan and settled into running a hardware store. It was too far for Neil's wife, Chelsea, to come. There was no one else Glen trusted with the bookkeeping. Over the spring and summer months, Maisie had called with reminders about bills to be paid. His farm workers were paid by the hour and he sent the hours to Maisie bi-weekly so she could prepare the figures for him to write the cheques. By fall, so many things were falling between the cracks, it was becoming a bigger problem with each passing week.

They discussed many options. It was finally decided that Ruby would go down and interview several possible local bookkeepers. Glen thanked Maisie again for her advice, her shoulder to cry on and the ear she loaned him.

"Thank you mainly for being you. Honest and helpful. I appreciate your friendship, Maisie. I don't really have anyone else I can talk to." He kissed her cheek and left.

Ruby found a bookkeeper that seemed more than capable, but Glen found her too nosy and let her go. The next one seemed more interested in Glen than the work at hand, so she bit the dust also. Finally, it was arranged that Ellen would go down bi-weekly, do what could only be done there in a day, and bring the rest back to the office for completion. Glen would pay for her travel and accommodation expenses. It was a workable solution and they had continued in this manner, lessening the trips to monthly for the quieter winter months. Now here it was March and time to gather everything for the final preparation of financial statements for taxes.

It was not a great day for driving. The temperatures were hovering just below the freezing mark and the sky was dark with cloud. Maisie had made reservations at a hotel in Estevan for them to stay in overnight so they wouldn't have to drive back in the dark. The windshield wipers were leaving a fine layer of ice even with the heater going full blast. She was glad when she saw the turn-off to Glen's farm road. Hopefully, as the day progressed, the temperatures would rise above freezing.

When she pulled into the driveway, she took a deep breath. This was going to be difficult. Too many memories. Too many emotions to deal with. Her eyes took in the front porch, the swing, the house, the barn and silos. Her heart gave a lurch. *Come on girl, keep it together. Don't let Ellen see you falter.*

She heard Parker barking as they went up the steps. He pranced between her and Ellen with tail wagging and a soft toy in his mouth.

"Hi, Parker. What have you got? Are you giving me your toy?" Ellen obviously had made friends with the dog. When Ruby had brought her to the farm the first time, she had told Maisie that the girl was leery of this large dog wanting to lick her face and put his paws on her knees whenever she sat. Maisie smiled. Of course, she would have come to terms with the family pet during the regular bi-weekly visits.

Ellen had also become friends with Billy. Maisie had only seen him once since the accident, when Glen had brought him to Regina to see a specialist. The boy wheeled himself into the hallway when they arrived and smiled broadly when he saw Ellen. He seemed to be adapting to the wheelchair well, almost doing a wheelie as he moved into the living room.

Maisie gave him a jigsaw puzzle of the ducks on Wascana Lake in winter which she had picked up in Regina. The pieces were large enough to be suitable for a three- to five-year-old. She received a brilliant smile in return.

"Thank you, Miss Forbes. My dad read me a story once about the ducks and geese that stay there in the wintertime. Daddy, can I make it now?"

"Sure, Billy. I'll open it for you and you can work on it while the ladies and I discuss some business. But you're forgetting your manners. Didn't we have something to do first?"

"Oh, yeah." The little boy took Ellen's hand. "Come on. We have something for you in the kitchen. Come on Miss Forbes."

"I'm not moving a single step until you call me Maisie."

"My daddy says I'm never to call grown-ups by their first names."

Maisie raised an eyebrow at Glen who shrugged then crouched down to his son's level. "Maybe we can make a compromise."

"What's a com ... comp a mise?"

"It's like meeting someone halfway in an argument. You know. They give in a little bit and you give in a little bit. Maybe she won't mind if you call her Miss Maisie."

"Is that okay?" The little boy seemed delighted with the compromise.

"It's absolutely okay. I like it very much."

They all went into the kitchen where the table was set for four and a plate stacked with pancakes could be seen through the glass in the oven door. Bacon was sizzling in the frying pan.

"That was the best breakfast I've had in a long time, Billy. Maybe since the last time I was here. Thank you." Ellen folded her napkin and placed it beside her plate.

"I'll clean the table so we can get started with the book work."

Maisie started to remove the plates.

"Billy and I will do that. I think Ellen knows where everything is in the office, so you two can get working."

"Thanks, Glen. With luck we'll have everything together by evening so we can start back first thing in the morning."

"Glad to hear you won't be driving back in the dark. Lots of black ice on the highway at this time of year. I think we might even get a light blanket of snow overnight."

"We've got a room booked at the hotel in town. I'd much rather drive in the morning, when you can at least see what's on the road." She almost added "We don't need an accident" but blessedly caught herself before the words were out.

The women went through all the files, sorted and arranged everything in chronological order and made note of any missing items. Ellen used the adding machine and labelled receipts, till tapes, and small papers while Maisie made journal entries. By the end of the day, they were able to compile what they needed into one box.

Delicious aromas were emanating from the kitchen by the time they were finished. Glen's and Billy's voices could be heard with the occasional laugh. Maisie was almost tearful listening to them. She had worried that Glen might give up on the farm once he came to grips with the fact that his son would never drive a tractor or pitch hay and maybe never ride a horse without help. Father and son both seemed comfortable with each other. The little boy was a carbon copy of his mother: fair hair and blue eyes. The only thing she saw of Glen in his son was the strong jaw and cleft chin and the way he held it in such a determined way when he spoke.

Now there was raucous laughter followed by complete silence. The two women looked at each other, then tip-toed toward the kitchen. Glen was bent over the wheelchair while Billy whispered in his ear. They spotted the females and quickly put fingers over their mouths telling each other not to say a word.

"What's going on in here?" Maisie stood with hands on hips.

"Whatever it is, it's certainly not good." Ellen was peeking over Maisie's shoulder.

Billy tried to imitate his dad's wink and they invited the women to sit down. Billy showed them where they should sit and wheeled back.

As Maisie sat down, a loud sound of escaping air came from under her rump. She jumped up and the two males roared with laughter. They had placed a whoopee cushion on her chair under the seat pad.

She pretended embarrassment and Billy stopped laughing only long enough to say, "Oh, Miss Maisie, the look on your face was so funny."

She continued her frown then joined in the laughter. "Shame on you for trying to make a lady guest look foolish."

Ellen was bewildered by the prank and the familiarity the group shared. She always thought Mr. Grayson was rather reserved. He was always friendly, but she had never seen him as anything other than business-like.

The laughter died and Glen put a supper of ham and potatoes on the table. Maisie was overcome with the memory of the last time she had shared this same meal with Glen. She looked up and saw that he knew exactly what she was remembering. *So he prepared this on purpose.* The lump in her throat almost kept her from swallowing.

After supper, Billy asked if they could play a game of *Trouble*, a board game he enjoyed. Maisie was becoming increasingly uncomfortable with the cozy atmosphere and suggested that she and Ellen would help with clean-up in the kitchen before going to the hotel.

Billy was visibly disappointed. Glen suggested that Ellen and Billy play a round or two of the game while he and Maisie cleaned up the kitchen. Before Maisie could voice a disagreement with the idea, Billy was already wheeling into the living room to get the game board out. Ellen agreed that the boy would be disappointed if he weren't allowed a game before the women left. She said she was the one who had introduced the child to the game and they usually played at least one round whenever she came.

Maisie was not happy with this turn of events, but hid it by joking about thinking she was paying Ellen to work and all the while the girl was here playing games. Then she was all alone in the kitchen with Glen.

TWENTY-TWO

"I'M NOT GOING TO JUMP you, Miss Maisie."

"Then remove your hand from my back." She hadn't meant to sound so harsh.

He did so. Instantly she wished it were back. God, her mouth was dry.

"Dry?"

"What? What did you say?"

"Do you want to wash or dry?"

"Oh, I'll wash. You know where everything belongs."

"You are very quiet."

"I'm uncomfortable."

"Why?"

"I don't know. Maybe suffering a little déjà vu."

"So you did notice."

"Yes."

"Maisie, I …"

"Don't say it."

"What?"

"Anything. Don't say anything."

"Okay, I won't."

He quickly turned her to him and wrapped his arms around her. He pressed his lips against hers. Her body failed her. Instead of pushing him away, she leaned into him as if pulled by a magnetic force.

"Darlin', I have wanted to hold you in my arms and kiss you like that for seven years."

She didn't answer. Couldn't answer. What would she say? That she had wanted it, too? Ached for it even? He kissed her again and she slid her arms around his waist.

"Stay here tonight."

"I can't. We have reservations at the hotel. This can't ever happen, Glen. No one knows that you and I have ever been more than acquaintances. To my staff, you are a client. I'm your accountant … One that your wife hired." She moved away from him.

She could hear the television in the other room and the noisy clicks of the dice inside the bubble on the game board.

"That's what I am to your staff. A client." He lifted her chin. "What am I to you?"

"The man who ruined me for any other man years ago. There have been many times I wished I had never met you. Then there are times I am so happy to have experienced the love that gave me the memories I live on."

"We can make new memories. Maisie, you know I still love you."

She escaped his reach and filled her arms with dishes. "I can't go down that road again, Glen."

"What road?"

"The one that leads nowhere."

"You're wrong. The road you're on now leads nowhere."

"Would you expect me to give up my practice and move here to the farm?"

"Couldn't you run an accounting practice from here? There are any number of professionals who run their businesses from home."

"My home is in Regina. My business is in Regina. Ninety percent of my clients are in Regina. It's difficult enough doing ten percent of it long distance. I can't imagine reversing it and having ninety percent of my clients there and me here."

She was scrubbing the dishes so hard, she was almost taking the pattern off the plates. He dried them in silence.

"It seems we're back to the same old argument." He laid the towel on the countertop.

"Yes, and we can't even blame my mother this time."

"If you can't — or won't — run your business long distance, can we at least try having a long-distance relationship? Does it have to be all or nothing? Can we at least see each other sometimes?"

She pulled the plug in the sink and watched the water eddy as it disappeared down the drain. Was that symbolic? She took the towel from him to dry her hands.

"I'm not sure that will be enough."

"It's better than nothing. Anything is better than nothing."

Everything raced through her mind. Billy. Shelley. Her mother. The travelling. The staff. Her mother. She looked at him and wondered for the millionth time if she really did love him. If she did, would a part of him not be better than none of him? Would that be enough for her? She thought of her lonely existence. The futility of it that she felt sometimes. Wouldn't it be nice to have him visit her from time to time? For her to come here from time to time? She thought of the nights alone. How many nights had she cried herself to sleep from pure loneliness? Hadn't she once cried in joy from the feel of him in the bed next to her? Wouldn't she love to feel that again? She looked at the man standing there waiting for an answer. Did she really want him part time? *Hell, yes.* She took his face in her hands and pulled it down to whisper in his ear. "Okay."

"Okay?"

"Yes."

"Just like that. Okay. Yes?"

"I don't know what I'm letting myself in for. What I'm letting you in for. I'm not sure it's the smart thing for us to do. I can't help but feel we'll be sorry at some point."

"Can we go back to just plain okay?" He lifted her chin with a forefinger.

She looked directly at him. "Okay."

"Will you stay tonight?"

"No."

"Damn. I was hoping I'd get another okay."

TWENTY-THREE
1972

"DO YOU KNOW WHEN YOUR exam will be, Ruby?"

"Not yet. Soon, I hope. It's been a long haul."

"I'm sure it seems that way to you, but really, you've done amazingly well. Passed every single exam along the way. That's commendable."

"I've been extremely fortunate to have had you tutoring me, Maisie. You've always given me responsibilities that are one step ahead of each phase of my program. You ensure that I'm well prepared for each exam. My poor old brain wouldn't have been able to cope with it all if it weren't for you."

"Nonsense. You've a brilliant mind and a natural aptitude for numbers. You've been working in this business for so long, everything comes easy to you." Maisie sensed an uncertainty in Ruby. "I suppose you're wondering about your future once you have those initials behind your name."

"Well, yes. I've been somewhat concerned wondering what your plans for me might be once I have my accreditation. I don't think it's presumptuous of me to expect a fee increase at that time. I don't mean to sound greedy, Maisie. You've always been generous with me. I know you will be fair and give me whatever salary you can afford."

Maisie walked to her desk and sat down.

"To clear the air, you won't be on salary after you receive your designation." She smiled at the concerned look on Ruby's face. "I'm hoping you won't be swayed into joining some big company once you have the credentials to do so. I happen to know you've been offered more than one job over the years working for one company or another. You have a good reputation among our clients, and they've passed that along to friends. I've been worried. So much so, that I quit bragging about you to others in the industry. I want to keep you as my own little secret, but I won't be a bit surprised if you haven't already been wined and dined by another accountant or two. In order to head them off at the pass, I'm willing to offer you a full partnership along with the financial uncertainty that entails rather than a regular salary."

"A partnership?"

"Yes. Let's sit and talk about it."

It was after hours and the office staff had gone home. Maisie motioned to the sofa and Ruby took a seat.

"As you're aware, I've been taking on more and more clients from the Weyburn and Estevan areas over the last couple of years. I've been seriously considering opening a branch office in Estevan but can't afford financially to be away from this office enough to make it feasible. Once you are a fully licensed accountant, you will be able to work on your own. I know your capabilities and I'm completely confident you can carry on with me being away several days every other week. I think we can work out terms agreeable to both of us. We would split the income from this office fairly, on an increasing scale for you, as I build a practice in Estevan and work less and less from here. We will work out bonuses for any new clients you bring to the firm on your own. We can expand on our bookkeeping staff also. You will need a private office. I was thinking we might expand into the empty space down the hall on this floor."

She stopped talking, taken aback by the surprised looked on Ruby's face.

"Surely you must have known you would have a place here."

"I had hoped, but a partnership! I never dreamed …" Tears glistened in Ruby's eyes. "I never dreamed, never hoped for more than being an associate. Maisie, I don't know what to say."

Maisie took her friend's hand in hers. "Don't say anything yet. Just pass the damn exam. We'll figure out the details later."

For the past two years, she had been travelling the highway between Regina and Estevan at least monthly, occasionally a couple of times a month. Glen would drive to the city as often as he could, sometimes bringing Billy with him. Maisie moved into a larger apartment in a building with an elevator. Billy loved coming to Regina where he would watch the geese and ducks in Wascana Lake. Winter and summer.

Her mother had been absolutely beside herself when she found out that Glen and Maisie were seeing each other. She had not warmed to Glen nor to Billy no matter how hard Maisie tried to unite them as a family. Madeline had flatly refused any invitations to do so. Maisie knew that deep in her mother's heart, her mother blamed Glen for the death of his wife. Now that her daughter and Glen had become a couple again, the determination of proving he was a criminal became uppermost in her mother's mind. The fact that the driver of the other vehicle had never been found only enhanced the distrust the older woman had of Glen. She questioned Maisie about it intermittently, as if bringing it up would remind her daughter she could be keeping company with a murderer.

Glen and Maisie had agreed to take it slow. At first, Ruby and Ellen just knew they were having dinner together whenever he came to the city. They were not aware that Glen was an overnight guest in

Maisie's apartment. They assumed that Maisie stayed in a hotel in Estevan when she went down there "on business". Billy knew she stayed at their house but not in the same bedroom. Her mother was certain they had been sleeping together all along. Gradually, everyone came to accept that the couple was more than just friends. Everyone was happy except Madeline. With each passing month and year, she distanced herself more and more from her daughter.

Trying to maintain clients spread over much of south-eastern Saskatchewan, keeping a somewhat tenuous relationship with her mother, and seeing Glen and Billy as often as possible, was taxing Maisie mentally and physically. She also knew that with Billy starting school this year, it would be more difficult for the two to make regular trips to Regina. The seed of the idea of making Ruby a partner had taken root as her bookkeeper entered the final phase of her accounting program. She had full confidence in Ruby being able to maintain the Regina portion of her practice. Every one of their clients knew that at some point Ruby had done work on their books and many had already come to think of her as an accountant. They laughed and joked with her as an equal and would ask for her when Maisie wasn't around. If Maisie could remain in Estevan for a full week each trip, it would make the drive less of a burden. She would gradually move more of her clientele to Ruby's desk, maintaining only the largest accounts herself. This would allow her to grow the Estevan office into a full-time business and possibly to hire support staff there also.

She often felt her mother should be satisfied that her career as an accountant and her financial independence were assured. Her mother's dream had been fulfilled. The threat of Maisie becoming a poor over-worked farmer's wife was non-existent. However, with the woman's continued dislike of her relationship with Glen, she came to understand it wasn't just Glen's choice of profession but the man himself that was the cause of her hostility. In her mother's eyes, he had won. Behind her back, that beast of a man had enticed her daughter into a relationship against her wishes.

Madeline had been increasingly vocal that Maisie's visits to Weyburn were just stops on the way to and from Estevan.

"I hardly see you anymore, Maisie. You used to spend weekends with me. Now I'm lucky to have an hour of your time on a Friday or Sunday evening. And even those are becoming few and far between."

"Mom, I can't run a successful business without spending some weekends in the office. And before you start spouting off about my time with Glen, he only sees me the same weekends you do."

"But you used to …"

"I used to come most weekends because you were struggling on your own. I had to help you physically to maintain your independence in your own house. Over the last few years, you've become less dependent on me. You even come into the city on your own now and stay with Ruby. You've developed hobbies and you've met new people both here and in Regina. You are not as needy as you once were."

Madeline snorted as she turned her back to Maisie. "Needy? I never realized I was such a burden to you. And you know why I stay with Ruby."

"Mom, for heaven's sake. You know I wanted to help you as much as I could. I got an education. As you wanted. I built a career. As you wanted. I planned my life exactly as you wanted. I even gave up romance. So now if I want to share some of my time with a man I care deeply about, I don't think that's too much to ask. I'm thirty-two years old. How long do I have to wait before I can think about the possibility of a husband and children without feeling guilty about neglecting you?"

The hurt in her mother's eyes was almost too much to bear. She felt herself about to apologize but managed to keep her lips closed.

"I guess I could move closer to Jeremy and Jeanne. Then you wouldn't have to worry about me."

"Stop it. Listen to you." Maisie was angry now. "You wonder why I don't visit more often or stay longer? This is why. You don't make the visits pleasant."

She started toward the door then turned. "Where is that happy woman who was making regular trips to Regina to shop and enjoy the restaurants and theatre? Ruby was asking me, just the other day, why you don't come as often as you used to."

"Tell her I'm avoiding the chance of coming face to face with a murderer. Why, I don't even want to stay in the same apartment that you allow that ... that ..."

"Murderer? You really think he's a murderer? You really want me to tell Ruby that? You really want me to say those words to her?"

"Why not? It's true. You know very well if he had been at home where he belonged that evening with his wife and child, she wouldn't have been out on the highway in icy weather."

"That makes him a murderer, Mother? Then I guess I am an accomplice to that so-called murder since I was the reason he wasn't at home. I've listened to you put him down for nine years and I'm growing weary of it. I walked away from him once because of you and I refuse to do it again."

"I believe you walked away from him because of your career not because of me. Now I'm beginning to think you never walked away from him at all. I wouldn't be surprised to learn you've been carrying on with him all these years even while his wife was alive."

"I'm leaving now. Think what you want."

She considered going back to Regina. *I can't let Glen ever find out my mother thinks he murdered Shelley. I don't think I can face him right now.* The knowledge that she had two clients waiting for her in Estevan forced her to turn the wheel in that direction. She had always been able to put a smile on the face that Glen saw all these years after her strained visits with her mother. She could do it one more time. *Besides Billy's waiting for me too.*

The thought of Ruby and her mother already having had a conversation about Glen's possible involvement in Shelley's death crossed her mind. The two women had become close friends. It wasn't unlikely that her mother might have confided her feelings to Ruby. If Madeline had ever felt the need to talk to someone about her fears or misgivings, who else would she have the conversation with but a trusted friend who knew the people involved. Would she have also told Ruby that Maisie and Glen had been lovers in the past? Ruby had never brought it up in conversation, nor had Maisie. Maisie felt it better left in the past.

It was late in the evening when she turned into Glen's driveway. Maybe Billy would already be asleep. She had grown to love the little boy. Even more so since she knew he would never be the strong, healthy farmer his father had anticipated in a son.

The flood light came on displaying the driveway and the well-kept yard. She sat for a moment looking around. It was a postcard. The rustic split rail fence surrounding the fields closest to the house including the large barns and silos. The well-maintained old farmhouse with its recent additions. The freshly painted bunk house out back. The two-car garage peeking out from behind the corner of the house. It had oversized doors to accommodate the machinery he was always repairing. He had every reason to be proud and possessive of this stately old farm. She pictured him as a laird, protector of the land around him and all who lived on it. She knew it was a never-ending struggle for the smaller farmers fighting to maintain their place among the corporate farms. She tried to picture his ancestors — the families who had broken the first soil and laid the first log of the original cabin. She envisioned Glen and his brother, Neil, playing in the yard and sitting on the fence watching their dad and the hired hands work the fields. She could almost smell the pies and bread coming from his grandmother's cook stove that still stood in the corner like an old matron sneering at the small electric range trying to impose itself on her domain. As if that little upstart could compete with the natural aroma of meals prepared above burning wood.

A knock on her car window broke her reverie.

"Are you going to sit out here all night?"

Glen was frowning at her. It was then she realized tears were streaming down her cheeks.

TWENTY-FOUR

"WHAT'S WRONG, MAISIE? WHAT'S HAPPENED? Your mom okay?" He had the car door open and was reaching for her.

She shook her head. "No, everything is fine."

"Why were you sitting out here so long then?"

"I ..." She turned away from him, walked to the front of her car and leaned against a fender. She swept her arm in an arc to show him what she had been looking at. "I was admiring the view, all these beautiful old buildings, the fields, trying to picture how it might have looked a generation or two ago."

"That's what made you cry?"

"I really don't know what made me cry. Really. I could almost smell the aroma of fresh baked bread and apple pies. I was thinking about you and Neil growing up watching your dad in the field."

Parker was probing her hand with his nose looking for a rub on the top of his head. "You must have had a dog even then." She stooped to let the aging dog lick her cheek.

"We did. His name was Rosco. He was the most beautiful mongrel a boy could ever want and went everywhere with Neil and me. When we had to go in different directions it used to drive him crazy trying to choose which of us to follow."

"How did he choose?"

"I think he played eeny-meeny in his doggy brain. We seemed to be pretty even in winning his company. At least until Neil started bringing Chelsea around and Rosco got tired of playing second fiddle. Then he was all mine."

They had walked to the front porch and Maisie, wanting to stay outside and enjoy the evening, took a seat on the swing.

"You never talk much about your mother. I wasn't able to fit her into the imagery."

"You know that my mother died from a heart problem while helping my dad with the haying."

"Yes, and I know you were barely out of your teens. You've shown me pictures of her, but you've never really talked about her. What was she like?"

"She was as quiet as my father was boisterous. That didn't stop her from being forceful in her own way. She made sure we all took our boots off outside the kitchen door. The front door was for company." He stopped and looked into space. "Damn it. I had forgotten about that back door."

"What was special about it?"

"Nothing. It was the same as everybody else's screen door. It was the way it sounded when it slapped shut. The spring would pull it closed behind you. Mom used to holler at us to close it slowly but somehow, we were always in a hurry. I remember how she used to put her hands on her hips and shake her head. I don't even recall when it was replaced. God, I wish I could hear it slap one more time."

"Was she strict?"

"She had come from a strict Methodist background and insisted we attend services on Sundays at the United Church in town. We always gave thanks for our food at the main meal every day. Good manners were instilled in us early, even though my dad did his best to make men out of us when we were out of her earshot. We learned most swear words from him along with dire warnings of what he would do if we showed disrespect to any female no matter her age, by using those words in mixed company. He loved my mother and showed it, which was not always common back then. My mother didn't have to demand our respect, it just came naturally. She was so gentle there was no way my brother or I would intentionally cross her. She was the best cook. I'm so glad that she was also a dedicated records keeper. She not only kept books on the farm finances and household expenses, but after she was gone, I found recipe books where she had written notes on how to make just about everything she put on the table. She had written inside the cover that they were for future Mrs. Graysons." He took a deep breath and smiled. "She was planning for the care of her sons' stomachs even then. I think she knew she wasn't going to live a full life."

"Are they still around?"

"Her sons' hungry stomachs?"

"No, the recipe books."

"They're still in the cupboard above the fridge."

He slapped his thigh and stood. "I wish she could have … Oh, well, I can wish all I want, can't I? I was luckier than some who have no memories of their mother at all."

Maisie's breath caught. Could he be thinking of his son whose memories of his own mother were already becoming foggy? She brought her hand to her throat and her heart went out to him. In that instant she knew she loved this man with all of her being.

"Let's go in and I'll fix you something to eat." Glen's voice broke. He went to the car to bring in her bag.

The next morning, she woke to the sound of Billy's laughter and Parker's barking. The little guy's sounds were no longer those of a toddler but distinguishable now as those of a young male child. When had that happened? Even Parker's barks were those of an older dog.

They didn't have the same sharpness as a few years ago.

If they are aging, so am I!

There was a knock on the door. "Maisie, are you up yet?"

"I am now. Come inside."

The door opened and Billy wheeled his chair into the room.

"Dad says if you can get ready in twenty minutes, we'll have enough time to make it for the time trials at the track."

Maisie had an appointment in the afternoon with a client. "What time is it?"

"It's almost nine-thirty."

"Will I be back for three-thirty?"

"Sure. I think they're finished around noon, but we have to leave like, right now."

"I'll be ready in two shakes. Can you throw a slice of bread in the toaster for me?"

"Sure. And you already look nice, so you don't have to spend a half hour putting goop on your face."

"Spoken like a real man. Get outa here and let a girl get ready."

He snickered and shouted from the hallway. "Twenty minutes."

She was ready in fifteen. Glen had the station wagon ready by the time she'd finished eating her toast. They were on the road in the requested twenty minutes. Billy had become a fan of the stock car races and was always excited when he got to watch the time trials.

They watched as a couple of the drivers stopped and chatted with Billy. He had a small book he'd bought at Woolworth's in which he kept their autographs. He had it ready when a driver, new to the circuit, wandered by. They always wrote encouraging comments along with their signatures. "Look, Dad. Number 24 said that one day soon they'll make racing cars that I can drive." He looked hopefully at his father. "Do you think that's true? Will they make cars for guys in wheelchairs?"

"I can't honestly answer that, son, but there's no harm in hoping. They adapted cars about twenty years ago so you can shift the gears without using your feet, I understand they can now make them so you can control the speed and brakes by hand. I don't know about racing cars, though, but it's a possibility."

Later Maisie asked Glen about the wisdom of raising false hopes.

"I don't think any hopes should be considered false. As long as he can hope for something, it keeps the possibility alive. If we give up hope, then what is there? Dreams are built on hope."

"What about the chance of disappointment?"

"Billy is going to face many disappointments but that shouldn't stop him from dreaming and hoping. I can't raise him to not hope. He must have something to aim for rather than just sitting in his wheelchair saying 'poor me'."

"You are a wise, caring man, Glen Grayson. Billy is lucky to have you for a father."

"I don't know about that, but he deserves whatever bit of luck he can get."

She was back at the farm in time to change into a blouse and better slacks and drive to her client's place by three o'clock. She had been using the den at the farm as her office, but as she passed through the downtown area, she couldn't help but eye-ball buildings that might house a small accounting office.

Two hours later, she had her briefcase full of work and was on the way to the farm again. Her new client, a building contractor, had been recommended to her company by his cousin, a local farmer. She was gaining a good reputation and it appeared there was business to be had. She, selfishly, hoped that Ruby would receive her designation soon. She was certain Glen would welcome any extra time she could spend with him.

The drive back was pleasant. Glen's farm was bigger than that of many of his neighbour's. He had been attending meetings on the wisdom of diversifying his crop. Staying on top of all the latest trends in wheat and other grains was how he managed to keep one step ahead of some of the other farmers. He had changed the type of wheat he planted a couple of years earlier. Maisie only knew it had completely changed the planting cycle, something about a spring wheat. She wasn't sure what it entailed and now he was entertaining the thought of changing to canola. It was a different kind of farming altogether, but it looked quite promising. He was looking at the results of studies being done on the future of it. His farm always looked so clean. He was cutting back on the number of beef cattle he raised also. He stayed on top of everything by reading and attending seminars all over southern Saskatchewan. Whatever, he was doing, he was doing right. His bottom line had stayed strong even in years others had somewhat dipped. The best part was, she never had to step foot in a field or clean out a barn. His house had all the latest appliances and a housekeeper came at least once a week. A physiotherapist was a regular at the house, helping Billy keep his muscles working and strengthening.

The boy would be going into Grade One this year, which would be a change for him. He would attend regular classes even though there were no buses for handicapped students available in their area. Glen would have to drive him to school each day.

When she arrived back at the farm, she was surprised to see the Grayson males, senior and junior, all cleaned up and dressed to go out for dinner. "Why didn't you tell me you wanted to go out? You guys could have just met me in town."

"What? Do you think we want to go out with you in your work clothes? We're going somewhere special. You better dress up."

"Yeah. You better dress up." Billy was grinning from ear to ear.

"Well, I hope I'll be given longer than twenty minutes since it's so special. It will take that long just for my curling iron to heat."

Glen rolled his eyes and Billy followed suit.

"Do we have reservations?"

"We don't need them. They know us where we're going."

"Yeah. They know us."

"I see. Now you have me intrigued. Maybe I should wear my diamond tiara instead of my rhinestone one."

"Well, it must be special because my dad said he changed his under wear even though the month isn't up yet." He burst out laughing when Glen pretended to cuff him on the ear.

Glen ushered them out the door and got Billy settled in the back seat, wheelchair stowed in the rear of the wagon, then he bussed Maisie's cheek as he made sure everyone's seat belts were fastened.

They didn't go into Estevan. Instead, Glen followed a secondary road for a distance until they came to a gate where the man inside a small office waved them through into what appeared to be a campground. *Strange.* After Glen backed the vehicle into what Maisie was sure was a trailer site, he told her to remain in the car while he removed Billy's wheelchair and got the young fellow out of the car. Then he removed a cooler and placed it on his son's lap. Next, he took a large, covered, wicker basket, opened Maisie's door and reached for her hand. When she was standing, he locked the vehicle, put the keys into his pocket with a wink at his son, and then extended his arm for her to walk with him.

Billy started across a patch of grass that was surrounded by trees. As she and Glen followed, Maisie saw they were on the banks of a small lake, and a picnic table was near the water's edge. Another table nearby was occupied by an elderly couple who had a small white dog on a leash attached to a peg in the ground. A beige camper trailer was barely visible through the trees behind the couple. Obviously, the couple were enjoying a camping holiday. They looked over and nodded as Billy approached the empty table.

"Have a seat, madame." Glen took Maisie's arm and had her sit at the table on the bench closest to the water.

He set the basket on the other bench then spread a tablecloth, and set plates and cutlery on the table. He placed a hurricane-shaped candle holder with a large white pillar inside it on the centre of the table. Billy handed him the cooler and Glen took out a large bottle of ginger ale. Billy took three wine glasses from the basket and placed them on the table.

Maisie smiled but said nothing.

Next came a small transistor radio, and Glen made a production of finding soft, easy-on-the-ears music. A couple of covered Tupperware containers and one platter were placed on the table. Finally, Glen unfolded napkins and placed one on his own plate, then on Billy's. "Allow me," he said as he unfolded the third and spread it on Maisie's lap.

He took the lids off the Tupperware containers to display potato salad, a vegetable salad and the removal of the cover from the platter revealed sliced cold roast of pork. He then poured the ginger ale into the glasses.

"Time to do the toast, Dad?"

"Of course, as long you don't use any of the swear words you've picked up in the bars."

This elicited another snicker from the boy. His smiling face turned reflective as he seemed to search for words. The picnic had obviously been orchestrated in advance.

Maisie wondered why the formal attire but they must have had their reasons. She glanced over at the other campsite and the couple appeared mesmerized. They had turned their chairs, no doubt to watch the weird picnic being played out next to them.

Billy cleared his throat in true toastmaster style and raised his glass. "Miss Maisie, I want to make a toast to tell you how special you are to me."

His serious face made Maisie smile even though she felt a "but" was about to follow. What was going on here? Was Billy going away or something? Maybe Glen was sending the boy away to school and this was a farewell picnic. No. He wouldn't do that. He would have discussed it with her. What, then?

"I know my dad has liked you for a long time and I have, too. You seemed like a ... well, like a really nice auntie and I loved it whenever you came to visit."

Loved. Came to visit. Past tense. Wasn't she going to be visiting anymore? Or wasn't he going to be there anymore?

"But now, I don't think I like you anymore."

Wait. What's he saying? She had a knot in her stomach. Why was Glen smiling and nodding?

"What? Why?" Maisie really wasn't sure what was coming. Had Glen found someone else? Was this a joke of some kind?

"What I mean is, I don't just *like* you anymore, I ... I ... Well, I love you." He blushed. "I want to make a toast to wish us more love." Now he really blushed and looked to his father for help.

"You are doing fine, son." Glen winked at Maisie, who didn't know what to think.

Billy looked at his father again and said, "Can't I just do it now?"

"I thought we agreed to wait until after we ate. In case. Well. You know. Just in case."

"I can't wait. My stomach is going to be sick, I'm so nervous."

Glen lifted his shoulders in a *What can I do?* shrug, looked at Maisie as if begging for understanding.

The old couple leaned forward in their chairs.

Then Glen nodded to his son. "We can't have you getting sick all over our picnic. Go ahead."

Billy dug into the bottom of the picnic hamper and came up with something that he hid from view. Then he turned to Maisie and said, "Maisie, will you please marry us? I mean marry Dad?" He opened a jeweller's box in which sat a narrow gold band with a diamond solitaire glinting in the rays of the evening sun.

Maisie swallowed hard. Now she understood why the formal wear.

TWENTY-FIVE

A MILLION THOUGHTS CREATING A million scenarios flashed through Maisie's mind. Again, her mother was in the mix. *I shouldn't. What's wrong with things as they are? I love them. They love me. We're doing just fine.* She focused on the anxious faces of the two males in front of her. In the background she heard Al Green singing "Let's Stay Together". What kind of perfect timing was that? It was surreal. Even the elderly couple at the table across the grass seemed suspended in time waiting for her reply. The young boy in front of her looked about ready to cry.

"Okay."

"Okay?" Glen and Billy replied at the same time.

"But ..."

"But?" They were sounding like a chorus.

"Only if you are part of the deal, Billy, because I love you, too."

"Okay. I'll be part of it. Does that mean yes?" He was beaming.

"Daddy, I think she means yes."

She heard applause. A dog began barking.

As she bent to down to kiss Billy's cheek the old gent whistled.

Glen took the ring from the velvet box and put it on her finger. "I hope I get a kiss too."

"Oh, are you part of the deal?"

He muffled her laugh with his lips, then said, "I guess we're a threesome. Only, Shorty here, doesn't get to come on the honeymoon."

"But, Dad …"

"No. Definitely not."

"We'll take you on another honeymoon when you get a school break." Maisie patted Billy's hand.

Glen stood and introduced his fiancée and his son to the other couple. They shook hands all around.

The old woman hugged Maisie. "Oh dearie. You had me in suspense it took you so long to answer." She turned to her husband. "Harry. Get the camera. You have to have a picture. Oh, that's the most romantic proposal. Harry. Hurry. Get the camera."

Harry had already opened the door of their trailer. He returned with a Polaroid camera in his hand. They had to re-enact the scene with Billy holding up a glass of ginger ale, then again, with Glen putting the ring on her finger.

They all oohed and awed over the snapshots as they passed them back and forth.

"Is that apple pie I smell?" The old man peeked into the picnic basket.

"That's the celebration dessert. Will you join us?"

"Daddy made it from my grandma's recipe."

The lady looked at Maisie. "I'm glad you said yes. A man who can bake apple pies shouldn't be left on the shelf."

They ate the pie first with their uninvited guests then the main course while the old couple went inside to make coffee for everyone.

They turned the music up later and everyone danced on the grass — even the couple's dog. All four adults joined hands and danced around Billy, who sat beaming in his wheelchair. The last they saw of the couple, the woman was wiping her eyes with a napkin.

In the car on the way home, Maisie asked why they had chosen a picnic spot for this fancy dinner.

Billy answered. "Daddy said it had to be done somewhere that you couldn't get up and run away. I saw you lock the car, Dad. I guess you weren't taking any chances."

"I see."

"I also told my son that picnics were traditionally recognized as romantic settings in movies and books."

"I see."

"Are you disappointed we chose a picnic to pop the question?"

"No. You were probably right on both counts."

"Would you have run away?"

"Mmm. Maybe. Probably not. But I'm glad I wasn't given the option."

She turned to see Billy's grinning face.

"I suppose you ordered that full moon to complete our romantic evening?" They were sitting on the porch swing, Billy tucked into bed with the picture of his grand toast on his bedside table.

Glen slid his arm around her shoulders. "I guess it wasn't the most romantic proposal a woman could get. A six-year-old. Elderly lookers on. A barking dog. Ginger ale instead of champagne."

She snuggled into his embrace. "I wouldn't have wanted it any other way. It was unique to our situation. It was extremely romantic." She patted his chest with her ring finger hand. "I will let you in on a little secret."

"What's that?"

"I've never, ever been on a picnic before."

"Never?"

"Never."

"Not even as a kid?"

"Nope. My mother always said it was too much work to pack up a meal and drive out among the bugs and flies just to put a meal on the table when she could do it in the kitchen much more easily. Picnics were never in the picture."

He heard the tremor in her voice. "Do you want to talk about it?"

"Not tonight. I shouldn't have brought it up."

He kissed her forehead. "I promise you a picnic at least once a month."

After a few moments of silent staring at the sky, he kissed her again. "I was really afraid you were going to say no."

"If you had asked me two days ago, the chances are pretty good I might have."

"What difference did two days make?"

"When I arrived here and was sitting in my car the other night, I saw — really saw — your farm for the first time. It was like a vision that came to me. I told you I envisioned life here. Not just now but how it must have been for your parents and grandparents. When you came out and we talked about your childhood, your dog, your mom. I came to understand you. To value you. To know the depth of the love I have for you." She kissed him passionately. "I am so sorry for all these years we've lost."

"We have many more ahead of us, Maisie. We'll plan a future instead of dwelling in the past."

"There is so much to talk about."

"The first is the wedding date. Then a honeymoon. Then the rest will follow."

"It's weird because just this week, I promised Ruby a full partnership in the firm when she gets her designation. I told her she will be responsible for the Regina branch and I'll concentrate on the Estevan branch."

"Oh, so you already had plans to move here? Damn."

"What's there to swear about?"

"If I'd known I wouldn't have wasted my money on an engagement ring." He tried to duck her soft shoulder punch.

"Well, to live here part time anyway. I still have to spend time in

Regina. There are clients there that will only deal with me. But I think I'm ready to think of this as home and Regina as the away office. I can't do anything until Ruby writes her exam, though."

"No chance of just turning it over to her completely?"

"No. She needs time to get the feel of complete responsibility for clients' accounts. She will still need coaching and guiding for a while."

"When does she write her exam?"

"In two months."

"Then we can set a wedding date for soon after that?"

"We can set a wedding date for any day you want. Tomorrow."

"Really? You don't want a large catered affair?"

"I want you, my love. I don't need all the frills of a fancy gown and an exhausting reception. I can ask Ruby to be matron of honour. What about you? What are your thoughts?"

"I just took for granted you would want a reception of some kind. You know, with your mother and brother and his family, your office staff and friends. My brother and Chelsea would come. I have a few buddies that always enjoy a good party."

"Would you be content with less?"

"You mean like a judge in the courthouse?"

"Or a minister in a small chapel and a nice lunch after?"

Glen rose and walked across the porch, staring toward the fields and barns then looked out from the steps across the front yard.

"Maybe we could have it here. Decorate the yard a bit. Have a caterer from town bring the lunch."

She strode up behind him and put her arms around his waist. "Oh, Glen, that sounds perfect. I love your yard with its white fences and the old trees."

"When?"

"Are you familiar with the minister at the United Church in town?"

"He married Shelley and me. Christened Billy. Buried Shelley. Are you sure you want the same man to marry us?"

"Do you like him?"

"Yes. He's a good guy. He dropped by many times to help me find my way through the tough times after Shelley died and the worries with Billy."

"Then let's do it. You can talk to the minister tomorrow and I'll get on the phone and check out caterers. As soon as I find one that's free on the same day as the preacher is available, we can set a date and let our families know. Hopefully, within a month."

"Billy's birthday is next month."

"I know. So is mine. Would you rather wait until the following month?"

"I can't think of a better birthday present for him than our getting married during his birthday month. Just not on the same day. So his birthday remains his own day." He moved closer to her and brushed a curl from her forehead. "He really does love you, you know. He asked me if he can call you Mom after we're married."

"How do you feel about him calling me Mom? I don't want him ever to lose the connection with Shelley. She's his real mother."

"I'm glad he has accepted you in every way. I think it's not a case of just *wanting* to call you Mom. I think he *needs* to call you Mom. He feels that close to you. I don't mind at all."

"Considering what's been thrown at him in his short life, I can't believe how cheerful and loving he is. You've done an excellent job, Glen. I'm sure it hasn't been easy for you."

"We get by. We — as in he and I —don't look at him as being handicapped. Instead of saying, he *can't* participate in some sports, we look for something else he *can* do, then he still enjoys his first choice, but as a spectator. That way, he has two new sports to be interested in. He can't play T-ball, but he's the best ping pong player in the county. When he couldn't try out for Tom Thumb hockey, he joined an air hockey group and has won a couple of trophies already. He's learned to adapt."

"He's amazing. You're amazing. I'm happy I was asked to join your family. I love my two men with all my heart."

"Then let's hit the sack. We have a lot to do tomorrow and I'm sure Billy will want to be in on the planning. Do you mind?"

"Do I mind that he loves me instead of resenting me? Not a bit."

TWENTY-SIX

AS THINGS WORKED OUT, THE best date for the wedding appeared to be Saturday, September 16. Maisie's thirty-second birthday and a scant three weeks away. Hardly time to get the house painted or even thoroughly cleaned. Invitations would have to be sent immediately. Immediately *after* Maisie could give the news to her mother. Glen wanted to go with her to share their news, which she wavered on, but finally decided to go by herself.

"What do you mean you won't come, Mom? It's my wedding day."

"You expect me to stand there and watch you give your life away to that womanizer and murderer? And on the anniversary of the day I brought you into this world? Maisie, how could you?"

"Would it have made a difference if it was the week before or after my birthday?"

"No."

"That's what I thought."

"You have not only broken my heart, you are laughing in my face by choosing the date you were born. Both of you. He must be having a good laugh at my expense. He waited it out, went behind my back and then reeled you in."

"I am not a fish that he hooked and landed. And neither one of us is laughing in your face. I am inviting you to attend my wedding to the man I love with all my heart. A good man. A man who loves me and treats me with the greatest respect and devotion."

"Until he decides he doesn't want or need you anymore. Are you forgetting how he treated his first wife?"

"With love and respect."

"With bruises and broken bones."

Maisie took several deep breaths. "Mom. I dearly want you to be at my wedding, but not with such hate in your heart. I've given you the date and the time. Glen and I would both like you there. There is a beautiful little boy waiting to meet his step-grandmother. If you decide to share my joy, let me know and I will arrange for you to be there. You are welcome to stay at the house or I will reserve a hotel room for you. I …" She didn't know what more to say. She started for the door then retraced her steps and hugged the stiff body of the mother who, she was sure, would one day be very sorry for missing this important day in her daughter's life.

As the door closed, she could hear her mother's shrill voice. "That man's son will never be my grandson. Never."

The drive back to Estevan was the longest and saddest hour of her life. Why did her mother harbour such hatred of Glen? She knew it had to be more than just his being a farmer. Was it because he had dared to eat the forbidden fruit? Was her mother that vindictive that she would ruin the lives of everyone just because they had gone against her wishes? Surely, she couldn't possibly think that Glen was a murderer. He had loved Shelley. Maybe not with the same passion he loved her, but he had respected Shelley, had treasured her ability to help him run the farm. He'd appreciated her support. She had been an excellent wife and mother. As far as Maisie knew, the woman had made only one mistake, but it had been a fatal one. As for the bruised and broken arm, Maisie could only take Shelley's word for what had caused it. Glen, himself, had retained doubts but there was never anything to refute it.

As she approached the outskirts, she turned right off the highway to the secondary road that would take her home. Home. She prayed that Ruby would pass her exam so Maisie could leave her Regina office in the hands of someone she trusted. It would mean more time with Glen and her stepson. Lord, how she had grown to love that little boy.

Billy was waiting on the front porch for her. "Is Grandma going to come for the wedding?"

The excited grin on the little face tore at Maisie's heart. "She's not feeling well, Billy. Hopefully, she'll be better by then."

The smile faded, then brightened. "She can stay in our house. She can have the room across the hall from me so she won't have to climb any stairs. You're moving upstairs with Daddy anyways so that room will be empty. It would be fun having my grandma staying right across from me. Maybe she would like to play some checkers with me."

Glen had had an addition built on the back of the house with two ground floor bedrooms and a spacious bathroom. Before she had come into their lives, he and Billy had been sleeping in the addition so that the stairs were never a problem for the boy. Glen had suggested that Billy was old enough now for Maisie to move upstairs into the master bedroom with its own bathroom. He said Maisie, being a female and all, needed more space for her own girl stuff. It was right at the top of the stairs where they could hear him. Maisie had even suggested that if Billy had two wheelchairs, one for upstairs and one for downstairs, they might be able to install an electric seat to take him up and down. She had seen one in an office building she had once visited. The owner of the business was an old, arthritic man and couldn't get to his office upstairs without it.

Right now, Maisie had a difficult time keeping the rage from her eyes. Glen's shoulder droop told her he understood. There would be no step-grandmother at the wedding. No step-grandmother staying in the room across from her grandson and playing checkers with him. Glen mercifully came to Maisie's rescue.

"Ya know, sport, when old people aren't feeling well, they really like to stay in the comfort of their own bed. Maybe Maisie's mother can come for a visit later on, when she's feeling stronger."

"Can I just phone her and tell her I'll take care of her in case she really wants to come?"

"I don't think it's a good idea to put pressure on her. Maybe you can send her a picture of the wedding afterward, so she'll feel like she was here."

"Okay. I guess that's a good idea." His disappointment was visible.

Just then the caterer arrived to go through the house and see what decorations, food, china and cutlery would be needed. Maisie was grateful for the interruption. It saved her from Glen's questions and Billy's suggestions. For an hour or so anyway.

Maisie had picked up some preprinted invitations in Weyburn so she and Glen sat and listed the guests each would invite. Maisie included her mother on the list just in case; her brother and his family, who lived in Swift Current; her friend Jessica and her husband in Centretown; Ruby; the other staff members, including Ellen; and the owners and the spouses of Whittier Whittier & McLean; and some of her previous co-workers.

Glen's list was short: Neil and Chelsea, and a couple of neighbouring farmers plus two buddies he had gone through school with and their better-halfs. There would be about thirty guests. They found the addresses of the locals in the Weyburn phone book. Maisie suggested visiting the library to find the out-of-town addresses.

Two days later, after sharing her news with Ruby by phone, she was on her way back to Regina. As she passed through Weyburn, the thought to stop in at her mother's once more was dismissed. *Better to give her some time to think.* She arrived at the office in mid-afternoon and dumped a couple of boxes of work on the floor of her office. Ruby wasn't there. Ellen explained that it was a quiet afternoon, so Ruby had taken advantage of the free time to go home and study. After showing her ring to the remaining women, and receiving hugs and congratulations, she checked her appointment book and saw that the following day was a busy one. Better to take the time now to sort mail and check files so she'd be ready to work immediately upon arrival in the morning.

TWENTY-SEVEN

THREE DAYS LATER RUBY KNOCKED on her office door and asked for a few minutes of Maisie's time.

"I hope you brought coffee with you."

Ruby nodded and placed two cups on Maisie's desk.

"We need to talk." She fidgeted with the sleeve of her blouse.

"What's up?" Maisie was worried about what was to come. She hoped there wasn't a problem with her accounting course.

"Madeline called me last evening."

"I hope she's okay." Ruby still hadn't looked above Maisie's chin.

"Maisie, she's not okay at all."

"My wedding?"

Finally, Ruby's eyes met hers.

"Yes. She is really despondent. I'm worried about her."

"I was hoping she would accept the inevitable after thinking on it for a few days."

"I had no idea she felt so strongly against Glen. I thought everything was fine and that she'd be happy for the two of you. Quite frankly, I'm shocked."

"Ruby, I don't know why she has such a dislike of Glen. She had always warned me about marrying a farmer. My education and independence were always in the forefront in her eyes. Well, I have achieved both. I thought that being in my thirties and successful may have earned me the right to marry a man of my choosing, not hers. I'm no longer a naive teenager who is easily misled. I have known Glen for many years and finally came to the realization that I love the man deeply. Why can't she accept that?"

"I don't know if it's my place to say anything, but you're my friend, after all. However, I'm your mother's friend, too. She seems worried about … Well. Not just about your happiness. It seems she's more concerned about your safety." Ruby stood and paced around the office several times. "Is it true that he physically abused his first wife?"

"Oh, for heaven's sake! My mother had better be careful about what she's saying. And to whom."

"Maisie, I do remember Mrs. Forbes coming into our office one time with a broken and bruised arm. She was very agitated during that visit, to the point of rudeness. It stands out in my memory because she was always so soft spoken and polite and then, well then, it wasn't long after that she died."

Maisie pushed her chair back and walked to the front of her desk. "Ruby, let's sit down." She motioned to the sofas. Ruby remained standing for a few seconds before easing onto one them.

"Now. Let's clear the air. Glen is not a wife beater. He was as concerned about her feeble excuse for a broken arm as others were. He told me he couldn't believe that she wouldn't tell him what really happened. He said she stuck to the falling down story no matter how much he questioned her. He was worried there was more to it than that, but just didn't know what to think. He even watched her for signs of drinking which, of course, just wasn't in the picture at all. Again, when she was killed in the accident, he wondered about her state of mind and health, surprised that she hadn't buckled Billy in when she had bought the new vehicle only because it was equipped with seatbelts. She was a good mother. Glen was a good husband. A good father. Her bruises and broken bone were not caused by him. He adored her, and totally respected her as his wife and as a good mother for his son. He still talks about all she did for him and the farm. He keeps reminding his son about her so that the vague memories of his mother will be good, loving ones for him to grow up with. Believe me when I tell you that I know Glen is no abuser. I have never known a more gentle man."

"I had the feeling that your mother knew more than she was letting on."

"What my mother knows about Glen, Shelley and Billy, she has heard through rumours and innuendos. She lives in a small community that thrives on gossip. Because she does not like Glen, everything is exaggerated in her mind. He has been nothing but kind and respectful to her, by the way."

"I didn't think they knew each other very well. You seem to have kept them distant from one another."

"The distance has been put in place by my mother, not by me."

"She told me she won't come to your wedding."

"That breaks my heart but I can't let it stop me. If Jesus himself were a farmer instead of a carpenter, she would declare herself an atheist rather than worship a farmer."

"Your father was a farmer."

"I know. It's the hard life she had at his side, during the worst years in the history of farming, that she dwells on. Not on how much they loved each other. Or on what a good man he was."

"Maisie, I just don't know what to think. I've always found Glen to be polite and friendly. It's hard to picture him as an abuser."

"Trust me, Ruby. I know him better than my mother does."

"She said you are blinded by his good looks and charm."

"I'm a grown woman approaching middle age. I have met many good-looking, charming men and I haven't been wooed into a false sense of romance with any of them. Even with Glen, it took a long time for me to recognize that what I felt for him was no longer friendship but love. Deep, true love."

"Do you think Madeline will change her mind?"

"I can only hope, Ruby. I can only hope."

That evening Glen called to tell her that housecleaners would be coming three days before the wedding to give the old place a thorough cleaning. "I even remembered to have the septic cleaned yesterday. Don't need any surprises the day of the wedding."

"Now that's something I would never have thought of. Guess I've been away from rural living long enough to have forgotten about important things like that. Good thing you are on top of everything."

"Several replies have come back. So far they're all positive."

"Great. Ruby is shy about being matron-of-honour, so I asked Jessica and she's delighted."

"I didn't take Ruby for the shy type. Oh well, obviously Jessica doesn't mind being second choice."

"She doesn't know she is. Second-choice that is."

"Okay. My mouth is zippered."

"How's Billy?"

"If he could jump, he'd be two feet off the ground. Instead he's doing wheelies! Are you able to come down this long weekend? He's hoping you'll help him pick out some school clothes."

"I'm planning on it. He must be excited about starting school. A lot for the little guy to handle. After that I'll come back for a few days to get as much work done here as I can. Then I'm all yours until after the wedding."

"We haven't even talked about our honeymoon."

"Glen, I know your farm will keep you busy into October so we have lots of time to talk about that."

"You don't want to get away after the wedding?"

"Maybe we can take Billy somewhere for a few days."

"I said honeymoon. As in the bride and groom having some time by themselves."

"Why don't we wait until the crops are in and the fields turned over? Then we can take a real vacation. Maybe go to Banff Springs or somewhere."

"That sounds good. Let's look into it."

"We will. I'll look forward to it."

They hung up without her telling him that Ruby would attend the wedding even though she felt it might hurt Madeline if she were to stand up for the couple. He had been upset enough that her mother was not attending. It had really bothered him that he was causing a breach between mother and daughter. She had assured him that, while it hurt her, she was not about to turn her back on a future with him because of her mother's interference again. "I'm looking forward to a life with the man I love, not pining away for him for the rest of my life because of a bitter old woman who has more hate than love in her heart."

TWENTY-EIGHT

AS USUAL, MAISIE HAD SLEPT in the guest bedroom the night before the wedding where her dress had been carefully kept from the groom's view. Glen's friends had taken him into town to celebrate his last night as a free man after the little rehearsal party. Jeremy, her brother, had arrived to give his sister away and was out at the stag party with Glen and would be staying overnight. Her sister-in-law, Jeanne, had remained at home to look after the animals in the veterinary clinic so Jeremy could get away. Maisie and Billy had played checkers until it was his bedtime. She had heard him in his room playing music until quite late. Appreciating that he might be too excited to fall asleep quickly, she hadn't suggested he shut it down. They'd had a long discussion earlier in the evening about her role in the household dynamics.

"You guys have been used to having the house to yourselves for a number of years. I know I've been here off and on but I'm sure it's going to be hard to put up with a female crowding your space on a more regular basis."

"Gosh, no, Maisie. I'm gonna love having you around. Dad already explained I will have to be on my best behaviour all the time. So I've been practising."

"How do you practise best behaviour?"

His face turned red and he shifted in his chair. "Well, you know, just using good manners and not acting like a goof."

"How do goofs act?"

"Ah, Maisie. You know how guys are when no women are around."

"If we're not around then how would we know?"

He leaned forward and looked around as if revealing a big secret. "You know, like not farting. And not going around the house in your underwear or scratching your uh … your bum. And not swearing or making fun of girls. You know, guy stuff."

"So you have to stop doing all those things now that I'm here."

"Yeah. Well. We didn't do them *all* the time. Just sometimes."

"When?"

"What do you mean?"

"When were the times you did them?"

"Just sometimes when we were alone and too lazy to put on our pants on Saturday mornings. Or sometimes when we had beans for supper, we'd see who could fart the loudest."

"And the swearing and making fun of girls?"

"Well, sometimes Dad would use a bad word if something didn't go right. Or he hit something the wrong way with a hammer. Things like that."

"And did you use those words too?"

"Not really."

"What does not really mean?"

He shifted around in his chair. "Maybe sometimes, when I didn't think Dad could hear me. Or sometimes I'd use them if Parker wouldn't listen to me."

"What words did you use?"

"I don't want to say them. Dad would kill me. He said if you respect a girl, you don't use bad language in front of her."

"I see. So it's just girls you don't respect who you and your dad swear in front of and make fun of?"

"I guess. No. I don't know. He said I wasn't to make fun of any girls and especially you because you are gentle and respected."

Maisie felt a twinge in her mid-section.

"Why would you make fun of me?"

"I wouldn't. Not really. I …"

"That's okay, Billy. Sometimes girls are kind of silly. Sometimes we do things that men might find funny and poke fun at. I get that. But I hope he told you not to ever make fun of how a girl looks or is built."

"He did. One time I told him there was a fat girl in my class at school and he really gave me what for for saying that."

"Do you know why you shouldn't say that?"

"Yes. Because maybe she can't help it. Just like I can't help it that I can't walk."

"He said that?"

"No, but I know that's what he meant. Some people just can't help the way they are. It's not their fault."

Maisie squeezed his hand as he reached to move a checker.

"So let me get this straight. Starting tomorrow, there is to be no passing gas, no swearing, no underpants showing, no scratching you're uh … bum, no rude comments about girls. Right?"

"Right."

"So what are you going to do for fun now?"

"I don't know. Be a square I guess."

"A square?"

"My dad says a square is a boring guy who doesn't understand a good joke or how to tell one. No pers … person … ality."

"A square, eh? No personality." She hugged him. "That doesn't sound like fun at all. We won't let that happen. Time to go to sleep now, sweetie. We have a big day tomorrow."

TWENTY-NINE

SEPTEMBER 16 ARRIVED IN A blaze of fall glory. The morning dawn set the lawn twinkling as if a thousand fireflies were dancing across it. The autumn dew dried in time for the decorators to set the chairs and the flowered arch on the lawn. There was a promise in the air of a hot, sunny day.

She hadn't heard Glen come in during the night. Hopefully, he was upstairs and not hung over too badly. She had anticipated a visit from him before he went to bed. *He probably didn't want to act like a goof and try to see me on the night before our wedding.* She smiled, remembering her conversation with Billy.

Jessica and her husband, Doug, arrived in time for breakfast. The girls ate lightly before driving into town to get their hair done. When they arrived back at the farm, Glen, Neil and Doug were busy helping the caterers set up. Billy was in his room going through his daily exercise routine before showering and getting dressed. He had insisted on waiting to eat with the men, so he was running behind schedule. Maisie's nephew, Scotty, Jeremy's son, had come with his father and was watching Billy go through his exercises. Scott was five years older than Billy and the boys had only met once before, but had hit it off and got along quite well.

"Are you and Doug staying in Estevan tonight?"

"We weren't going to, but Doug decided he didn't want the drive back to Centreville after all the drinking and celebrating. Besides, it will be kind of nice to have a night in a hotel to ourselves."

"I guess it's a rare opportunity for you to be away without the kids."

"Yes. It was nice of you to include them in the invitation, but we decided to make your special day a special night for us. We will have been married fifteen years next week, so we decided to take the occasion to celebrate our anniversary a few days early."

"How nice! Wow, fifteen years. By the time Glen and I are married that long, I'll be forty-seven, much older than you are now."

"Glen is older than you, isn't he?"

"Ten years, so he'll be an old man of fifty-seven."

"That's not old." She gave Maisie a tight hug. "I am so happy that you and Glen are finally getting married. Doug and I both felt that you two were meant to be together from that first night you met at the barn dance. It took you a long time to get here, but at least it's finally happening.

"When you and Glen dropped by last year on your way from Regina, we couldn't have been more delighted to see the two of you together. You guys always look so happy."

Maisie stepped back and smiled at her friend. "We are happy. You have no idea how many times I have kicked myself for taking so long to realize how much I love that man. I should not have listened to my mother."

She shrugged her shoulders and shook her head. "I'm not sorry I got my education, but I know Glen would never have stopped me from my career. I was almost finished my schooling when we met, and it wasn't that many years after my graduation that I went out on my own. I could have opened a practice in Estevan just as easily as in Regina."

"It's your mother that kept you from marrying him?"

"Yes. She won't be here today. It became almost a crusade for her to keep me from marrying a farmer. Nothing Glen or I could tell her about modern day farming would change her mind. I gave in to her rather than battle with her every time we were together.

"I wasted too many years of my life living my mother's dream rather than my own. I never blamed Glen for marrying in the meantime. Shelley was a good woman for him and I'm glad they had a few good years together … and of course, she gave him a son. Billy is such a sweet, loving boy and never lets his handicap stop him from living his life to its fullest. I feel so blessed that the two of them are accepting me into their close-knit family." She fought the tears shimmering in her eyes and threatening to ruin her make-up.

"Oh, my. We'd better change the subject and start getting dressed before I have to fix my face all over again."

"Where is your dress?" Jessica looked around the room.

"It's getting so hot outside, I'm glad I went for a dress rather than a gown. I thought it more appropriate for an afternoon garden wedding anyway." She opened her closet and removed an ivory sheath with spaghetti straps and a matching sheer, short-sleeved bolero.

"Oh, Maisie. It's beautiful and it's the perfect shade to bring out the auburn highlights in your hair. Where are your shoes and jewellery?"

"I have satin pumps that were dyed to match. I was worried about walking in high heels on the grass but with Glen at six feet four inches to my five feet six inches, I thought we might look like Mutt and Jeff." She opened a small jewellery case and removed a pair of gold earrings with small diamonds. "Glen gave me these for Christmas last year."

Jessica helped the bride pull on her dress without mussing her hair, then helped her place hairpins to hold a small pill-box hat with a short puffy veil on her head.

"Our bouquets are in the fridge. You'll have to get them when we go out."

There was a knock on the door. "Room service."

Jessica opened it to let Doug bring in a small tray on which two glasses of iced tea had been placed. He gave a wolf whistle when he saw Maisie, then commented on how well his wife's beige capris matched the bride's ensemble.

"Thank you for the drinks and the sarcasm but you can leave now. As you so kindly pointed out, I still have to get dressed." Jessica pushed him out the door. "And don't you go telling Glen what Maisie is wearing."

Maisie had noticed an inconsistent banging sound coming from outside the kitchen. "Doug, what's all that noise out back. It sounds like a door banging."

"That's Neil and Glen. They're installing an old screen door on the kitchen entrance that they found out in the barn this morning. It seems to have some memories for those guys. They keep letting it go so that the spring slaps it shut. Neil was pretty impressed with it."

Maisie smiled, remembering Glen's fond memories of that door. *It must really be important to him to be installing it on his wedding day.*

Before Doug disappeared, Maisie asked if he would check on Billy to see if he needed any help.

"Glen's taking good care of Billy. Scotty is with them, too. We'll make sure he has the rings and that his fly is zipped. Glen's too."

When the organist started playing, Glen and Neil were in place beside the flower bedecked arch. Jeremy was waiting on the porch and offered his arm to his sister. A knowing eye exchange passed between them before he squeezed her hand. He knew how much it hurt Maisie that their mother wasn't there to share the joy. He had even stopped in on his way through Weyburn to try one last time to talk her into coming.

Billy was waiting at the bottom of the stairs where Jessica joined him. The procession made their way down the aisle between the lawn chairs. Billy first in his best Sunday suit, then Jessica in a robin's-egg-blue, two-piece dress that added the right amount of colour to her fair complexion and long blonde hair. Doug winked at his wife and gave her the thumb's-up.

Maisie's heart skipped a beat when she saw Glen in a brand-new, light-brown suit, the sunlight glinting off the silver that was creeping through his brown hair. He looked like a handsome movie cowboy complete with his shiny western boots.

The ceremony was over too quickly. Maisie felt that after waiting all these years to get to the altar, it should have taken longer. They took time for pictures in the garden, then by the cake, and then it was time to sit for lunch with a toast to the bride. They had thought about having finger food, a cold buffet type of meal, but decided to go for a regular lunch with their guests seated at tables under a large open tent. Many had travelled a couple of hours to get there, so they deserved to be fed.

Maisie insisted that Glen help Billy get his wheelchair comfortably up to the table. She remarked that the boy might be feeling left out with Glen giving all his attention to his new bride. By the time Glen finally pulled his own chair out, all the guests were seated and waiting. As he lowered himself to his chair a loud *rrrrrip* could be heard. Startled, everyone under the tent, including the wait staff, stopped breathing as a hush settled over the crowd. A loud laugh came from Billy sitting in his wheelchair beside his father.

"What the?" Glen bent and pulled a whoopee cushion from under the chair pad. "Billy?"

The boy was laughing so hard he could hardly talk. "Not me, Dad."

"Then who?"

The boy pointed to Maisie who was nonchalantly unfolding her napkin.

Glen turned. "I don't believe it. Maisie? You did this?"

She stood and said, "And that, ladies and gentlemen, is exactly how I was welcomed at my first dinner in the household of these two men."

The crowd roared as she winked at Billy who gave her a thumb's-up. Ellen stood up at her table and announced "I can attest to that. I had always thought Mr. Grayson rather a prude until that night."

Maisie kissed her husband on the cheek as he mumbled something about some people really know how to harbour a grudge.

Later, as she danced around the floor with her step-son in his wheelchair, Billy told her how cool it was that she had played that trick on his dad. She leaned down to whisper in his ear, "Let it be known I won't have any goofs or squares living in my house."

Before she knew it, they were cutting the cake, taking a last whirl around the dance floor, thanking everyone for coming then driving away in Glen's well-preserved 55 Chevy.

"Are you sure Billy wasn't upset about not coming with us?"

"Are you kidding? His grandmother always spoils him rotten when he's there."

"It's nice of Shelley's mother to take him so we can have a night away."

"She loves that he comes to visit. Their house is totally handicap accessible so he can move freely around their place. When I told her I was remarrying, she was afraid she'd lose access to him. I assured her that would never happen."

"She's not resentful that you have another woman in your life?"

"To be honest, I think she's among those who feel we were carrying on an affair while Shelley was still alive, so I think she kind of wrote me off a long time ago."

"Does she think we were having a romantic dinner the night Shelley was killed?"

"She hasn't said so, but it wouldn't surprise me. She's been cool towards me but keeping Billy in her life has meant keeping me in it as well. And we do have Shelley in common. After all, she was my wife."

Maisie thought about that and wondered if Mrs. Thompson was also of the opinion that Glen had something to do with Shelley's death.

"Where are we going?" It was late afternoon, so they had three hours before dark. Mrs. Thompson had asked if Billy could stay two nights. Glen had agreed, so now they had two nights for themselves.

"Not into town. Everyone will be looking for us there."

They drove for about an hour after crossing the border into North Dakota. Glen finally turned into a resort-like facility on a lake. Maisie noticed the sign advertised fishing, golf and horseback riding. She wondered which activity Glen had in mind.

It didn't take long for her to see that what Glen had planned involved neither fishing nor golf. They did go out for a boat ride and they did go horseback riding. She hadn't ridden a horse since her father was alive. Theirs had been more a work horse than a rider but her father used to put a saddle on it and she and Jeremy would take turns riding it around their farm.

She and Glen went out on a few trails around the resort. The food was excellent in the dining room and they enjoyed watching glorious sunsets two nights in a row.

"You never talk much about your father." Glen took her hand and kissed it. "You said he fell in love with your mom on first sight and that he worked hard on his farm, but that's all I know about him."

"I guess my mother has been in the forefront of my thoughts for so long, I've let him fall into my distant memories. You're right. I haven't talked about him." She sat back in the deck chair outside their room and lifted her feet onto the railing. "There really isn't too much to tell. He was out working the fields and looking after the livestock from morning till night. I'd see him at breakfast and again at supper. Sunday was the only day he'd take any time off and that was only half a day for us to attend church. He was very strict about that."

"Where did you attend church?"

"In Weyburn. My mother wasn't brought up in any particular church, but Dad's family had attended the Presbyterian Church, so that's where we went. I learned the Bible at Sunday school and we pretty well lived by it."

"Was he stern? Did he have a sense of humour? You must have inherited yours from someone and I don't think it's from your mother."

"I always found him gentle. I think my brother felt his belt a couple of times, but he never struck me. Both of my parents seemed always to be too tired to show any kind of emotion. It was only when Jeremy learned to drive, and he and I could go into town a couple times a month, that I learned what fun was. My father was the one that usually suggested going to a rodeo or the sulky races a couple of times over the summer. My mother loved those events. She seemed to come to life when we went. He would take us to a couple of hockey games in the wintertime. My brother joined a curling league when he was old enough.

"Dad spoke kindly to my mother and often thanked her for a meal or a favourite cake. I would say he was polite rather than loving. But I don't think Mom ever encouraged any physical interaction. Our farm wasn't like yours. The house was old and our fields were only about a quarter the size of yours, fences broken in many places. They had seasonal workers, but mostly Mom and Dad worked it themselves. Jeremy had to help Dad on weekends from the time he was about ten or twelve. He likes animals so preferred looking after the livestock rather than working the fields. That's why he went after a veterinarian's degree. He worked the farm plus weekends at the hardware store in town. He managed to save enough for room and board at school and Dad gave him the tuition fee the first year. After that, Jeremy got summer work with a vet that worked out of Weyburn.

"Dad died the year after Jeremy graduated. Mom sold the farm and that was that. Dad was just a memory. I do remember he was very handsome. When he got dressed up on Sundays and we went into town, I used to notice the ladies looking at him. He was polite to them, but I remember he always kept my mother's hand tucked into his arm."

"Did you know your grandparents?"

"No. My grandmother was dead before my parents met, and my grandfather died when I was a toddler. I think that's when life ended for my mother, too. My father took over the responsibility of the farm and felt it his duty to do not only his own share of the work but his father's, too. From what I understand, my grandfather prided himself on running a family farm and didn't use too much outside help. Only at harvest time. I believe my father thought he would let his father down if he didn't do the same. So he worked himself into an early grave and my mother became a bitter widow. I can remember sitting with her, patching bedsheets and mending pillowcases. I learned how to darn socks when I was still a child. My mother only brought out her hand-embroidered tea towels and her crocheted tablecloth if anyone dropped by after Sunday service. Which was almost never. Otherwise, we used the tea towels made from bleached flour sacks and a worn-out tablecloth that had been a wedding gift from an aunt. That's when she first started her mantra warning me not to marry a farmer."

"But you did and I will see that you never regret it."

"If she could see the difference in farming today — and even the difference between my father's farming style and yours — I think she would have had no cause for alarm."

"I wish I'd known your father."

THIRTY
1975

MAISIE HAD GIVEN UP ON her mother. For three years she had had high hopes of the possibility of a reunion with the woman. She finally accepted defeat. Even Billy had long since come to the conclusion that his new grandmother was not going to be a part of their lives.

Billy had asked if it was his handicap that was the problem. Maybe Maisie's mother couldn't deal with it. In his young years, he had more than once experienced rejection by adults and children who didn't have the patience or compassion to accept an invalid into their midst. When Maisie learned that Billy blamed himself for Madeline's not coming to see them, she became even more angry with her mother. It took a while, but Glen assured his son that it was Glen the woman didn't like, not Billy. Glen had explained as best he could that Maisie's mother had lived through a difficult time on a farm so she didn't want her daughter going through the same kind of hard life. That somehow she blamed Glen for talking Maisie into going against her mother's wishes and marrying him. He explained that sometimes when you love someone very much, you become upset when they don't take your advice and maybe put themselves in harm's way.

"But we don't want to harm Mom."

"No, we don't, but her mother thinks I've brought her into a situation that might be harmful to her health. Sometimes when people are older, they are so set in their thinking, you can't change their opinions no matter how hard you try. All we can do is ask God to help her see the light and maybe one day she'll learn that Mom is happy on our farm living with us."

Maisie relied on her brother and Ruby to keep her up to date on Madeline's well-being. Ruby went to Weyburn to spend weekends with Madeline several times a year, and the older woman would visit Ruby in Regina as well. Madeline would never come near the office and never asked Ruby about Maisie.

It was early in the spring of 1975 that Ruby first reported a change in Madeline.

"She seems on edge about something, Maisie. I know she's never liked Glen, but she's never really said anything specific against him since you were married."

"And she is now?"

"We were watching something on television about the farmers hoping for a good crop this year. All indications are for extremely wet weather for planting season. She mumbled something about that murderer finally getting his just dues. I wasn't sure I heard her right, so I asked her what she said and she shook a pointed finger at the television and said 'You'll get yours, Glen Grayson. You'll get yours.'"

Ruby seemed almost reluctant to go on but, after a deep breath, she said, "I was wondering if Jeremy might have noticed it and said something to you or, there's the possibility I'm just imagining things."

"What kind of things?"

"She just seems forgetful sometimes and once or twice I thought she might be a bit confused. Occasionally, I think she forgets she's here in Regina and not in Weyburn. One time, she put on her coat and said she was going to walk downtown to the grocery store. When I reminded her she couldn't walk all the way downtown from where I live, she seemed startled then clearly embarrassed. Another time, I heard her crying in her room and when I asked her what was wrong, she said she hoped God would forgive her for raising a daughter who turned into a whore. I couldn't help but wonder if she might be on the verge of dementia. Then she seemed okay for a while. We talk on the phone at least weekly and most times she's her old self. Once, when we were talking, out of the clear blue she said something about Glen not waiting until his wife was dead before he started carrying on."

Maisie was spending the day at the Regina office that Ruby pretty well managed on her own now. A good number of Maisie's rural clients had switched to her Estevan office. Ruby had developed a full clientele of her own and was doing quite well financially. Maisie now came to the city only once a month for a few days of work and appointments with a few faithful city clients.

She had even given up stopping in Weyburn a couple of years earlier because it only upset her mother and lord knows it didn't do her own well-being any good, either. Maybe it was time to try a visit on her way home.

"I'll give my brother a call and see if he's noticed anything different about Mom. She was getting so upset by my attempts to visit that I quit trying. I'll see if Jeremy thinks I should stop by on my way home."

"I hope it's just me and there's nothing going on with Madeline's mind. I know now that Glen isn't a murderer and that he was happily married. Since I've gotten to know him better and had conversations with him, he has always spoken proudly of his first wife. I know she was a good mother, too. The couple of times she brought their little fellow to the office he was happy and well-behaved. I worry about these things popping out of your mother's mouth again. I know she didn't like you marrying a farmer and thought those things she said at the time of your wedding were just because of her own life on the farm. She never mentioned them again until recently."

"If she won't see me, maybe Jeremy can arrange for her to see a doctor and be tested for dementia. Thanks for letting me know, Ruby. I appreciate it."

"She's my friend and I do worry about her."

"I know. You and Mom hit it off from the first day you met. You've been a good friend to her. I'll look into it because if she's not thinking responsibly, she may need help with decision making — which means my brother will have to look into her affairs. I hope she's remembering to take her medications and to pay her bills."

"Maisie, she's fine almost all of the time. There have only been a few incidents when she appeared to be uncertain about things."

Maisie caught Jeremy at the clinic and he agreed, yes, maybe she should stop in and try to have a conversation with their mother on her way home to Estevan. They could discuss it then and take it from there.

"Mom. It's me. Maisie. Please open the door."

"Get away from my door, you hussy."

"I came to see how you are. Won't you let me come in for five minutes? I love you and want to see you."

"If you don't leave right now, I'll call the police."

"Mom, for heaven's sake. I'm your daughter. Please open up."

"Go back to your wife-beater husband."

"Glen is not a wife-beater. He's never laid a hand on me except in kindness and love."

She could hear her mother's footsteps then the bolt slide in the lock on the inside door.

Thank goodness.

Then it opened and a thin, frail Madeline poked a finger at her from the other side of the screen door. "No, he wouldn't touch you. Why would he? You helped him get rid of the woman that was between you and him. I'm surprised the police never figured that out."

"Mom, will you give up on that? Glen did not kill his wife. Nor did

I. You have to quit saying such horrible things."

"I don't have to quit thinking or saying anything. Go away. You're not the girl I raised. Go on. Get out of here." She slammed the inside door closed and slid the bolt back across.

When Maisie arrived home, she called Jeremy and explained the conversation — or non-conversation — between her and their mother.

"It doesn't sound good, Maisie. Maybe I'll take Scotty to Weyburn on the weekend. It's been a while since he's seen his grandmother. I only hope it's a pleasant visit."

She waited until after Billy had gone to bed before she explained the situation to her husband.

"I'm so worried someone might actually believe her one day."

"I can't believe she's continuing to hurt you this way. I really don't know what I've done to her. Can't she see that farming isn't the way it used to be? You are not overworked, nor have I interfered with your business."

"Of course, she can see that. She's just felt the hate for so long she can't let go of it. I thought when she started coming to Regina and seemed to be enjoying life a little more, that she'd give up on her spiteful feelings toward farming. She and Ruby have had some fun times together. It's like she's two different people."

"Well let's see what your brother finds out on Saturday."

"We're in Weyburn. Do you have room for Scotty and me tonight if we come to your place?"

"Of course. Did you see Mom?"

"I'll tell you about it when I get there. We'll see you in an hour."

"Was that Uncle Jeremy?"

"Yes. He and Scott are coming here for the night."

Glen put the newspaper down. "Did he see your mother?"

"He said he'd tell me about it when he gets here. I hope everything's all right."

"Good." Billy enjoyed the occasional visits of his cousin. "Scotty and me can watch the hockey game together. The Leafs are playing tonight."

"Scotty and I." Maisie corrected him.

"Yeah. You can watch it with us, too. We can all watch the hockey game together."

He chuckled when she gave him The Look.

"I'll clean my stuff off the bed in the guest room for him."

When he left the room, she sat on the hassock by Glen's chair. "Jeremy sounded rather solemn. I hope Mom is okay."

Glen reached out to pull her to him for a kiss. "Your mother is closing in on seventy. Considering her hard life, she's been pretty healthy up until now. She's been lucky."

"I know. She's always been frail and, of course, her lumbago gave her reason to complain, but she's lived this long without ever being hospitalized for anything. I just hate to think that her mind might be going. I would rather it was something physical that can be fixed."

"Most times, physical deterioration is painful. Dementia isn't."

"I know." She sighed. "I'll go peel extra potatoes for our supper guests."

As she was pulling the pan from the oven, she heard Glen welcoming her brother and nephew. Billy's voice soon drowned out the others. He was always happy to see his cousin even though Scott was a few years older. They all made their way into the kitchen and rubbed their bellies when they saw the table covered in platters and bowls of hot roast beef and gravy, boiled cabbage and steaming mashed potatoes.

"Hey, sis, that smells good."

"Sit and eat. Billy's happy to have company to watch the hockey game tonight."

"Yeah, the Flyers are playing the Leafs." Billy was sporting a blue jersey with a white maple leaf on the front.

After everyone had finished eating, the boys took glasses of chocolate milk into the living room to watch the hockey game while the adults drank coffee in the kitchen.

Jeremy was the first to speak. "I ended up taking Mom to the hospital today. They decided to keep her overnight to run tests. She'll probably go home tomorrow."

"What kind of tests?"

"Let me start at the beginning. When I got there, she was really happy to see me but it took a few seconds for her to recognize Scott."

"What? How long has it been since she saw him? It can't be that long."

"Maybe a couple of months. Once she remembered him, it was all okay. We had a nice visit and I was ready to pass it off as just a momentary lapse on her part. It happens."

"Did something happen to change your mind?"

Jeremy glanced at Glen as if unsure about continuing.

"If you would rather talk to Maisie alone, I can join the boys in the living room." He started to rise.

Jeremy took his arm. "No. Sit."

"I don't mind. If you're more comfortable without me here, I'll just sit with the boys."

"That's not it." He sipped his coffee. "It's just that my mother started talking about you, Glen."

Maisie interjected. "Let me guess. She accused him of being a wife-beater."

"Worse. She accused him of killing his first wife."

Glen shifted uncomfortably. "I remember she was upset that Maisie and I were having dinner together at the time of Shelley's accident. She had it in her head that it was more a romantic liaison than a business dinner."

"Exactly. She told me that she knows you killed your wife and she's worried you'll do the same to Maisie."

Maisie frowned. "She spoke to me about Glen being a killer, but she didn't tell me she was afraid for me. On the contrary, she told me he would never hurt me because I was his accomplice. She told Ruby she prays for God's forgiveness because she raised a whore and was afraid I might have been in cahoots with Glen for Shelley's murder. If she told Ruby her thoughts, I wonder if she's told anyone else."

"She has." Jeremy frowned and took his cup in both hands. "She's been to the police."

"What?" Glen almost choked on a mouthful of coffee.

"She told me she went to them after you were there the other day, Maisie."

"Did you talk to the police?"

"From what I can gather, they told her to go home and they'll check into it. In fact, they drove her home. I have the feeling they merely listened but didn't take her seriously."

"When I asked her why she would tell the police something like that, she got quite upset. She said somebody has to stop Glen before he kills again. She appears to have lost sense of time, though. She's talking like this happened recently. She grabbed her purse and wanted me to go with her, saying they'd believe her if I went with her. She opened the door without a jacket and became quite agitated when I tried to stop her. She screamed that I didn't care what happened to you or to her. She said Glen might come and kill her because she knows too much. She said the police have to believe her before it's too late."

"Were you able to calm her down?"

"I got her to put her jacket on and get in the car. Scotty was nervous and I think frightened by her. I drove the few blocks to the hospital and sent him in to get someone to come out and help us. An orderly came out and opened the rear seat door. She was confused but went in with him. When she got inside and realized it was the hospital and not the police station, she got almost violent, screaming that no one believes she knows who the murderer is. They gave her something to calm her and I sat with her for an hour or more. They questioned me about this murder she was screaming about. I explained that she's not herself. That she seems to be fantasizing."

He rubbed his chin with his thumb and forefinger. "I had made Scott sit in the waiting room while the doctor examined her. I was worried about the long-term impact this might have on his perception of his grandmother. The doctor gave her a cursory look and said he would order an immediate CTScan and blood work, then perform cognitive testing in the morning."

Maisie stared down at her clenched fists. "Do you think she may be bordering on dementia, Jeremy?"

"I don't know what to think. She certainly isn't the same taciturn woman she was before."

"I guess we have to wait and see what the doctor says tomorrow. Do you want me to go with you?"

"If you would like to come, sure. We may have to make a decision about her and it's better we do it together."

A loud cheer was heard from the living room. Obviously, the Toronto Maple Leafs had scored.

THIRTY-ONE

WHEN MADELINE SAW JEREMY AND Maisie walk in together, she glared from one to the other. "Are you ganging up on me?"

"Nobody is ganging up on you, Mother. We're both concerned about you." They had agreed that it might be best if Jeremy did most of the talking.

"Where's Scott?"

"He's in the waiting room."

"What are you doing here? I thought I told you to stay away from me." She all but sneered at Maisie.

"I was hoping you might have changed your mind."

"Has your husband turned himself in?"

"For?"

"Murdering his wife."

"Mom, we both know that Glen did not murder his wife. We were at a business dinner when the accident happened."

"That's right. You were his alibi. Just like you planned it."

Jeremy moved between them. "Have you seen the doctor today?"

"He was in. He thinks I'm a crazy woman."

"Why would you say that?"

"He X-rayed my head with some newfangled machine last night. Then he had somebody else come in and give me a bunch of little kids' puzzles to do."

"Has he been back since all of this was done?"

"No."

Jeremy slipped out of the room but was back within minutes.

"The nurse on duty said he's in the hospital making rounds and will be in soon. Maisie will wait with us until we know if you'll be allowed to go back home today."

"Why wouldn't I be?"

"They may want to run more tests."

"I won't do them. There's nothing wrong with me."

"Well, there she is. Good morning, Madeline." The family doctor Madeline had seen regularly since moving to Weyburn breezed in the door and pulled up a stool by the bed. "So what's this I hear about you causing a ruckus last evening?"

"I didn't raise a ruckus. I raised my voice because people wouldn't listen to me."

"Are you feeling calmer now?"

"I've said my piece and now I'll go home."

"Well, Madeline. I don't see any reason why you can't go home. I read your scan and the blood test results. I looked at the report also from the "little kids' puzzles" as the nurse said you called them. There is an area of mild concern with your cognitive skills."

"What does that mean?"

"It means that you got the puzzles done correctly but not in the prescribed time frame. You were slow figuring them out and then following the instructions."

"I don't understand. I've always been a good reader and I got them done right."

"That's true. However, your processing of what you read is slowing down."

"Doesn't that happen to everybody as they get older? Everybody slows down."

"To a certain degree, yes. I'm going to change one of your medications. We'll see if that helps. You're also having trouble with short term memory, which, again, happens as we age. We just want to keep an eye on it and see that it doesn't progress too quickly."

"Are you saying I have dementia?"

"I would say you have a tendency in that direction. We'll do what we can to slow it down. It may not get any worse, but we want to keep an eye on it. So, you can go home today with a different prescription and I want to see you in my office in six weeks. These new pills will replace the ones you take at night."

He turned to Jeremy and Maisie. "When you take her home after getting this prescription filled, will you remove the red pills she takes at night? You can return them to any pharmacy for disposal. I don't want her getting them mixed up."

"Yoo-hoo, I'm over here, Doctor. You can talk to me."

"I want to make sure you only have the proper medication in your cabinet, Madeline. Don't get snarky with me." He patted her hand and winked at Jeremy and Maisie on his way out.

"I'll take you home, Mom. And maybe Maisie won't mind going to the drug store."

"I can do that." Maisie took the prescription from the night table and turned to Madeline. "I'm sorry you had to spend the night here, Mother. I hope the new meds will do the trick for you."

"They won't make me forget that you outright disobeyed me and married that murderer."

Maisie literally bit her tongue as she turned to Jeremy. "I'll pick these up and meet you at her house. I can take Scott with me if you like. So you can tend to Mother's release."

An hour later, Maisie had delivered the meds and Scott to her mother's house. She had not been allowed inside so she thanked her brother for his help, returned to her car and headed home. She was relieved that it wasn't anything worse with her mother. Ruby would be waiting to hear from her.

Somehow, she couldn't feel the concern that she should have felt about her mother's mild dementia. A few years ago, she would have been beside herself with worry. She had since built a wall that the hurts her mother directed at her couldn't permeate. Had it also built a defense against the love she should have felt toward her mother? It stood to reason the shield would work both ways. All those years of weekly car trips between Regina and Weyburn to see to her mother's needs seemed to belong in another dimension. Could the relationship be saved? Would her mother ever accept Glen and Billy as her family? The miles slid by and she turned into their driveway before she was ready for it. She knew Billy would be waiting to tell her about the hockey game at the rink after church this morning. Billy loved the game. He couldn't play, but the coach had taught him how to look after the time clock at the practices. Billy was happy being involved and was always eager to share all the plays and the conversations with the players when they were in the penalty box. He took his job seriously and it was a rare occasion when they had to reset the clock because he was slow turning it on at a faceoff.

She knew Glen would be waiting too. He had been more than kind over the years. He never seemed to harbour resentment that her mother disliked him with such a passion and now there was this new issue with her openly accusing him of murder. Madeline had tried desperately to talk Maisie out of marrying Glen and when that hadn't worked, she had turned downright hostile. Now it appeared she was telling anyone within hearing distance that her daughter, the whore, had married a murderer — had even colluded with him on it.

She sat on the back steps listening to the braying of the cattle. She loved this farm. She wondered how long her father might have lived had he owned a modern spread like this. She remembered Glen asking about her father. Her memories of the farm had been more associated with her mother than with her father.

One fond memory came to mind. It was a Sunday when she was so young she barely remembered it. They had come home from church. She recalled that Jeremy had stayed in town to play at a school friend's house. She had sat on the back steps and watched as her dad hitched a horse to their wagon before calling her over to join him. He had picked her up and set her on the seat beside him. When he snapped the reins, the horse started off down the worn path that bordered their property. The sun had been shining and the breeze had played with her hair, blowing it into her eyes. She remembered how her dad had laughed at the expression on her face when he had slipped his arm around her and let her take the reins in her own hands. It was probably the only time her dad had taken only her with him in the wagon like that. She frowned now, remembering her mother's anger when they came back, because the lunch she had prepared had been kept waiting for half an hour.

Oh, Daddy. I know you tried. Lord, how you tried.

The slapping of the screen door woke her from her reverie.

Billy was indeed waiting with his play-by-play of the game. Glen was nowhere to be seen.

"Where's your dad?"

"He said he had some work to do out in the barn."

"I'll get supper going. Did you get to church?"

"Yeah. You know Dad doesn't let me miss unless I have a really good excuse."

Billy followed her into the kitchen. "Ya want me to peel potatoes?"

"I was thinking we might have spaghetti. There are meatballs in the freezer."

"Sure! I love spaghetti and meatballs. You make the best."

"How about you wash some vegetables for salad?"

Glen hadn't returned by the time the meal was ready, so she sent Billy out to the back porch to ring the dinner bell.

A few minutes later, he sauntered through the kitchen door and planted a kiss on her cheek. "How did it go?"

"Okay, I guess. She's back at home. The doctor said her tests showed a slow progression toward dementia but not serious enough to worry about her living alone yet. He changed her meds and told her to come back in six weeks."

"Did she talk to you?"

"You mean did she yell at me? Same old same old."

Glen turned her to him and wrapped his arms around her. "Are you okay?" He kissed her forehead.

"I guess. I am so sorry that she won't let this thing go about you."

"What thing has Grandma got about Dad?"

Glen turned to Billy before Maisie could answer. "You remember how I told you she wasn't happy about Mom marrying me because I'm a farmer?"

"Yes."

"Well, sometimes when people get older the things that bother them seem to grow in their imagination and they get fixated on them." Before he could finish the sentence, Billy interrupted him.

"What does fixated mean?"

"Look it up in the dictionary, son." He ruffed the boy's hair. "Anyway, your grandmother is getting older and her mind doesn't always see things in their proper light. She didn't like me when she was younger and that dislike is getting worse in her mind. She can't help it. It's just the way our brains work as we age."

"I wish she'd come here and maybe she'd see that it's fun living on a farm."

"I'm sure she would too, my boy. That's one more thing for you to pray for."

The next day, Maisie called Ruby at the office and gave her the complete story of the past few days.

"She may be feeling alone. I'll call her tonight to chat. Maybe it will cheer her up."

"Ruby, thanks again for bringing this to our attention. My brother acted quickly on it and hopefully the doctor can help slow the process down. He was quite confident she'll have no problem living on her own for a few years to come."

That evening Ruby called shortly after 8 o'clock to say she had talked with Madeline and everything went smoothly. No complaints, no confusion and no loss of memory.

THIRTY-TWO
1977

IT HAD BEEN AN UNSEASONABLY hot spring and Maisie had experienced an exceptionally busy tax season. Business was booming. It was mid-May and she was on her way to Regina for the second time in the past four weeks. She had suggested to Ruby that they hire another accountant to take some of the load from both of them. Not only was she busy with her business, she was becoming increasingly involved in the community's affairs. She sat on several boards of various not-for-profit organizations in Estevan, and had only recently declined the position of president of the Chamber of Commerce.

Billy was happy that she volunteered when and where she could in some of his activities. There were more and more opportunities for paraplegic children and teens to participate in hobbies and sports. At eleven years of age, he was intent on developing his upper body strength, not just to help his mobility, but to enable him to participate in more sports. He had graduated from darts to javelin and was playing wheelchair basketball, both of which required amazing arm strength. His school grades were excellent, which helped because he would never be eligible for an athletic invitation to university. A lot of Maisie's time was spent on fundraising for and awareness of the various organizations that offered recreation, rehabilitation and research for the handicapped.

It was not even 9 o'clock and the warmth of another hot day could already be felt. The crops were promising an early harvest as long as this sunny weather didn't stretch into drought conditions. Ruby had short-listed several potential applicants for a junior accounting position, two recent CGA graduates among them. Forbes & Sawchuk Accountants had earned a good reputation for themselves and there was always a list of graduating accountants jockeying to become a part of their firm. The first appointment was scheduled within the half hour.

Maisie pulled into the parking lot and felt the heat of the pavement hit her as she exited her car. She was surrounded by two- and three-storey commercial buildings. Their office was situated on 11th Avenue a few blocks from the main business section of downtown Regina, allowing for ease of parking and a quieter atmosphere. She liked Regina, and couldn't help the occasional wish that she still lived here. She rented a room in a downtown hotel for the few days she spent there. Ruby had offered her a room in her apartment, but Maisie liked to kick off her shoes and relax alone when she left the office. Because her time was limited in the city, she crammed a lot of work into long hours and wanted complete downtime once she left the building.

She entered their office space and immediately was met with the face of someone she assumed was an expectant applicant. Ruby had spaced the appointments a half hour apart and obviously, this one had arrived much earlier than his allotted time, possibly hoping to impress

— or was perhaps anxious to get it over with. She asked the receptionist to accompany her into her office.

"Alice, please hold all my calls for the next two hours. Would you be so kind as to bring me a cup of coffee and the files of the applicants I'll be seeing this morning? Also, you can let Ruby know I'm here now if she wants to talk before we start the interviews."

Alice was the latest in a procession of receptionists. Ruby had let Tess go years earlier. The woman had not changed her cavalier attitude about showing up for work when it suited her, plus Ruby had never been comfortable with the way she seemed to listen in on conversations. Nowadays, it seemed young people applying for entry-level positions didn't stay around long enough to build any real loyalty. The first time they felt hard done by, they would leave and a new one would move into the slot. Maisie had been lucky that Ruby and Ellen had stayed all these years. Ellen had taken short leaves after the births of her two children but had returned ready to work after only a few months' absence each time. Fortunately, the grandmother was a willing babysitter. Ruby and Maisie had been surprised when the young woman chose to continue in her role as bookkeeper rather than become an accountant. The young man she had chosen to fall in love with and marry had a good job with the government so they felt secure in their financial future. Her earnings as a bookkeeper would be set aside for their children's education and retirement. She had no plans to leave anytime soon. Maisie had hopes for Alice as well. She had been with them almost two years now and seemed happy enough. Now they just had to find a suitable accountant to complete the staff.

The interviews produced two obvious front runners. After weighing their pros and cons for another half hour after they left, Ruby seemed most impressed with the very first candidate. Since it was Ruby who would be working more closely with him, Maisie agreed to bring him on board. His name was Craig McDermott and he was a recent graduate from the University of Saskatchewan in Saskatoon. His family background was farming, so Maisie was hopeful he might eventually take over some of her rural clients located in the

Regina area, and maybe even pick up a few from his family's home area up Highway 6.

The women went to a nearby haunt for lunch. Maisie expressed her hope of Craig's taking some of her clients. She offered to come up and help with his training to familiarize him with their files. Ruby was relieved she wouldn't have to give up any of her own clients so was more than agreeable. It had been decided the young man would start the beginning of June, which would allow him time to find living accommodations and have a bit of a vacation before he started full-time work.

"I'll arrange things in Estevan to allow me more time up here until Craig is familiar with all my clients. I'll see if I can get an inexpensive room rental here for my more frequent visits."

"I don't know why you don't stay with me. It would save you a bundle."

"I appreciate your offer, Ruby, but I need my own space for down time. Besides, Billy may want to come with me the odd time in between his own sports schedules."

"How's he doing? He seems so involved in everything."

"He is so well-adjusted, you wouldn't believe it. Smart in school and involved in sports. He loves music. Did I tell you he started trumpet lessons?"

"No. How does he find the time? You and Glen must be worn out driving him to everything."

"We've arranged for him to be picked up for some of his events but it's hard when you live in the country. We're just so happy that he's involved in all these activities, that we don't mind trying to get him there."

"If you're going to be spending more time in Regina, will Glen be able to pick up the slack?"

"We'll have to talk about it for sure. One good thing is that many of my own committee involvements take a break over the summer. That will free up some of my evenings. Billy wants to come to Regina for lessons with one of the music schools up here, so maybe he won't mind giving up one of his activities at home to do it. I can schedule my office hours here around his classes if we can get him enrolled."

"It's probably none of my business, but you and Glen have been married for a few years now. Are you not planning on having children of your own?"

Maisie put her fork down.

"I consider Billy my own child. He calls me Mom and hardly remembers Shelley. So for all intents and purposes, I am his mother. However, Glen and I have never really done anything to stop us from having another child. It just hasn't happened." She picked up her fork again. "With our upcoming schedules, maybe it's just as well."

"I suppose. Besides it might be hard for Billy to adjust to a sibling who could do all the things that he can't."

"There's that, too. Although he has asked if he'll ever have a brother or sister." She looked at her watch. "I'd better get back to the office. I have several appointments this afternoon. If I can get all my work done, I really want to head home this evening."

"Maisie, I didn't want to bring it up earlier, but do you think you might find time to stop by your mother's place on your way home?"

"Is there a problem?"

"When I chatted with her last night, she brought up Glen again. She hasn't mentioned him in over a year but out of the blue she said she was going to go to the police station today to see if they have done anything more about arresting him. She said it was past time they put the cuffs on him."

"Oh, dear God. Did you mention I was coming here today?"

"I never bring your name up. Sorry to say, it usually upsets her, so I avoid talking about you at all."

"I'll call my brother from the office. I don't want to go if it will only set her off again. She has been relatively good the last couple of years. Jeremy visits her every six weeks or so and she's been fine."

In the end, Jeremy thought it best if Maisie went straight home. He would talk to Madeline, and if she brought up Glen's name at all, he'd try to diffuse it.

When Maisie arrived home at 10 o'clock that night Glen gave her the message to call Jeremy.

"Did he say how Mom is?"

"No. He was rather abrupt. Just said for you to call him."

She checked her watch. It was late but he had asked her to call.

"Jeremy? It's Maisie. Has something happened?"

"The police in Weyburn called me and asked me about Shelley's accident. Mom had gone to them and insisted they reopen the case. She said she knows Glen was responsible and that it wasn't an accident at all. When I mentioned she was suffering from mild dementia they told me she seemed perfectly lucid and was quite candid about the events surrounding the accident — including the interview they conducted with you at her house. She told them she can prove he did it."

"What? Surely, they aren't taking her seriously."

"They told me they assured her they would look into the file again. When I asked if they actually were, they said there was a new division in Regina that looks at old files that have remained open."

"It can't still be open after all these years."

"Apparently, because the hit and run driver was never found, the file has remained open. It's what they call a cold case file."

"So you're telling me they're actually going to look at it?"

"Yes."

THIRTY-THREE

"I DON'T BELIEVE THIS."

"Glen, I am so sorry. Who would have thought that my mother's bitterness and dementia would cause the police to reinvestigate an eight-year-old accident?"

"But why? Why would they listen to the ravings of a demented old woman?"

"That's the point. She didn't present herself as unbalanced. They told Jeremy that she was lucid and recited the events of that evening in a clear concise manner. When they pulled the file and checked it, they found it to be exactly as she described."

"She said she had proof? What the hell is she talking about? What kind of proof?"

"I don't know. There is no proof." Maisie shook her head.

"I just hope they realize what a mistake this is before it goes any further. I don't want Billy disturbed by any police investigation."

"Oh. Billy. Of course. That poor boy has enough on his plate without his mother's death being brought to the forefront again."

Two days later, Glen received a phone call from the Weyburn radio station asking him his feelings on the reopening of his deceased wife's accident file.

Maisie called Jeremy and asked if he had spoken further to their mother, and if it was possible she was the one who had leaked gossip to the radio station.

"I don't think she would know who to call at the station, Maisie. Why don't you call the Weyburn police and see what's going on? I have five surgeries at the clinic today so that'll keep me here. I won't be able to follow up with Mom for a couple of days."

"Glen is quite upset. He, we, both of us, are worried that Billy will get wind of this and we don't want him distressed by lies about his mother's death."

A phone call to the police revealed only that it was being looked into but no information could be given out at this time.

"I think it's time we paid your mother a visit."

"I don't know if she'll even let us in, but it might be worth a try. Do you think we should send Billy to his grandparents' for a couple of days until this is taken care of?"

"I'll ask the Thompsons if they can take him. I was thinking I should give them a heads-up about this anyway. They'll be devastated to have Shelley's accident front and centre in the news again. I'm sure they'll want to keep Billy protected from any gossip, too."

Maisie called Ruby with the news and their plans to take a run to the Weyburn police and to try to talk to her mother.

Within the hour, a surprised but happy Billy was left with his grandparents. His granddad had bought him an archery set and was going to teach him how to shoot it using hay bales behind the barn.

A visibly distraught Glen and a worried Maisie continued up the highway to Weyburn, undecided whom to talk to first: the police or Madeline Forbes. The only comfort was that the Thompsons were on board with trying to keep Billy away from the radio, television or newspapers, from which he might learn about this investigation, until it could be stopped or quelled.

Glen parked the pickup outside City Hall, which housed the Weyburn police station in the basement. He and Maisie asked to speak to someone about the Shelley Grayson case file. After several intercom conversations with several unseen people, the officer at the desk asked them to have a seat. After a brief wait, they were ushered into a small room with a table and several chairs. Soon, another officer entered and took a seat.

Glen and Maisie introduced themselves and explained the reason for their visit and concern. The officer was surprised to learn that Maisie was the daughter of the woman who had asked for the file to be reopened. He made a note that Mrs. Forbes was under the care of her family doctor for dementia and that she had been seen and treated at the hospital two years prior for hysteria brought on by concerns about this same case. After a half hour of questioning and notes, Glen and Maisie left with assurances that everything would be done to keep any news of the investigation away from the media out of concern for the victim's paraplegic child. They were advised not to talk to Mrs. Forbes, whom they would inform not to discuss an ongoing investigation with any news people. Glen was assured that he was not considered a suspect unless or until any new evidence to the contrary might be discovered. However, he must understand, that because a witness had come forward with supposedly new information, an investigation would be conducted and old witnesses questioned again.

Glen had been unnaturally silent the whole drive home. It had been her experience that when he became angry, he became quiet. The angrier he got, the quieter he became. Maisie reasoned he had cause to be angry with her mother. His way of handling anger was exasperating for her sometimes, especially when she was riled up for a good fight and he would clam up and walk away. He'd disappear for hours and come back calm and most times apologetic.

When they arrived home, Glen dropped Maisie at the house and told her he was going to work in the barn for a while to clear his head.

She went inside and called her brother to explain what had transpired during their visit to Weyburn.

"Maybe Mom will be satisfied that she's done what she can and will let the police deal with it now."

Maisie wasn't so sure. "Do you really think so? I'm wondering if maybe her meds have to be increased. Do you think her dementia is getting worse and distorting her memories of the past?"

"I'll call Doc Miller's office and try to get an appointment. How's Glen taking all this?"

"He's remaining calm but of course it's upsetting him. We've taken Billy to his grandparents' house for a few days trying to keep him from getting wind of the rumours and news reports."

"Did the police give you an indication of their thoughts on it?"

"The officer we spoke with said they have to investigate any reports of new evidence, but in most instances, it's just different versions of what they already have. They're also going to tell Mom she shouldn't speak to the news media about an ongoing investigation."

"I wonder what she meant when she said she could prove Glen's guilt."

"Jeremy, you saw how she was that night at the hospital. She is so full of spite and hate for Glen — and me for *disobeying* her — that I'm sure she's imagining all kinds of things. Even the night of the accident is all wrong in her head. She's always been determined that we were having a romantic dinner instead of a quick business meeting at a highway café that was a convenient location for both of us."

"Do you think the police might be persuaded that it was a tryst instead of a meeting? I mean you guys *did* have a history and you *are* married now. They may look at it the way she wants them to."

Maisie couldn't believe what she was hearing. "For God's sake, Jeremy. We were not romantically involved. Glen loved his wife. They were happily married. Believe me."

"Mom said he had broken her arm just a week or so before."

"He did not break her arm."

"How *did* she break it?"

"I don't know. She told me she fell."

"They all say that."

"Who all say that?"

"Women who are victims of abuse. They always say they've fallen or walked into a door to explain bruises and broken bones. We even get pet owners who explain their cat's or dog's broken limbs that way."

"Are you accusing Glen of lying? You think that he actually abused Shelley?"

"Maisie, I'm not accusing Glen of anything. I'm just saying it sometimes happens — even accidentally."

"I don't think I want to continue this conversation. I can't believe you are even saying these things to me."

"Look. I'm sorry, sis. It's just that something has Mom all upset and I have to ask."

"Goodnight, Jeremy. We'll talk again after she's seen the doctor."

She set the phone down and fell onto the bed. *He can't actually believe Mom. Can he?*

She fell asleep and when she woke up the house was in darkness. She searched for Glen and wondered if he had eaten. Nothing seemed to have been used in the kitchen. A glance out back showed the lights on in the barn. She opened a can of soup, placed it on the stove and set about making sandwiches. After placing everything on the table she went out to the porch and rang the dinner bell. When Glen didn't respond, she walked out to the barn and called out to him. No response. She walked to the big garage where he had a workbench and often worked on tools and equipment, but he wasn't there, nor was his pickup around.

He must have gone into town to have a beer with the guys.

She came back in, turned the element off under the soup and ate her sandwich alone. She was already in bed when she heard Glen's truck in the driveway. When he didn't come in, she looked out the window and saw the light still on in the barn.

THIRTY-FIVE

THE SOUND OF THE PHONE ringing woke her up. It stopped as she rolled over to answer it. She was alone in bed and it appeared she must have been alone all night. The radio alarm beside the bed said it was 10 o'clock. How had she slept so late? Glen called to her from downstairs that her brother was on the phone.

She got up and went downstairs. *He'd better be calling to apologize.* Glen didn't look well as he handed her the phone.

"Maisie. It's Mom." Jeremy's voice was shaky.

"What's the matter with her?"

"She's dead."

"Dead. Dead? What? What are you talking about? Where is she? Is she in the hospital?"

"She was found dead in a lane just off the street. It looks like she was beaten and robbed."

Maisie moved the phone from her ear and looked at it like there was something wrong with it. "When? What lane? Off what street?"

Glen placed a mug of coffee on the small table beside the phone.

"They figure it happened sometime last evening. She had been at bingo and they said it looks like someone attacked her as she was walking home."

"Who said? Who found her?"

"A milkman was making his rounds early this morning and saw her lying in the lane that runs off the street behind her house. Her purse was missing. I'm leaving to go there now. Can you meet me there?"

"Yes. Yes, I'll get dressed and come. Are they sure it's her?"

"The milkman knew her. She was a customer of his. Take your time. I have to go to the hospital to make positive identification before I meet you at her house."

Maisie hung up the phone then whispered "Goodbye" to the dead receiver.

Glen lifted her into his arms where she sobbed on his shoulder until her tears ran dry.

"Go and shower. I'll fix you something to eat before we go."

"You'll go with me?"

"Of course." He kissed her forehead then patted her bum as she turned toward the stairs.

She sat naked on her bed after her shower, staring at a picture of her and her mother. They were cheek to cheek and laughing at the camera. It was one taken by Ruby during a supper they had shared to celebrate Madeline's sixtieth birthday. *We had such fun. When did it all go wrong?* She hugged the picture to her chest. Remembering. *When I started seeing Glen again.*

"You just about ready, honey?" Glen was in the doorway.

"I will be in about ten minutes." She quickly dressed and touched her cheeks with some blush, a little mascara on her eyelashes and she was good to go. "Should I pack an overnight bag do you think?"

"It probably wouldn't hurt in case we get delayed. Maybe throw a change of underwear and my toothbrush in the bag as well."

They had driven about twenty minutes in silence when Glen said, "I remember the first time I met your mother. We took her to a rodeo, and she seemed to have fun that day. I even saw her smile a time or two." He put a hand on Maisie's knee. "She sure knew her horses and riders. She could pick a winner before they were two seconds out of the box."

"She and Dad used to follow the circuit news around the area and would get to at least one rodeo close by. Their big dream was to one day go to the Calgary stampede." She wiped her eyes. "They never made it."

"Did your mother work before she and your dad married?"

"She worked at a restaurant in Estevan. That's where my dad saw her and fell in love. He said she was the most beautiful girl in all of southern Saskatchewan. They were married within months of meeting."

"It was your grandfather's farm when they got married, right?"

"Yes. Daddy's father owned it, but he died early, too. I never thought about it before, but I wonder if it wasn't a hereditary heart condition. My mother never forgave my father for dying and leaving her."

"Your father was right. Madeline was a good-looking woman."

"He was a pretty good-looking guy too. My friends used to tell me how handsome they thought he was."

"So you got your beauty from both of your parents."

"I guess. If you say so." She blushed at the compliment. "Everyone always said I resembled my father and that Jeremy took after her."

"Neither of your parents had siblings? I've never heard you mention extended family."

"My mother was an only child and Dad had a sister who married and moved to California. He never talked about her much. He would get the occasional letter, but never any pictures or anything. And we could never afford a trip to visit. Nor could my parents have left the farm for that long. When you really think about it, my parents led a pretty lonely existence. I guess my mother had reason to be bitter."

"They must have had friends. Other farmers? People from church? Parents of your friends?"

"I don't recall too many occasions when they entertained. We would attend the church picnics and rodeos and the odd baseball game in town, but Jeremy and I didn't have too many friends until we went to high school. I got into tennis then when some of the kids were able to drive and we got out to socialize more."

"I wish we'd met back when we were younger, but I was just that much older than you that we weren't at the same events at the same times."

"Our farm was much smaller than yours so I don't think our parents would have even known each other. Probably no one outside of our immediate area would have known us. My mother never mentioned that your family name was familiar."

They entered the outskirts of Weyburn and Glen remembered the way to Madeline's house. To Maisie, the little bungalow looked shadowed and forlorn even though the sun was bright and high in the sky. Jeremy's car was nowhere in sight, but when they approached the front steps, a policeman opened the door and asked who they were.

When Maisie explained the family relationship, they were allowed to enter, but told not to move or remove anything. That's when she and Glen came to realize that Madeline's house was being treated as a crime scene.

"When Mr. Forbes gets here, you both can go through her things together to determine if anything is missing."

It wasn't long before Jeremy arrived. Maisie hugged him tightly and they sobbed in each other's arms. Glen gave Jeremy's shoulder a comforting pat. He was totally unaware of the conversation in which Jeremy had hinted at his own suspicions about Glen abusing Shelley and possibly being involved with Maisie at the time of Shelley's death.

They went through Madeline's jewellery and items that someone might think had value. They couldn't find anything missing. The woman had not owned much except for her wristwatch and a few pairs of earrings. The rest of her things were costume jewellery and a couple of Royal Doulton figurines Maisie had bought her. She owned no sterling silver flatware. No coin or stamp collections. Everything seemed to be intact. There was dark dust over a number of things in the bedroom and around the doorknobs. The policeman explained that they had dusted for fingerprints, so Maisie, Glen and Jeremy would have to give theirs at the station. A search for any notes or papers that might have been threatening or suspicious in nature had also been done.

A second officer arrived, and they had Jeremy sign papers. They left saying they were through with the house investigation. There had been no sign of forced entry, so since nothing was missing and nothing unusual found, it was concluded that whoever the perp was, he had not gained entry to the house. It was a case of assault resulting in death and the theft of Madeline's purse.

Jeremy told Maisie that the coroner at the hospital said it looked like she had put up quite a struggle. "That would be Mom." Maisie replied. "She wouldn't give up without a battle. Poor woman."

"They need to know what we want done with her body."

"I believe you are the executor, Jeremy. Whatever you decide is fine with me."

"I think a family service in the funeral home and a private burial beside Dad would be appropriate. I don't want nosy people and reporters coming and gawking at her in an open casket."

"That sounds fine with me. The sooner the better."

"Will you go with me to choose a casket? And maybe you could pick out a nice outfit or something for them to dress her in?"

"Of course. Do you mind if I invite Ruby to come to the service? She was a good friend to Mom."

"Certainly. There are a couple of neighbours that always looked in on her, too. I'll phone the pastor at her church. See if he'll come. Say a few words. Maybe he'll know if she was friendly with anyone from church."

"Don't you think it sad that our own mother is dead and we don't even know who her friends are? Whom to invite to her funeral?" She burst into tears at her own words. Shame and regret were the cause of her outpouring of grief. *Mom, why did you have so much hate in your heart? I hope you are finding happiness in God's domain and that there isn't a single farm field in sight up there to dampen your spirit.*

She phoned Ruby and gave her the gruesome news. "I'll let you know what day the funeral will be if you want to attend."

"Of course, I'll be there. I wouldn't miss my friend's funeral. Poor Madeline. To die all alone like that. Who would do such a thing to a frail little woman like her? I hope the police catch him and throw the book at him, as they say."

The funeral was scheduled for two days later. They put a short obituary notice in the Weyburn newspaper only to find the story of her brutal death on the front page of the same paper. It also gave a graphic description of the unsolved murder of her son-in-law's first wife and how suspicion had fallen on him at the time. They made a point of reporting he had been having supper in a restaurant with Mrs. Forbes' daughter at the time of his wife's death. It was reported that recently, the deceased woman had claimed to have proof of Glen Grayson's guilt in the death of his first wife. Now the police would probably never know what that proof was or if it existed.

"Damn those bastards! Is it never going to end?" Glen threw the paper on the kitchen table and went out to the barn.

Maisie picked it up and swore also. Why were they so quick to pick up on the ramblings of an old woman suffering from dementia, and report it as fact? She felt sorry for Glen. She recalled her brother's tone in the telephone conversation they'd had a few days earlier. Did people really suspect Glen, and in effect, her, as well, of murdering Shelley? She tried to look at it through the eyes of others. Maybe their marriage really did make them look guilty.

Poor Glen. Such a gentle man to be looked at as a killer and wife abuser. She couldn't recall his ever raising his voice, let alone raising a hand to her. He was frustratingly calm at all times. There were incidents when she thought he would blow up and get angry, actually wanted him to do so, but instead, he chose to walk away and finish the discussion after she had time to cool down and talk without screaming. The only time he showed real passion was in bed. His lovemaking was always an experience of intense emotion and love.

He made sure she enjoyed it as much as he did. That had never changed. They enjoyed their sex life as much now as when they first met.

Billy was another area of great passion for Glen. He was proud, almost to the extreme, of his son's accomplishments and had no patience for anyone who couldn't understand that people with physical handicaps didn't necessarily have mental ones as well. Billy was ahead of his age group in school. He could very well enter high school at the age of twelve if they let him. He read everything he could get his hands on. He enjoyed music as much as sports. Glen was quick to point out he must have inherited it from his mother, giving Shelley full credit for his son's intellect.

No. Glen was not a killer. He didn't have the killer instinct. He was maddeningly perfect and she loved every maddening inch of him. She was lucky that he had still wanted her when opportunity knocked the second time.

The ringing of the phone broke her reverie. It seemed to be doing that a lot lately.

"Hello?"

"This is the Estevan Mercury calling—" She broke the connection.

THIRTY-FIVE

WERE THEY GOING TO SUFFER the wrath of the news people who were not allowed inside the closed doors of the chapel in the funeral home? Time would tell.

Ruby Sawchuk and Ellen Webster were the only staff members from the office invited to attend. Several members of Madeline's church and a half dozen neighbours were there as well. Jeremy and Jeanne with Scott, and Glen's brother, Neil, with his wife, Chelsea, and their daughters all sat in the front pews. Maisie was surprised to see the Grayson family had come all the way from Saskatoon when they had never even met her mother. Then understanding dawned. They were showing their love and support of Glen. Jessica and Doug Boyle arrived just in time for the service. Glen had not wanted Billy to attend since he had been excluded from his grandmother's life. Add to that the fact he was afraid the press might be there, and he didn't want his son to be witness to any scene that might create. The boy had argued he was old enough to deal with death and really wanted to participate in at least this last tribute to the grandmother he had never known. In the end, Glen relented and Billy sat in his wheelchair at the end of the second pew beside his cousin.

The service was brief. When the casket was removed from the chapel to be taken to the cemetery, the pastor asked the reporters to please step back and allow the family privacy in their time of grief. A police car was waiting at the entrance to the cemetery and refused entry to any but the cars with tickets on their windshields. The family served light refreshments to the invited guests at Madeline's house after the interment. It was all over in less than four hours.

Jeremy and Maisie had decided to spend a couple of nights at the house to get all the paperwork done. Jeremy had been listed as executor of their mother's will. Since their mother had no estate to speak of, it didn't require a lawyer to probate the will. All she owned were the contents of the house and less than a thousand dollars in a savings account. Maisie and Jeremy had covered the cost of the funeral.

They agreed that most of her things, including her clothes, could be given to the Good Will store. Maisie asked for her mother's costume jewellery and the Royal Doulton figurines. Glen took a quilt Madeline had hand-sewn and her favourite teapot.

"We can call the people from Good Will to have a truck pick this all up tomorrow. Do you want to arrange for someone to come in and clean the next day after it's all out? Or do you want me to do that? The landlord can list the house for rent then."

"Yeah, okay. I'll do it."

In going through Madeline's things for garbage pickup, Glen came across their school report cards and a newspaper clipping listing Maisie's graduating class from the CGA program. "Maisie, look at this."

He was holding their mother's photo album with a few pictures from the farm days. There was only one that showed them as a family unit. It must have been taken by someone visiting. They were all sitting by a Christmas tree decorated with popcorn and crepe paper streamers. A star cut from cardboard and covered with foil sat at the top. "I will take this and have a copy made so we will both have it. It's probably the only one ever taken of all of us — besides the one in your office. It must have been the year Dad invited the pastor and his wife for a visit on Christmas Day."

"You're right. I think I was seven and you must have been twelve. I remember Mom was so put out because her fruit cake hadn't turned out that year and she was embarrassed by only having shortbread to offer." She stared at the picture for several minutes. "Do you ever remember Mom and Dad kissing or hugging each other?"

"I don't know. I never paid attention to that kind of stuff at that age. Why would you even ask something like that?"

"Mom was always affectionate with us and certainly respectful to Dad, but I don't remember any real affection exchanged between the two of them."

"Those were hard times for them, Maisie. The farm barely brought in a living and it took both of them working it just to get by. I'm sure they were too tired by day's end to laugh and have any real fun."

"Oh, yes. Mom certainly reminded me of *that* often enough." She shrugged and handed the picture to her brother. "Her words 'never marry a farmer' were a mantra I listened to almost daily after Dad died. She never forgave me for disobeying her."

"She's gone now, Maisie. You can enjoy your marriage to your farmer without hearing those words again."

Maisie thought she heard a slight tinge of sarcasm in her brother's tone but let it pass.

Jeremy suddenly reached for the picture again and stared at it. "You know, now that you mention it, I remember Mom saying something like that at Dad's burial."

"What?"

"I was holding her while she was leaning over to kiss the casket one last time. I remember now. She said 'Damn you, Ernie. Damn you for leaving me like this. I swear on your grave that I will never allow our daughter to marry a farmer. Never.'"

"I never heard her speaking."

"She was whispering. I only heard her because I was holding her. She was shaking and almost ready to collapse."

"That explains a whole lot. My marriage to Glen betrayed the oath she made on Dad's grave. That's why she couldn't forgive me." She fell back on her haunches and took the picture from her brother. "That poor sad woman."

They stayed until the house was completely emptied, cleaned, and the key turned over to the landlord. A couple of neighbours had dropped by with food for them to snack on while they worked. A plainclothes policeman came by to ask more questions about their mother's daily habits, possible debts, questions about any run-ins with neighbours. Did she have any male friends? No one had seen or heard the actual attack but a neighbour a block over remembered hearing vehicle tires squealing as if burning rubber in a hasty getaway. He had only caught a glance of a truck before it disappeared out of view. It happened so fast, he couldn't even remember the colour of the vehicle. Could have been kids though. They're always squealing their tires around the neighbourhood.

"A few months ago, someone had complained about a man hanging around the bingo hall. After a police warning, he was not seen again. Probably someone hoping to grab a winner's take."

"Had my mother won anything that night?"

"One of her neighbours who had been there said she won a $50 bingo that had to be split three ways. Not enough, really, to attract a vicious attack."

"Her purse hasn't shown up?"

"No. We were hoping the perp might have taken any money then tossed it, but no sign of anything."

"I'll stop by the police station when we're finished to let them know the house is empty and the landlord has the key. They may want to keep an eye on it until there are new renters in it." Jeremy shook hands with the policeman as he left.

"That's a good idea." Maisie looked around at the little house. "I can't imagine what it would be like moving into a house that belonged to someone who was recently murdered. I'm anxious to get home and back to work. It's been hard being in Mom's house these last few days. Difficult to hold back the tears. I just want things to return to normal."

"Would it not be similar to you moving into a man's house whose wife had been murdered?"

The question hung in the air.

"What?" Maisie couldn't believe her ears.

"Look, sis. I'm sorry. I ..."

"Jeremy, is there something you want to get off your chest? Something bothering you?"

"No. Yes. Maisie, I'm not the only one who has that lingering doubt about Glen's guilt or innocence. I'm sorry. It's just a doubt — a fear really — that won't go away."

"Who else is suffering from this 'doubt or fear'?"

"Well, the police for starters. They've never been satisfied that Glen is totally innocent."

"If you ... and the police ... are questioning Glen's innocence, then you must be questioning mine also."

"Not me. Not at all. Glen's position in this does not mean that I doubt you for a minute."

"But?"

"Just for shit's sake, even he is guilty, you wouldn't necessarily have to have been involved. In fact, I don't believe you were involved at all. You were an innocent victim. It could have all been arranged without you knowing what part you would be playing in it."

"Just for *shit's sake*, Jeremy? Just for *shit's sake*?" She put one hand on her waist and brushed her forehead with the other. After taking a few steps away from him then turning and walking back to put her face in front of his, "Do you honestly believe that Glen is capable of murdering his wife? That whatever plans he might have had would include killing his child? His own son?"

"He may not have known Billy would be in the vehicle with her."

"I can't believe what I'm hearing. From my own brother no less. I ... I don't know what to say, what to think."

"Sis, I shouldn't have voiced my fears." He reached for her, but she stepped back. "They're just fears, you know. I like Glen. I can't imagine him doing what people think he might have done. But I can't help fearing for you. What if? Do you ever think of that? What if he is guilty? I don't think he's a cold-blooded killer. But he could have snapped. Maybe they were having problems no one is aware of. And if he snapped once, he could do it again! His wife did have an unexplained broken arm and bruises. Maybe Mom was right and he was an abuser. I just worry about you, Maisie."

"I can't listen to this. Are we done here?" She went into each of the bedrooms and the bathroom. "I think everything has been done that needed doing. I'm going home."

"Maisie, I love you. I guess I got carried away with my big brother role. I wish I could take my words back, but I can't. I'm sorry."

"Keep me informed about the police investigation." She went out the front door without looking back.

She was halfway home when she had a flashback to Glen checking his watch several times during their infamous dinner.

The phone calls from the various media slowed then stopped after several months of no new developments either in the death of Shelley or Madeline. There were innuendos every once in a while about the convenience of the death of the only person who might have had clues about the murderer in the first death. The police received numerous calls concerning her mother's death. All had new clues. New information. A blue truck seen hanging around her house. A beige car that had always been parked out front. A man she was seen with in the beer parlour. Someone had heard screaming in her house on several occasions. No one was happier when the phone calls and whispers stopped than Glen. Billy had gotten wind of some of the gossip and questioned his father and Maisie about them. So far, they had been able to satisfy his curiosity without revealing everything.

The new accountant in Regina was learning quickly and Maisie's clients had taken a liking to him. By October, she was able to cut her days in Regina to just two a month. Which was a good thing because her life was becoming hectic in Estevan. When she did go north, she took Billy with her for music lessons with one of the most highly acclaimed music teachers in the province.

Appointed to several boards in Estevan, she spent a good part of each month attending meetings and fund raisers. She seemed to be out more evenings than she was home. They had to hire a new housekeeper to come in and clean weekly. The other one had left with no notice. Glen was becoming pretty well the sole driver for Billy.

It was close to Christmas and Maisie was pretty well done in. She had attended several social events on her own because Glen was driving Billy to his meets, lessons, gym classes and social events. Her business was booming, and she had been asked to run for town council in the next election. She had declined, joking about her marriage possibly ending in divorce if she accepted one more responsibility.

It wasn't far from the truth, she was afraid. Glen was becoming impatient with their evenings no longer being spent together. Even Billy had complained that he hardly saw her anymore and couldn't remember the last time they'd watched a movie together.

"Maisie, you do realize that you are nearing the age of forty."

They had just made love and Glen was bussing her shoulder with kisses.

"What brought that on? Am I not as pleasing as I used to be?"

"That's not it at all. Your body is as desirable as it ever was, and it still responds to me in a way that drives me crazy."

"Then why the age reminder?"

"I was just thinking about all the years we've been having sex pre and post marriage. We haven't talked in a long time about having another child. I'm just wondering if it's going to happen before we're using canes and sitting in rockers on the porch."

"Glen. You know I don't use any form of birth control. I've done nothing to prevent a pregnancy. I'm as surprised as you that it hasn't happened."

"At the age of thirty-seven, you don't have too many baby-producing years ahead. Do you think it might be time to see if there's a problem?"

"I ... We've talked about this before."

"Yes, and you said to just wait, that you were sure it would happen when we were married and more settled."

She wondered how long he had been stewing about this while saying nothing. She recalled how important it was to him, to his heritage, that there would be someone to take over the farm, to carry on the family tradition. Maybe it wasn't her age, but his, that bothered him.

"I know you want another child and I do, too. I'll call the clinic in the morning and arrange for an appointment with Doctor Poulter for me."

"I'm not blaming you."

She took the back of his hand to her lips. "I know you're not. However, you have already produced a son. It's nothing you're lacking so it must be me. It could be something that's easily fixed and you're right, I'm not getting any younger. I don't want to have to deal with teething and diapers when I'm in my forties."

Glen was whistling as he fixed breakfast for her. The crops were harvested and sold so there wasn't the rush for him in the morning as there was for her. Billy's bus had picked him up for school already. There were three other special needs children in the district that required transportation to school, so the bus had a large territory to cover and Billy was always first on and last off. It made for a long day for him, but he never complained.

"Will you pleasure us with your company at supper tonight?"

"I'll call once I get to the office and see the schedule." She detected a slight frown, but he kissed her cheek when putting her plate on the table. "I'll try."

THIRTY-SIX
1980

THE AUTUMN RAIN WAS HITTING the bedroom window in waves. It almost sounded like sleet. Maisie moaned and pulled the blankets over her head. *So much for weather forecasts. I thought it was supposed to be sunny this weekend.* It started up again, louder. She finally had a weekend with no commitments and now it was going to be miserable out. Glen had been growing quieter, almost retreating within himself these past months. She had grown worried when he'd failed to respond to her touch in bed a few times. She knew he was losing patience with her increasing evenings at work and meetings. Never one to complain, he would just withdraw and spend more time in his workshop building outdoor furniture.

It had started with him teaching Billy how to build bird houses years ago. They used to spend hours out in the shop together. They made so many, they started selling them at the farmers market in town. Then they had progressed to weathervanes but their work together came to an end when Billy was accepted into high school a year early. He had done well in school the previous year even though his teacher had made Glen and Maisie aware of an unsettling restlessness in class. It had grown to the point of disrupting classes with unruly behaviour when he finished his work ahead of everyone and then had nothing to do. Glen had threatened to pull Billy out of some of his leisure activities if he got one more complaint from the teacher.

The guidance counsellor at the local high school happened to be an assistant coach of Billy's basketball team. When Billy told the guidance counsellor that his father had threatened to take him off the team, the man had called Glen to discuss the problem. It was he who suggested that Billy might be just plain bored in school. He asked permission to discuss the situation with Billy's principal. After a great deal of back and forth conversations, Billy was tested and found capable of passing most of the tests for entrance into high school. For the balance of his grade seven school year, he took English, math, and science classes with the grade eight students. The following September, he was accepted into grade nine. He found it required a great deal more studying —and piles of homework — which meant less time working in the shop with his father.

Maisie knew Glen missed the time with his son and more than once, she felt a twinge of guilt about not being able to give Glen a second child. She had undergone testing and had suffered through a series of hormone replacements and other procedures that took the life right out of her and left both her and Glen increasingly despondent about her inability to conceive. She had turned forty this year, so the chances of pregnancy were pretty slim. They had discussed adoption, but it had been made clear that she had to be a stay-at-home mom, at least until the child was old enough to be in school full days. They had argued for a while about her having to give up her career with Glen insisting she could work from home for a few years. She argued she had worked too hard over the years to build her practice only to give it up. She would never get those clients back again.

They had never really overcome the problem, and she knew it upset Glen that their home life was not at all the way he had anticipated.

"You knew I was a career woman when you asked me to marry you."

"What if we'd been able to have a child of our own? You would have had to stay home then."

"Only for a short while, then we could have hired a nanny to take care of the baby. She could have even helped with Billy. We wouldn't have had to conform to the legalities of adoption."

This had been an ongoing argument since they first learned that Maisie was incapable of having children. Eventually Glen had conceded rather than have it come between them. So she tried to spend as much of her rare free time with Glen and Billy as she could. Now here she was with a free weekend to spend with her boys, and it was raining, possibly sleeting, outside.

It had stopped again. Or had the wind just shifted. She got up and opened the curtains to bright sunshine. "What —?"

She bent back as something hit the window again. Sand. It was sand. *What's going on out there?*

She looked down at Glen standing below their window with another handful ready to let loose. He motioned for her to open the window.

The sash slid up easily and the cool morning air brought goose bumps to her arms. "What are you doing?"

"Trying to get my lazy wife out of bed."

"Why didn't you just come and get me?"

"I'm all muddy. Put some warm clothes on and come down."

"What for?"

"I want to show you something. Hurry."

She quickly donned a pair of jeans and a sweatshirt and went downstairs and out the back door.

"Go back and put a jacket on."

"Where are you taking me?"

"You'll see."

"Where's Billy?"

"You'll see. Grab the camera."

They started off across the field on the Honda ATV. Glen had bought two a couple of years ago and had had one of them adapted for Billy to drive. They would often go three-wheeling out on the fallow fields. Maisie was not fond of the contraptions, as she called them, thinking they were "tippy", but she was just a girl and didn't know about boys' toys.

They were travelling across the freshly plowed fields. It was the kind of fall morning that poets wrote about; a mist on the ground and the unmistakable fragrance of autumn in the air. The sun was trying its best to warm the crisp air and probably would by mid-afternoon. It seemed like they had already crossed more land than she thought they owned when she caught a flash of colour in a copse ahead as they went over a slight rise. The leaves on the few trees were a brilliant orange. Billy was sitting on his ATV waiting for them. As they drew closer, she could see he was grinning from ear to ear.

"Hey, Mom. Come and see." He was shouting and waving frantically.

If it weren't for the grin, she might have thought he had had an accident with his tippy vehicle. As she and Glen pulled up and he cut the engine, she saw there was something on the ground behind her son's bike.

"Look, Mom. Look. My first deer."

On the ground was a good-sized buck with an arrow through its chest.

"Oh, my. You shot it yourself?"

She knew his grandfather had been teaching him archery, but she hadn't realized he had advanced to the hunting stage.

"Yep." She could hear the pride in his voice "I want you to take a picture of it so I can show Grandpa."

She looked at Glen who was beaming. He usually got a deer for their freezer sometime in November, but she knew he hunted with a rifle.

"We got out here early and were able to sit in the camouflage until it came by." The boy's smile hadn't left his face.

"Stay there and I'll try to get both you and the buck in the photo."

It was mid-afternoon by the time the animal was ready for hanging from the rafters in the barn. Glen had called his former father-in-law who was on his way over to see the game his grandson had taken. The carcass had been dragged home on a tarp behind Glen's ATV. The rest of the day was spent with more picture taking, skinning, and finally, hanging the sides. Glen and the older man drank a few beers in the process.

Glen phoned a local butcher to arrange for the meat to be cut up in about ten days. Maisie thought that was awfully long to leave meat hanging, but apparently the longer it hung the more tender it was supposed to be. Then she remembered her father slaughtering cows on their farm and leaving the sides to hang forever.

Maisie invited Billy's grandfather to stay for supper, but he declined. It was already dark and promising to turn cold overnight. He had only stayed to help his grandson finish the job properly.

"Thanks for coming, Grandpa. You taught me how to shoot real good."

"I'm proud of you, boy. Deer are one of the hardest animals to shoot with a bow. You have to get closer than with a gun and they usually turn and run before you're close enough."

Maisie noticed the old man shake hands with his grandson but turn his back on Glen's extended hand.

In spite of this, it was still a better weekend than anything Maisie could have planned for her men. They watched the CFL's semi-final game between the Stampeders and the Blue Bombers that night.

When she went in to say goodnight to Billy, he asked her to sit for a moment.

"Mom, do you notice that Grandpa isn't all that friendly with Dad? It seems like he's polite but not, well, you know ... friendly. They never joke with each other or laugh together or anything. Don't they like each other?"

Maisie looked at her son and took his hand in hers. "I think this is a conversation you should be having with your dad."

"I've tried but Dad just says I'm imagining things. That being around Dad just makes Grandpa sad because of my mom dying and all. Don't you think he would have got over that by now?"

"I don't know, Billy. Maybe he's a little resentful that your dad got married again. Maybe he thinks your dad has forgotten about your mom."

"But that's not true. Dad hasn't forgotten her. He still takes me to her grave on Mother's Day and on my mom's birthday and even sometimes in between. I know he goes there by himself sometimes, too." Maisie almost did a double-take. She wasn't aware that Glen spent time at Shelley's grave except for the times he took his son there. "He talks to me about her whenever I ask. He's always telling me how pretty and smart she was."

"Your mother was all of those things. I think you forget that I knew her, too. She was very pretty — just like your dad says — and she took really good care of you. I think your grandma and grandpa are just lonely without her, and don't understand that your dad misses her, too. Her death doesn't mean he quit loving her."

"I know. I just wish my grandpa and my dad could get along better."

"Goodnight, Billy." She kissed his cheek and gave his shoulder a pat.

Before she went out the door, Billy asked, "Mom, do you think now that I'm in high school you and Dad could call me Bill instead of Billy?"

"Sure, darling. Is that what they call you at school?"

"Yeah. I kind of like it. It sounds more grown up than Billy."

She bumped into Glen who was just about to enter the room. "I thought there was a party going on in here and I wasn't invited."

"I was just telling Mom, now that I'm a teenager and in high school, I kind of like being called Bill instead of Billy."

"So my little boy is growing up."

"Dad, I haven't been a little boy for years."

"You're right, son. You are growing into a fine young man." He gave his son a thumb's-up as they left the room.

That night, Glen's lovemaking was more intense than it had been in a long, long time. When Maisie commented on it later, he winked at her and said, "I guess I had to prove I'm not aging just because my son is."

"And who did you have to prove that to? Me? Or you?"

"I guess a little of both."

He pulled her to him and they lay spooned most of the night.

THIRTY-SEVEN

THE DOORBELL WOKE EVERYONE UP on Sunday morning just after 7 o'clock. Glen opened it to find two uniformed police officers on the porch.

"Mr. Grayson? Mr. Glen Grayson?"

"Yes."

"You recently traded in a pick-up truck in Estevan?"

"Yes. Is there a problem with the ownership or something?"

"Or something."

Maisie came to the door to listen.

"Well, you better come in and tell me what the problem is." Glen motioned for them to come into the kitchen.

Billy wheeled into the room.

The two officers looked at each other. "Can we talk in private?"

Glen was about to protest but Maisie said she and Bill would go into the living room so they could talk.

"What do you think is wrong?" The boy sounded worried.

"I don't know. Something about the truck he traded in at the dealership in town."

She turned the television on so it covered the conversation in the other room. She didn't want Bill hearing anything that might upset him.

"You don't have to protect me, Mom. I'm not a child anymore."

She was startled, but it was true. He was fourteen and his voice was even showing signs of maturing. "I think your dad deserves some privacy. He'll tell us what it's about after the police have left."

She found a sports channel that gave a complete account of the scores from all the games played the day before. Twenty minutes later, one of the officers came and invited them into the kitchen. Glen stood red-faced looking at Maisie as they entered the room.

"What is it, Glen?"

"It seems they found something that looks quite incriminating against me in their case about your mother's death."

"What? I didn't know the case was still open."

The other policeman spoke up. "When the cleaners started working on Mr. Grayson's truck that he traded in, they found your mother's purse stashed up in the frame under the seat."

Maisie just stood with her mouth open. "I … I don't understand. I … Glen, do you know what they're talking about?"

"No, Maisie, I don't. I have no idea at all. What's more, they're taking me into custody."

Bill wheeled his chair toward his father. "What? What are you saying? Are they taking you to jail? Are you taking my dad to jail?" He looked ready to bound up out of his wheelchair and pounce on the man closest to him.

"We're taking him into custody for further questioning. We need some answers that might explain how the purse got there. You might want to get a lawyer."

"Maisie, Billy. I swear I have no idea what's going on here. Best you call Stan Lawson and see if he can get a proper lawyer for me. There's an explanation for this somewhere, we just have to find it."

"No. You can't arrest my dad. He would never hurt anyone. You can't just take him away like that."

"Sorry, son. He'll be held until a bail hearing in a day or two. Ma'am, I advise you to get that lawyer."

"But surely to God you can't arrest him on just that!"

They put handcuffs on Glen and led him out. "I love you, Maisie, Billy. Trust me. I don't know how some purse got in my truck."

THIRTY-EIGHT

THEY HAD TAKEN HIM TO Weyburn and were holding him for questioning pending a charge of first-degree murder in the death of Madeline Forbes. Their family lawyer, Stan Lawson, helped with retaining an experienced criminal lawyer from Regina, named Wesley Cullen. Glen was being held in custody while they investigated further to see if he was culpable in the death of his first wife.

Maisie cancelled all her appointments for the next ten days. Ruby had been one of her first calls, not only because Madeline had been Ruby's closest friend, but because she wanted the staff to know before the news hit the papers and television. Maisie's clients in Regina were to be rescheduled as well. Together, the women drafted a formal notice to the effect of "due to a private family matter, Maisie Forbes is forced to reschedule ..." It would be given to the staff and only the clients who asked. Most of the clients in Regina knew Maisie only by her maiden name, which was still on the door of the office. She had not changed it, for business purposes.

The story of Glen's arrest made the next day's newspapers throughout Saskatchewan, and the evening news the next day. The radio stations began broadcasting almost immediately. The implications of Maisie's involvement weren't long in following. Billy was allowed a brief absence from school. Work would be sent home for him to do on his own.

Neither Maisie nor Billy could go beyond the end of their driveway before microphones and cameras were shoved in their faces. It was big news across the province — maybe the country — that a suspect had been arrested after a three-year investigation into the brutal murder of sixty-eight-year-old Madeline Forbes in 1977. What was making the case even more interesting was that the suspect was the son-in-law of the victim. Further investigation was taking place concerning Grayson's possible involvement in the unsolved death of his first wife in 1966.

Darlene, Maisie's secretary in Estevan, gave her the first sign of a spin-off from Glen's arrest when she called on the morning of the second day after the police had taken him away.

"Maisie, I'm so sorry to bother you with business, but I think you need to know what's happening."

"What is it, Darlene?"

"There have been telephone messages left from two of your local clients who want their files returned to them immediately by courier. They are, in effect, giving you notice that in light of the pending police investigation, they will be cancelling any contracts or agreements with you."

"So the man has already been tried and found guilty." Maisie put her head in her hand and hesitated for a few seconds. "All right. Prepare their files and include an invoice for the time I've spent on their work. There's nothing else we can do at this point. Let me know if any others decide to pull out, too."

"Is everything okay, Mom?"

"Yes. Well, no, Billy ... Bill." She took a few deep breaths. "Some of my clients are hesitant about my doing work for them while a criminal trial in our family is a possibility and they've asked for their files to be returned. I do look after their finances and I don't blame them for being uncomfortable." She thought it best not to sugarcoat it. If the boy was old enough to handle a man's name, then he was old enough to handle the problems they were about to face."

"Do you think they'll release Dad?"

"They will have to sooner or later. They can only hold him for a few days, I think. If they charge him with first-degree murder, his bail will probably be quite high. That's what we're paying Mr. Cullen to work on. I'm not all that familiar with the laws surrounding murder."

"Somebody planted that purse in Dad's truck. I know they did. There's no way he would ever hurt anyone — let alone your mother. She was an old lady. Why would he want to kill her? They're crazy if they think he did it."

This was not the time to fill him in on all the history surrounding her, her mother, Glen and his marriage to Shelley. Bill knew that his grandmother had not liked Glen, but he knew nothing about her accusations of Glen killing his mother. Nor the accusations that his father had been having an affair with Maisie and had indeed been accused of enjoying a romantic dinner at the time of the accident that had killed his mother and crippled him. *O, what a tangled web we weave when first we practise to deceive!*

"You know that and I know that and the police will soon come to realize it also. Mr. Cullen is a well-respected trial lawyer. He'll be sure to find all the evidence to set your dad free. We have to leave it in his hands."

The phone rang again and Billy picked it up. It was another reporter asking for Maisie.

"Can't the police stop them from calling us? They're invading our privacy." He wheeled his chair to the front window. "Look at them. We can't even get to the mailbox."

"Do you want to stay with your grandparents for a few days? It's probably quieter over there. You might be able to concentrate on your schoolwork better."

"Then who will be here to look after you? I need to stay home with you, Mom."

Her heart went out to the boy. He had always been the one needing care. Now he wanted to be the caregiver. She couldn't love him more.

"I just don't want you to fall behind in your schooling. Your dad wouldn't want that either."

"I'm staying. I don't want those people bothering you."

She hugged the boy. *Please, dear God. Let this all be over soon.*

Ruby phoned with the news that three of Maisie's clients had called looking for reassurance that their files were safe and would not be affected by the police investigating Maisie's husband. She had assured them that their office was in no way affected by the events in Estevan.

"How's it going, Maisie?"

"Rough. Poor Billy is upset by all the attention of the news people. The phone is ringing steadily, and news vans and cameras are camped at the foot of our driveway. I wanted to send him to stay with his grandparents at least until Glen is allowed out, but he feels I need his company and protection. He's such a caring boy and is so fearful about his father's arrest."

"Any news on that? Have the police found anything more?"

"Not that I know of. There's nothing more for them to find. Except who the real killer is."

"Maisie, I … Never mind."

"Say what's on your mind, Ruby."

"Before she died, Madeline told anyone who would listen that Glen killed his first wife. Anyone who lives in Estevan or Weyburn that the police question will probably tell them what she said. I'm sorry, but she even suggested he was having an affair with you at the time of his wife's death. That he had killed her so he could marry you."

"Then we got married."

"Yes."

"Thanks, Ruby. I know it doesn't look good for him. His fine character won't be enough until they find whoever actually did it."

"Does Billy know about all that?"

"No. He knows I was Glen's accountant and friend but as far as I know, he doesn't know we were involved before we were married."

"You were? I didn't know that."

Maisie was sure her mother would have told Ruby long ago about her and Glen having a history. One that Madeline had interrupted.

"I thought you knew. I'm surprised my mother didn't tell you."

"I'm surprised *you* didn't tell me. So the police will have even more reason to suspect Glen."

"I met Glen at a barn dance and we dated a few times years before he became involved with Shelley. My mother made it almost impossible for us to continue any kind of romance, so we broke it off. Actually, it was Glen who ended it when he met Shelley. I was still in school and working at Whittier Whittier & McLean. We never kept in touch and I didn't even know he had married until the day Shelley showed up in our office. That was it. You know my business was mostly with his wife. The first day he came to our office, he and I talked business over lunch. Then I met him for supper the night she was killed to turn over the tax files to him. The restaurant was on the highway that goes through Weyburn. It was convenient for us both. I was going to Mom's anyway that evening. That's it. That was our 'alleged romance'."

"He had probably been carrying a torch for you all those years."

"Maybe. I don't know. He was a nice guy and I had always wondered what might have been if Mom … Well. That's all water under the bridge now. He married a lovely woman, had a son, and life was going well for him. While Shelley was alive, Glen never gave me any indication that he wasn't totally and completely happy. He loved her and treated her well."

"You never wondered about her bruised and broken arm?"

"Ruby, please don't you start in on me about that, too."

"Oh? Have the police asked you about it?"

"My brother did. I guess Mom had talked to him about it. And no, I don't think for one minute that Glen injured Shelley. He does not have a single mean bone in his body. He really is a kind and gentle man."

"I have never seen him other than kind and polite. My next client is waiting so I better go. I just wanted to let you know that some clients are edgy."

"I've lost three local ones. I'm prepared for a negative response from the locals. I'm sure it will be temporary. Glen has lived here and been respected by everyone all of his life. There's only one farmer that ever gave him grief. Glen refused to sell out to a corporation that wanted both farms, his and this other guy's, or none at all. The other guy wanted to sell, Glen didn't. The man was furious. That's the only time I've ever known anyone to have reason to hate him. Except for my mother. As in any small town, though, gossip spreads quickly and the news reporters are painting him as a pretty despicable character. Call me later if anything new develops there."

Maisie revisited the idea of sending Bill to his grandparents. She wondered what Glen would have done.

THIRTY-NINE

ANOTHER DAY PASSED BEFORE THE police came with questions about the night of Shelley's murder. She almost asked what had taken them so long. Billy had been in the study working on his school lessons, but came out at the sound of the doorbell and voices.

She gave the police much the same account of her involvement with Shelley and Glen as she had given Ruby. If they probed further, she would simply tell them she would not discuss anything without her attorney present.

"Were you aware that the previous Mrs. Grayson had suffered bruising and a broken arm days before her death?"

"Yes. She visited my office wearing a cast."

"Did she tell you how it had been broken?"

"She told me she fell."

"Did she seem distraught or nervous?"

"I don't recall her being anything but her normal self."

"How was she when she was normally herself?"

"Pleasant. Friendly."

"If we were to question your staff, would they have the same presumption as you?"

"I can't answer for my staff."

"Did you ever see Mr. Grayson during the time you did the accounting for them?"

"He came to the office a couple of times but most of my dealings were with Shelley."

"Did you ever meet Shelley Grayson anywhere but at the office?"

Maisie was becoming increasingly uncomfortable with the direction this questioning seemed to be headed. She thought it might be better to end it before they brought Glen into the equation.

"I don't know why you are asking me these questions but I think before you go any further, I might like to talk to my attorney. My business dealings with Shelley Grayson never at any time had anything to do with the death of my mother. Good day, gentlemen."

"They may have had something to do with the death of Shelley Grayson."

"I don't know how. Please leave and don't come back unless my lawyer is present."

They left without argument. She answered Bill's questions the same way she had answered Ruby's. He had wondered why the police were asking about his mother breaking her arm. He had no recollection of that at all and it had never come up in conversation.

She decided it was time for him to go to his grandparents and wouldn't take any argument from him. The Thompsons were more than cool, almost to the point of rudeness when she arrived with Bill. He only went with the promise he could come back when his father was released. She and Bill hadn't been allowed to see Glen and they both wanted him home.

The reporters increased in numbers a few days later once formal charges were laid against Glen. There were several: the least of which was theft, and the most serious, a charge of first-degree murder. He was granted bail, which Maisie had to arrange and sign papers for at the bank. Bill insisted on coming home so he'd be there when his father got home. He had wanted to go with Maisie to pick Glen up, but she explained it might make his father uncomfortable for Bill to see him in that setting.

When they arrived home, father and son both broke into tears. Glen dropped to his knees beside Bill's chair and they hugged tightly for several moments. They had managed to leave the jail downtown without being noticed, but the news of Glen's being out on bail must have been released because they could see and hear an even larger number of vehicles at the end of their driveway. The house was only set back about a hundred and fifty feet from the road, so it was difficult to maintain privacy. Maisie closed the drapes across the front of the house and locked all the doors.

"This isn't fair to the two of you." Glen looked more than perturbed, he was downright angry. "If I'm going to cause all of us to be locked up in our own home, then I may as well have stayed in jail. I wasn't thinking."

Maisie slid her arm around his middle. "I don't want to hear you talk like that. We have you here with us again. We're together like any other family. Those vultures out there can go to hell. All we wanted was you back home again and here you are."

"Mom's right. Those guys are out there whether you're home or not. The only time they're going to leave is when the police find out who really killed Grandma Forbes."

The next few weeks brought no fresh news. It was mid-December when the police came with a search warrant and went through the house, barn and workshop. Bill was being tutored at home and had finished the work required for his first term. Uniformed police took a few papers and personal things of Glen's in plastic bags. One of the detectives, while searching the den, asked Bill if he remembered the time his mother had broken her arm. Bill said no, but when the man started to ask a second question, Maisie stepped in and said they were not to talk to him without their lawyer present.

"Why do they keep asking about my mother's broken arm?"

He looked at his father. His need for knowledge about his mother's death and the questions surrounding it were eating away at him.

"They have never found the vehicle or the driver that caused the accident. It's still unsolved, so they're wondering if the rumours are true or not that I was responsible for her death also. They are under the assumption that I may have broken her arm and caused the bruises."

"That's ridiculous. Why are they wasting their time trying to blame you for everything instead of looking for the real murderers?"

Maisie didn't want to tell him that her own mother's false accusations were the main reason.

Jeremy and Jeanne invited them to come for Christmas. Scott would be home from university and they thought it might do Bill some good to spend time with his cousin. Maisie remembered the conversation with her brother, when he questioned the possibility of Glen being responsible for Shelley's injuries and subsequent murder and then the murder of their own mother. She wondered if it was a good idea to take Bill into that suspicious environment. She approached Bill and Glen about it, but the boy wanted to stay at home and just have Christmas by themselves. When Glen and Maisie were alone, Glen expressed his relief at Bill's choosing not to go into that environment. He told Maisie that he wondered if their son wanted to stay at home because he was getting weary of being under a microscope. People were constantly looking into every corner of their lives.

The staff in Regina was, in fact, interviewed by the police, including the elusive Tess. Tess, who was always hanging around listening to conversations. Tess, who never seemed able to look anyone in the eye and who came and went as she pleased. When Maisie learned that she was being questioned, she prayed the girl wasn't capable of distorting anything she might have overheard through doors or by listening in on telephone conversations.

Maisie still had enough faithful clients to keep her busy at the office several days a week. Bill had been busy doing his schoolwork at home with his father, but now that his term was finished, she brought him with her to the office. She showed him how to do some of the office work such as filing and a few other simple procedures. He caught on quickly and seemed to enjoy the distraction of doing something different. Before long, he was using the calculator to add columns in ledgers and verify them by adding across the bottom as well. He was learning the basics of using a computer at school and told her she probably should take a course because his teacher said there would soon be a computer in every office. Maisie laughed and said that ledgers and calculators were doing the job just fine and probably would for a long time to come. She didn't want to undermine the words of the boy's teacher, but remained sceptical that any machine could accurately take the place of the human brain when dealing with numbers.

Their world was shattered a week before Christmas when Wesley Cullen called to tell them that Glen's trial was being delayed pending the outcome of the investigation into Shelley Grayson's death. The police were digging deeper and his culpability in that death would reflect on how his trial would be handled. They couldn't find enough evidence to make an arrest for that one yet, but they were deeply suspicious that he was indirectly responsible, especially since he appeared to have killed the only person who had claimed to have clues to his guilt. Maisie's name was being tossed around as an accomplice in both murders as well.

When that news hit the street, she lost almost all her clients in Estevan. She closed the downtown office until further notice, referring her clients to the posted phone number for information. A few days later, when she went to pick up some of her office equipment, she found that the window had been broken and nasty graffiti was painted on the front brick wall. The names she was being called would not exactly garner trust in clients. The office was trashed but nothing appeared to have been taken. Her file boxes had already been safely moved to the den at home. She called Darlene to come in and help her pick through everything, then Glen came and loaded it all into the back of his pickup. He brought plywood from home and boarded up the windows. She then locked the door, and left.

Mr. and Mrs. Thompson called to discuss the possibility of Billy's coming to stay at their home indefinitely. With all this publicity about his father and Maisie being broadcast daily, they didn't want their grandson put in danger from vandals.

"It can't be good for the boy to have to deal with the police and reporters coming and going all the time. It must be very hard for him to listen to it all and now that windows are being smashed, we are beside ourselves with worry." It was Bill's grandmother who had called this time, demanding he be brought to their house. Immediately.

"I'll discuss it with him and see what he wants to do. This is his home and I know he wants to be near his dad. You are right. It is distressing wondering who's ringing the doorbell each time and not wanting to answer the phone in case it's a reporter. Or the police."

"I don't think the decision should be left to him. Of course, he's loyal to his father, but he's not old enough to realize the consequences. What if people become unruly? He can't move as quickly as you to get to safety."

"The final decision won't be his, but we have to consider his feelings and where he is most comfortable. He is going through an extremely stressful time especially since his mother's death has been put back on the table. He feels safe here regardless of what's going on outside. I promise we'll discuss it with him and get back to you."

Bill did not want to go with his grandparents. He was determined he was staying in his own bed in his own home. They were a family and that's the way it was going to stay. And stay it did … Until Maisie got a call that Ruby had suffered a heart attack and was in the hospital.

FORTY

GLEN HAD RESTRICTIONS ON WHERE he could travel and who he could be with. It was ludicrous that he had been released into Maisie's custody when she was under suspicion herself. However, she was the one that had paid his bail and the police had absolutely no evidence to charge her with anything.

The problem was that she couldn't travel to Regina and leave Glen behind. It would be the three of them or none at all. The choice was not theirs. Ruby's ill health removed all options. They arrived in the city in the early evening just two days before Christmas. They took a small suite at the Saskatchewan Hotel — expensive but it was Christmastime and they were lucky to get any kind of room downtown. She had no idea if they'd be there days or weeks. She had reserved the rooms for a week. If they had to stay longer, she would deal with it then. No one seemed to know for sure the extent of Ruby's heart damage. She would give the woman's cousin a call in the morning. In the meantime, they would be in nice surroundings to celebrate Christmas at least. What little shopping she had been able to do was packed in a box, none of it wrapped. She had not enjoyed shopping in Estevan with everyone staring and whispering.

She had to meet with the staff in the office the next day. After that, the office would be closed until after January 5. She would see if Craig McDermott would come in for a couple of days between Christmas and New Year's to help her sort through what had to be done and decide which of them would do it. In the meantime, she would try to get her own clients' work done so she could concentrate on Ruby's clients in January.

The next morning, they had breakfast in their room then the boys agreed they'd keep themselves occupied in the mall while Maisie went to the office. Glen had some shopping to do and plans were made for them to take in a movie and see if the Pats were playing hockey over the holidays.

Ruby had bypass surgery the next day, Christmas Eve.

Maisie didn't sleep well. If Ruby couldn't return to work, what would be the next step for Maisie and her family? The Estevan business was all but finished. She and Glen were both being shunned. A trip to the supermarket was an embarrassing, if not painful, experience. Her hairdresser had been booked solid the last two times Maisie had called. *It's only a matter of time until my remaining clients pull the plug. Maybe I'd be doing them a favour by just shutting my business down and saving them the discomfort of having to search for reasons to take their business elsewhere.*

She finally got up and went to the window. She opened the heavy draperies slightly and looked at the city lit up below. The Christmas trees aglow on the streets dampened her mood. She found no peace or goodwill toward men. The bright colours and glittering windows of the businesses below reminded her of that Christmas night an eternity ago when Glen had given in to her mother's suggestions and had kissed Maisie goodbye.

Her thoughts came back to the present. Was there some way she could keep the office going here without Ruby? How could she do that when Glen couldn't be away from Estevan indefinitely and she had to be with him until his trial. *Whenever that was.*

The feel of his arms sliding around her were comforting. "Hard time sleeping?"

The door to the sitting room where Bill was sleeping on the pull out-sofa was partially open, so they spoke in whispers.

"I'm worried about Ruby and the office here."

"Ruby is still a young woman. She'll get through this and bounce back as good as new."

Maisie leaned back against him. "I hope you're right." She turned to face him. "I think I'm going to shut down the Estevan office completely."

"I guess there's not much left, is there?"

"Just a handful of clients."

He reached for her hand. "Maisie, I … I'm …"

"Don't say it. I know you feel responsible." She pulled his hand to her lips. "There is no way this is your fault. If anyone is to blame, it's my mother. You are a victim of circumstances."

"Circumstances. You're right. There's only circumstantial evidence. I just can't believe that everyone is so ready to find me guilty. People I've known all my life are turning their backs when I approach. I hate even going into town. Guys I used to drink beer with are crossing the street to avoid me."

"As soon as the trial is over, everything will get back to normal."

"Will it? What if they don't find another suspect?" He brushed his hair back. "I don't think they're even looking."

"What's going on?" Bill had wheeled himself into their room. "Are you guys having a party without me?"

Glen suggested it might be time for a card game.

FORTY-ONE
1981

BY MID-JANUARY, THE WORK IN the Regina office was on track. Ruby's surgery was deemed a success, and barring any unforeseen circumstances, she could resume light duties in about ten to twelve weeks. That meant she would be out of commission for most of the busiest months of the year.

Maisie packed up several boxes of files to take back to Estevan. They had moved into a smaller hotel right after New Year's Day because of the expense. Her men had managed to keep themselves busy, attending a couple of the Regina Pat's home games, catching up on the latest movie releases and visiting an indoor archery range and a local gymnasium. When all else failed, they bought several jigsaw puzzles to work on.

Future plans in Estevan were still up in the air. When they arrived home, their mail was waiting for them on the kitchen table. Gus Blondeau, the hand who had been hired by Glen's father, had brought it in each day. Among the envelopes were two from clients of Maisie's saying they would be taking their accounting needs to another service in town for tax filing.

Glen was to meet with Wesley Cullen in two days. Bill was already almost two weeks behind in his schoolwork for the second semester. He decided he would try attending classes and see how it went. Glen and Maisie assured him they would call his tutor to help him catch up on the missed work.

At the end of January, Maisie shut her business down completely, sending letters to the three sole remaining clients and making arrangements for them to pick up their files from her home office. No trial date had been set, and when Glen questioned his attorney why not, the reply was that the prosecutors were dragging their feet, hoping to implicate him in Shelley's death as well. No other suspect had been found for Madeline's death, so it was certain that Glen would stand trial for that, regardless. It was just a question of when. Wesley told him it could take year or more before it was brought to trial.

It was toward the end of their first week back home that Glen first talked to Maisie about selling the farm.

"Why, Glen? This is your family home. Your heritage. I can't picture you living anywhere else."

"You know as well as I do that the heritage will end with me. Bill can't run it even if he wanted to. It takes too much physical hands-on work. Besides, he doesn't really have an interest in it. You can see he's more hung up on numbers and he's enjoying that computer stuff he's learning." He smiled as he tucked a curl behind her ear. "He seems to have inherited more of his mother's traits than mine. The only outdoor activities he's shown any interest in are hunting and riding around on his ATV. He's not even indicated a desire to ride a horse. There's a therapeutic riding farm on the other side of town where they teach people with physical disabilities to ride. I asked him a couple of times if he'd like to give it a try and he just wasn't interested. Animals aren't his thing. Since Parker passed, he hasn't even asked about getting another dog."

"Shouldn't you be having this conversation with Bill? He's your son. The farm is his birthright. It's written in his ancestors' wills. You have another good twenty years of farming still in you. By then he may mature and decide he'll find a way to farm from a wheelchair just as he's found ways around many other obstacles."

"I have to be practical. I don't know if I'll be around to see this season through. I have to get everything in order now. I can't leave it until mid-season, and there's too much land to lie fallow for a year or more. Now is the best time to sell. We had a good year last year and the farm should fetch a pretty good price. I understand the prices for farm property are high right now. With my change to canola a few years ago, our profits have been steady."

"Then what will you do?"

"Wait for the courts to decide my future, for starters." She didn't like the droop of his shoulders and his downcast mouth.

"Glen, you are starting to sound like a quitter."

His eyes darkened and his grip on her arms tightened. "I can't help what I sound like to you. I thought I was sounding like a thinker. I thought I might be proactive in my thinking. It won't do you, Billy, or me any good if I'm hauled off to prison in the middle of a harvest." His voice grew louder as he spoke each word.

"And if you're not hauled off to prison? What then?"

"I can always get hired on with one of the corporate farms. Maybe by whoever buys this one."

"Is that who you would sell to? Your sworn enemy? A corporation?"

"They may not even be interested. When old man Duncan finally got them to take his farm off his hands, he really started blowing off steam about me keeping him from making real money. He sold it for half the price they were offering him years ago when they wanted both of our properties."

"So he expected you to give up *your* life so he could make some 'real money' before he died?" Maisie knew the man had died within six months of selling his farm several years earlier. "His farm was quite a bit smaller than this one. Maybe that had something to do with the price?"

"Yes, I have almost double the number of acres he had and that's more enticing to the big money people."

Bill's friends were a little kinder to him than Glen's had been. The boy flourished, finishing at the head of his class. Maisie wondered at the stamina the young lad had. He had matured in the last six months. Even his body was developing at a good rate. He worked hard at building — and keeping — his upper body muscle. He had a regular workout routine that he followed meticulously. He challenged his father to arm wrestling often and it was getting harder for Glen to put him down. The boy would grin each time and promise it wouldn't be long before the back of Glen's hand would be kissing the table.

Jessica and Doug Boyle came from Centreville and spent a weekend with them. They had remained good friends and had kept in constant touch. Jessica had been well aware of how Madeline had treated Maisie and Glen. She was angry at how the woman had caused such turmoil in Maisie's life, especially after Maisie had spent so many years taking such good care of her mother. The trips back and forth between Regina and Weyburn during the time Maisie was taking her accounting course had been selfless and generous on Maisie's part. The ungrateful old lady had repaid her by making her life miserable. They did not believe for one minute that Glen had killer blood in his veins.

The farm had been on the market for several months by the time school was out. A serious offer was pending and this helped lift Glen's spirits somewhat. He had been getting gloomier and shorter of temper with each passing month. His accompanying her to Regina regularly had helped him pass the time. Maisie had almost enjoyed being away from the farm for the intermittent weeks she'd spent in Regina. It was a city in which she felt at home. Ruby came back in mid-April but could only work half days, three days a week. Her surgery had taken more out of her than anyone had anticipated. When she spent too many hours in the office, she grew tired and short of breath. Maisie was spending two out of every three weeks up there. Craig had brought many new clients into the firm and was proving to be of real value. His billable hours were almost as many as Ruby's had been before her health deteriorated.

When Maisie was readying for her drive home from Regina at the end of June, Ruby asked how the sale of the farm was going.

"Glen is hopeful it will close any day now."

"What will you do then?"

"He's been looking at a smaller place closer to town. A bungalow on about ten acres. Just enough property for him to putter around in all summer. Plus, with it all being on one floor, it's more Bill friendly."

"I don't suppose he'd consider moving closer to Regina?"

"I doubt it. Why do you ask?"

"I'm seriously thinking of retiring. Maybe stealing a client or two from the firm to work on at home. I'm finding a full day at the office too much for me."

"Oh, no. Ruby. You are the life of the firm up here."

"I know you gave up your practice in Estevan. I was hoping you might come back up here now that Glen is selling. Won't Billy be going to university in a couple years?"

"He will. How soon are you thinking of calling it quits?"

"I'll stay through the summer if you like. I'll just work at home more. I don't want to drive to work in winter weather anymore, so September is the latest I'll stay. But I'd really like to go by the end of July if you can work something out."

"I'll talk to Glen and to Craig. Maybe another bookkeeper to help Craig with his load will help see us through." She hugged her friend who, she knew, was retiring reluctantly. "Ruby, you have helped me through so much, how can I not allow you the time you need? I'll do my best to work something out quickly. I am going to miss you dearly."

The farm was sold, not to a corporation, but to the married son of a family who had been farming near Swift Current for generations.

Glen's farm ended up being exactly what they wanted: a farm large enough to provide a comfortable living, but small enough for a family to operate. It pleased Glen — and Bill as well — that a young family who had farming in their veins would be moving in and taking over. Glen had talked to his son and they agreed it was unrealistic to think that Bill would ever take over the farm. In spite of both his parents having farming in their blood, he had no desire. He had asked Glen to try to sell it to a family like them who would treasure it the way they had. The moving date was set for mid-August, just in time for the harvest to begin. The bonus was that they wanted Maisie to do the farm accounting.

Glen was not happy about moving to Regina but when the dust settled, he agreed with Maisie that it might be the right move. It appeared they were heading for a trial date in late fall or early in January. The police had nothing more than suspicion to link him to Shelley's death.

"I can't go on much longer like this. I may as well be in jail. I'm living in limbo. I'm not free and everyone has me judged as a criminal. I go into town and they cross the street rather than rub elbows with an animal that could kill his wife, cripple his child, and beat an old woman to death. I feel so sorry for you and Bill. I don't how the two of you go on day after day with smiles on your faces. You even lost your business. I'm so grateful you've stayed with me even though I sometimes want to set you free. Tell you to go, get on with your life."

"I don't want to ever hear you talk like this. It's only the fact you've stayed strong that has seen us through. Your son and I know you're innocent. We know you aren't capable of doing the things you're accused of. If they send you to prison, we will fight it every day of every month until they set you free. We love you and when the real killer is found, all these people who turned their backs on you will have their own consciences to deal with. How many of them have asked you for help over the years? How many of them have you seen through lean times with small loans? They have short memories. We'll get through this Glen Grayson. Together."

They auctioned off most of the household furniture, keeping only the fine pieces of wood furniture that had been his mother's and grandmother's. They decided to rent a house inside the city of Regina until the outcome of Glen's trial was known. Realistically, they had to take into account that Glen may well end up in prison. Even a small place in the country would be too much for Maisie to contend with while trying to run an accounting business and take care of an invalid son. Bill was enrolled in school. He was able to take two final year courses since he had acquired two more third-year credits at summer school. If all went well, he could finish his final year of high school by the end of the following summer. He would be ready for university before his seventeenth birthday.

Maisie had continued to use her maiden name for business, so it was still Forbes that appeared on the door, stationery and advertising. Many of the clients in the Regina office had been brought in by Ruby and Craig, so most were not aware of the criminal investigation of her husband.

Glen had to report regularly, and he kept in touch weekly with Wesley Cullen. By September, they were told his trial was scheduled for January. He busied himself with odd jobs around the house but soon ran out of walls to paint and hinges to fix. His days grew in length to the same ratio that his nerves and temper shortened. He was becoming despondent and found fault with just about everything. The street was too noisy. The neighbours too close. The weather too damp. The traffic too heavy downtown. The only thing that seemed to make him happy was picking Bill up at school and the time they spent together.

Maisie's days were long and there were times she dreaded going home to listen to Glen complain. Then hated herself for being so selfish. One night in December, she awoke to find his side of the bed empty. When she looked for him, he was in the basement in his underwear watching an old movie on the television, crying. He didn't look up when she came down the stairs. He just sat staring at the television. She sat beside him and placed her hand on his knee.

"I could be put away for a very long time."

"I know."

"Will you be okay with Bill until he's old enough to be on his own?"

"Glen, don't. You know I —"

"Hear me out. I'm fifty-one. If they give me a life sentence, the very earliest I could be out is in twenty-five years. I would be seventy-six. There's always the possibility I won't make it that long. I have to think about Bill and you and the kind of life I'm leaving you. You're still a young woman. Too young to be living alone for the rest of your life. I want you to know I'll understand if you find someone."

"Stop it."

"Allow me this. If they put me away, I have to know that you aren't getting a life sentence also. I can't sit in there thinking about you working all day and coming home to an empty house night after night. You are too young and vibrant for that. I would hate it. Sitting there thinking about you growing into an old woman all alone."

She leaned on his bare shoulder then kissed his neck. She drew her hand up his thigh and leaned into him. There was no response from him. "You are the only man I have ever loved. Since the day I met you, you are the only man that has ever touched me. Did you know that? You have always been the only one for me. Even when you were married. I tried dating but I couldn't get interested in anyone. I always loved you, even when I didn't know it." She placed a hand on his tear-dampened cheek and turned his face to her then kissed his lips.

"Glen Grayson, you won't spend the rest of your life in jail because I won't allow it. I will hire the best detectives, the best lawyers. I won't rest until you are a free man again. I will spend every cent from the sale of the farm to do so if necessary."

One corner of his mouth turned up. "I guess I better get everything signed over to you then. Grandfather and great-grandfather be hanged. You'll need lots of money."

FORTY-TWO
1984

"NO, YOU ARE NOT QUITTING school."

"But, Mom. I'm not really quitting, I'm changing direction. You know I want to become an accountant. You did it, and you didn't finish university."

"Times are different now, Bill. It's important to have a degree. What if you want to go on to become a chartered accountant? You need a university degree. That's all there is to it. Besides, you are still in your teens. Most kids your age are just graduating high school, not finishing their second year of university."

"I feel like I'm wasting my time. I want to enrol in the CGA program."

"Continue with the computer courses. You say they're the future of the world. Conquer that aspect of the accounting field and you'll break new ground in our company. I know some accounting firms are experimenting with a new software programme designed for our use. It wouldn't hurt for us to move in that direction. Take financial planning. Fewer companies are offering pension plans than in the past, so more people are going to need guidance in setting money aside for their retirement. You could offer financial advice along with managing your clients' current finances."

It was an ongoing argument. One that started when she first took Bill on as a bookkeeper during the summer following his first year of university. He had found his place in the world. This is what he wanted to do with his life. It suited his physical capabilities and he loved working with numbers.

"I can do that with evening courses."

"You will do it with daytime courses. You know your father has his heart set on your graduating. No one in his family has done it. Your grandparents would be disappointed, too, if I allowed you to drop out."

Glen, to no one's surprise, had been found guilty of Madeline Forbes's murder. His charge had been reduced to second-degree murder because there wasn't sufficient evidence that he had pre-planned her murder. Wesley Cullen, his lawyer, argued that the most the court could charge was that he had lost his temper and her death was the result. Wesley had tried to get the charge reduced to manslaughter. Even if evidence should arise that showed he did, in fact, kill his mother-in-law, there was no evidence to indicate he had gone anywhere near her home with the intention of murdering her. Glen was given a life sentence with a chance for parole after fifteen years. In spite of what the judge had described as a heinous crime — the beating death of an aged, defenceless woman — Glen had a clean record prior to this offence; and because of the absence of a murder weapon, clearly Glen had not gone there with intent to murder his mother-in-law. The sentence was ten years fewer in prison than they had feared but still, fifteen years was a long time. He would be sixty-seven instead of seventy-seven when his eligibility for parole came about.

Maisie and Bill had stayed in the rental house. It was convenient for both of them. A handicapped-accessible bus had picked the boy up for high school and it was a short drive for Maisie to work. She could even come home for lunch if she chose to. Then he had gone to the University of Saskatchewan in Saskatoon. It had been a traumatic experience watching him go off on his own. But he had been determined to have some independence, and to give Maisie some as well. But he had looked so young when she'd left him in his dorm. He was young, younger than all of his classmates. She needn't have worried. He was a happy young man and the university had much to offer him mentally and physically. He joined many activities and made friends easily. His aunt and uncle lived close by and met him often for meals. Their home was not handicapped equipped, so it was easier to buy him dinner out or to meet him on campus.

There was no real loss of clients as a result of the trial and the guilty verdict. Only one farmer near Regina gave notification of changing accounting firms. This one had given her a tongue lashing for trying to hide her identity by using her maiden name. Otherwise, the business remained intact. Several of the clients Ruby had inherited from Maisie years earlier readily made the change back to her. They expressed concern about Ruby's health but appeared happy to be back in Maisie's fold again. She and Craig were the only two accountants, and they had a bookkeeper, a secretary and a receptionist between them. Bill had fitted in nicely over the summer: taking pressure off the bookkeeper trying to catch up on everyday work following tax season, then covering the summer holidays for all the staff, including Craig. Bill was young, but he was intelligent.

Glen was serving his time in the Federal Penitentiary outside Prince Albert. Maisie and Bill were able to visit him once a month, and after he'd been there a year, they were granted several three-day family visits in private quarters within the prison. The first time, Maisie and Bill went together to visit. Once, Bill had gone alone, and once, Maisie had gone alone. It was nice to be together under one roof as a family, but extremely difficult to leave after the three days of togetherness. Glen had written that he found it harder to face the loneliness of prison after those visits.

Maisie knew some of the despair Glen must have felt. The first time she went alone to stay with him, she cried for a week afterwards. Every time she went to bed and felt the cold, bare expanse where his warm body should have been, she broke into hysterical crying fits. She couldn't imagine what it must have been like for him.

Damn whoever had done this to them! Somebody had killed her mother, and somebody had killed Shelley. Was it the same person? Probably. Damn him. Or her. She would search for that person for the rest of her life. She felt she didn't deserve God's forgiveness for the hatred in her heart toward whoever had torn their lives apart.

But the one person she knew she could never ever forgive was herself. She was ashamed to even think of the times she had questioned, in her own mind, whether Glen really could be guilty. She had almost given in to those suspicions knowing the frame of mind he was in the night her mother had died. Those feelings had been strengthened by the fact that he had no real alibi for his whereabouts. He had been missing for several hours. More than enough time to go the hour's drive to Weyburn and back. Her brother had even placed the niggling seeds of doubt about Glen's innocence in Shelley's death. Could he have lost his temper and grabbed her arm? Shelley's excuse that she had fallen was what any wife who loved her husband would say. Yet she had seemed in a fragile frame of mind the last time she was in the office in Regina. She had clearly wanted to be out of there without being questioned too thoroughly. Had she been ashamed? Embarrassed?

After her brother's accusations, Maisie had found herself watching Glen whenever he got riled about something. Would he be capable of striking her? Was he capable of striking anyone? Then the guilt would hit her. He was not. How could she even suspect that he was capable of brutality? He was a kind, gentle man who would walk away rather than lose his cool.

These thoughts usually brought on more tears. She would absolutely die if he ever knew her thoughts, her doubts. They had to find who had done all this. Neither Glen nor Bill knew she had a private investigator on retainer to try to find out anything possible about Shelley's whereabouts the days prior to her death.

She was sure that whoever was responsible for the accident that killed Shelley and injured Bill was the same person who had killed her mother and planted the purse in Glen's truck. And it wasn't her husband.

FORTY-THREE
1986

"I WISH DAD COULD HAVE been there."

"I'm sure he feels the same way. He's so proud of you."

"You took lots of pictures to show him?"

"Yes."

Bill had graduated from university with a Bachelor of Science degree just months shy of his twentieth birthday. His hope, and Maisie's, was to continue with his accounting education. His plan was to take some time from formal education to work with Maisie in the firm for a year or so. He had been attending school year round since his first year of high school and he wanted the experience of putting his education to work for a while. He was undecided whether he would pursue an MBA, a CGA or a full CPA. He needed time to feel his way and be out from under the strain of constant studying.

"It will be nice to earn some real money for my efforts," he had told Maisie when she agreed to let him officially join the staff at her office.

He had enjoyed working with Craig between semesters. This worked out well for Maisie as she felt some male guidance might be good for the young man. Craig was in his thirties, an excellent role model, and young enough to better understand the workings of a twenty-year-old mind.

It was great having Bill home again. She had missed his upbeat attitude and ready smile. His stint at school in Saskatoon had been good for him. He learned complete independence and seemed to be well-liked by his fellow students. His handicap had proven to be a non-issue at school. There were so many activities for students, that didn't require physical prowess, that he never felt left out of things. Nor had his young age proven to be a hindrance to social life on campus. There seemed to be enough students who didn't drink for a variety of reasons, that being excluded from a lot of the campus parties was not an issue. His upper body strength and early training by his grandfather had helped him make the archery team through which he had won several awards.

Glen had come to terms with prison life. He, too, had kept himself physically fit and played third base on one of the prison baseball teams. At the age of fifty-six, the other players called him Gramps, but they respected that he could hit a ball as well as any of them. Maisie had continued her monthly visits, taking Bill with her whenever he was in the city. The detective she had hired had told her two years earlier to save her money, that he had exhausted all his investigative leads. He promised to keep his eyes and ears open and to let her know if anything surfaced.

"I'd like to spend a week or so with Grandpa and Grandma before I start work."

"Of course, sweetie. You haven't had a chance to spend much time with them."

The Thompsons were in their seventies and seriously considering selling their farm and retiring to a home in town. Bill wanted to see the farm one more time. Maisie drove him down to Estevan. The plan was for him to spend two weeks with his grandparents then come back in time to cover the summer vacations of the support staff again. They would also discuss where he would fit into the business in future.

He was full of promise and had some great ideas on how to grow the business. His training on computers and in financial planning was going to open areas not covered by their firm before. He told Maisie he was glad she had talked him into staying in school. They discussed the new direction in detail on their drive south. They even talked about purchasing their own building rather than continuing to pay rent. Maisie promised to keep her eyes open for any promising real estate that might come on the market.

As usual, the Thompsons were cool to Maisie as she helped her son bring his things inside their house. They had never forgiven her for marrying Glen. They truly believed she had been his lover while their daughter was alive. In their eyes, she was as guilty as he was. It had been a bad relationship that had deteriorated even further when Glen was found guilty of killing his mother-in-law. In their minds, it proved he had a killer instinct and was quite capable of murdering his unwanted wife. They had even tried at one point to get legal custody of their grandson. They'd only kept the relationship alive for fear of losing contact with Bill altogether. Maisie hated being put in the position of having to converse with them but they truly loved Bill and treated him with kindness.

It was barely into the first week of his visit with them when Maisie answered the phone to Bill's voice raised in anger against her and his dad.

"Bill, hang on. What has you so upset?"

"Why did you and Dad never tell me you were lovers while my mother was still alive?"

"Because it's not true. Who told you that?" Although, it didn't really take a genius to figure that out. The only question was "Why now"?

"Grandpa and Grandma."

"Why would they say something so horrible to you?"

"Maybe because it is true?"

"It's not true."

"You didn't sleep with my dad before I was even born? I don't believe you. How could you! No wonder everyone was so suspicious of my dad."

The desolation in his voice was heartbreaking.

"Billy … Bill, I think I better come down there."

"No. I don't want you here."

"You want me to wait until the end of your visit with them?"

"I don't want to see you, period. You and Dad lied to me all these years."

"We did not lie to you. Your dad and I had a relationship before he even met your mom. We broke up when they started dating."

"Then why did he go all the way up to Regina to have you do his accounting? There are lots of accountants down here."

"Oh, boy. Sounds like your grandparents have been filling your head with false assumptions."

"Don't blame my grandparents for this! They didn't fill my head full of anything. Why didn't your mother even like my dad?"

The only answer she could give him sounded lame. "My mother hoped I would not marry a farmer. She hoped I would marry a professional man. An accountant. Or a lawyer or something."

"That's not a very good reason. It had to be more than that. I think she knew he was fooling around with you while he was married to somebody else."

"Bill. That is not true." She was trying to think fast. "I'm coming down to talk to you and your grandparents."

"No. I want to talk to Dad first. I want him to talk to me man to man. I'm not a kid anymore. I want him to look me in the eye and tell me that he loved my mother and would never hurt her."

"Bill, I …" She was talking to dead air.

FORTY-FOUR

SINCE JUNE WAS A QUIET time in the office for the accounting staff, Maisie decided it might be a good time for a private family visit with Glen. She felt he should be aware of how the Thompsons were attempting to influence Bill's feelings. She made arrangements for it one week hence and let her staff know she'd be gone for several days. The evening before her scheduled departure for Prince Albert, she went shopping and bought a new matching outfit in pale green, Glen's favourite colour. She had just finished a bath and was about to put her pj's on when her phone rang. *Bill. Please let it be Bill.*

"Maisie. It's Wes."

Wesley Cullen.

"There's been a development in Glen's case. I don't have all the details but don't go anywhere until you hear from me again."

"I have a scheduled family visit with him tomorrow."

"Cancel it."

"He'll be disappointed."

"I'll call him tonight. Wait for me to get more details."

A few weeks later, Maisie and Bill were on their way to Prince Albert to bring Glen home. Not only had he been cleared of the murder charge of Madeline Forbes, he was free of any implication in the death of his first wife and the injury of his son. This lifted a heavy mantle from Bill's shoulders. He loved his father, but his grandparents had filled his head with *evidence* of his father's and Maisie's duplicity in his mother's death.

When Wesley had called the day after his initial phone call, he told her he was looking into an incident in Thunder Bay. A lawyer friend of his had learned that someone may have confessed to Madeline Forbes's murder. He said it might be the break they were waiting for, but the confirmation might take time. He would be seeing Glen in the morning to ask him some questions. Nothing was definite but it was hopeful.

Maisie didn't know what to make of it. She decided not to tell Bill until confirmation was received. She didn't want to get the boy's hopes up in case it turned out to be false information.

Within two days, national news broke the story that someone had been picked up and brought in for an unrelated incident in Thunder Bay, Ontario. Pending charges, the man had told another prisoner being held that, in his terms "He was scared shitless that the cops would find out about something he done in Saskatchewan years ago."

Hoping to win favour with the police, the recipient of the guy's foolish statement told his court-appointed attorney about the conversation.

That particular attorney worked for the law firm owned by Wesley's friend, Harry Winston, and remembered this case being discussed in their office years earlier. It had been such a big story at the time, that lawyers across the country had followed it closely and Harry had even given his pal Wesley some legal advice during the trial.

The arrested person in Thunder Bay had told his cell mate about a deadly hit and run he had been involved in in the '60s near Estevan, Saskatchewan. It had taken a week for an investigation and for the files from the incident to be pulled. At first, the guy, Stirling Frank, had denied he had said anything in the holding cell but had finally broken down and confessed. He said he was tired of running and looking over his shoulder every time he saw a cop. He had been finding it more and more difficult to live with his conscience. He felt even worse for the kid he'd crippled than he had for killing the woman, he said.

His story had to be corroborated and details verified, of course. He was not the only one implicated in the crime. In the telling, he confessed that it had been a criminal act, not an accident. The only accident was that he was just supposed to scare Shelley, and subsequently, Glen, into selling their farm to the conglomerate who wanted to buy his and the neighbour's farms. After hearing that part of it, everyone assumed it was the corporation who had resorted to scare tactics, but after more questioning, Stirling informed them it was a farmer named Duncan, who had paid him to do it.

Glen was telling Maisie and Bill the events leading up to his release on the drive back home.

"Mr. Duncan? I don't believe it."

"I found it hard to believe, myself. He and my father worked side by side. They helped each other when needed."

"I remember the day he was in your kitchen and told you that your father would have accepted the conglomerate's offer. He was one angry man."

"Yes. And that surprised me. I knew he was anxious to sell, but never dreamed he would raise his voice to me like that. Now I find out he was capable of murder."

"Glen, that was at least four or five years before Shelley's death. Were the big farming corporations still after your farms at that time?"

"They would come around every few years or even send letters sweetening the pot."

"Had Mr. Duncan ever threatened you directly?"

"No. But he refused to have anything to do with me for a few years."

"Then I wonder what made him so desperate as to threaten Shelley."

"Maybe we'll find out. The police are checking into this Stirling Frank's story. Apparently, Stirling is the one who broke Shelley's arm too. It was supposed to be a sign of what would happen if I didn't sell. If it's true, then old man Duncan's name will be dragged through the mud."

"Too bad. The man has been dead for years."

"The police will want to know if Stirling's story is true. They'll probably dig up any financial records they can find, for one thing. I don't know much more about it at this point. I just know they had enough to release me. Stirling Frank signed a confession and in doing so, he signed my freedom papers."

"I wonder why Shelley never told you who broke her arm. Or why."

"Knowing her love of the farm was almost as deep as mine, I think she didn't want me to know. I'd bet she thought it would blow over without me ever having to know she'd been threatened."

Maisie stroked Glen's arm. "That's love, Glen. She must have loved you very much to have suffered threats and physical harm and kept it from you so you wouldn't be coerced into selling the place. She knew how much it meant to you. That you intended to hand it over to your son when his time came."

"I know. I hate to think about what she was going through mentally and physically."

"But you were charged with my mother's death, not Shelley's. How does his confession to her murder release you of blame for that?"

"Apparently, he has confessed to that as well. Again, he was only trying to frighten her, not kill her. He got scared when he heard on the news that she was telling everyone who would listen that she had proof who killed Shelley." Glen shook his head and stared out the window briefly. "Usually when a guy bungles something, it's by not finishing what he set out to do, not by *over*doing it. Twice."

"I'm just grateful to be out of there. Wesley will fill us in on the details as they surface, I'm sure. He said he'll think about going after the system for a wrongful imprisonment settlement."

Bill had been sitting quietly in the back listening to his father talk. "Maybe we'll never know what Grandma Forbes thought she had on Dad."

❧

Glen remained in the passenger seat of the van after Maisie parked in the driveway at their house. He looked around the neighbourhood. It was the sound of Bill's asking someone to help him out of the back that broke Glen's reverie.

That night, as Glen watched Maisie undress, he asked if she would be willing to move to the country.

She smiled and replied, "You can take the man out of the country but you can't take the country out of the man."

"That's what they say."

"What do you have in mind?"

"Definitely not to farm again, if you're worried about that." He ran his fingers down the length of her hair. "I thought maybe a place similar to the one we looked at before we moved up here."

"You know that Bill will be working full time in the office now. Both of us will have to drive in to work."

"I don't know how the finances sit, but is the possibility of outfitting him with a custom-built van an option?"

"He's hinted at the idea a couple of times himself. I think it would be great if we can do that. It would certainly give him the independence to come and go as he pleases."

"It would give you independence as well, Maisie. Your life certainly hasn't been your own these past ten years." He pulled her to lie beside him. "Don't think I haven't thought about it night and day. Neither Bill nor I deserve you."

"You and Bill have given me a lot in return. A family for one thing. A reason for my existence."

"You've given us so much more. You've given us unquestioning love and devotion. I don't know how Bill and I would have survived without you." He kissed her temple. "I never stop thanking God for you saying yes at that picnic so many years ago."

She smiled. "I think I would have had to deal with the wrath of that old couple at the other table if I'd said no. That would have been unbearable."

She could feel the hardness of his need and nearly burst with joy at knowing her man would be beside her in bed every night. She'd felt the loneliness of an empty bed and no partner to lie with and share thoughts, dreams and expectations with for far too long.

"I love you, Glen Grayson, and I am so, so happy to have you back."

A couple hours later, they heard Bill come in the front door after having coffee out with a girl he had met at university. She had caught the bus over a few times, then Maisie had given her the keys to the van so the young couple could go out on their own. Bill always called a taxi for her to go home after.

"It's going to take me a while to get used to the realization that my son is a man and not a boy any longer."

He curled his arm around Maisie's waist and they lay spooned till morning.

FORTY-FIVE

BILL BLEW ALL TWENTY CANDLES out on his birthday cake. "Bye bye, teenage years."

He had been excited beyond words when he'd come outside that morning to find a fully customized van in the driveway. It needed further adaptions to fit his personal needs, but those would be minor. He also had to take driving lessons and pass a test before he could use it, but the thought of getting around on his own was almost too much for him to comprehend and this was obvious to Maisie.

His grandparents had been invited to share his birthday, but his grandfather was not good at travelling anymore. So it was the three of them, plus Craig McDermott and his wife, and Bill's young friend from university, Michelle Lacoste. They were in the dining room of the Hotel Saskatchewan, Bill's choice of location for his birthday dinner.

Glen and Maisie submitted an offer on a house on fifteen acres east of Regina off Hwy 1 near Balgonie. It was less than a twenty-minute drive into the city. It was mostly cleared, but a good number of trees remained, and a large pond sat on the property. A nice place to make a fresh start.

Glen thought he might like a couple of horses and possibly get into breeding in a small way. Once the papers were signed and the keys were theirs, the first thing was to have a contractor come and build ramps to the front and back doors, and to redo the main bathroom to make it wheelchair accessible.

Bill had talked about getting an apartment in the city so he could have a social life now that he had his own vehicle. He was still uncertain as to which direction his education would go in a year's time. For now, he'd continue to live with his parents, and ride to work with Maisie.

They learned as much from the newspaper as they did from their lawyer about the story behind the deaths that had affected all their lives so disastrously. The man, Stirling Frank, was sticking to his original story about the events leading up to the death of Shelley and the near death of Bill. After Glen saw the man's picture in the paper, he said he recalled him. He had been hanging around downtown a bit. Glen remembered he had been somewhat of a drifter with no education to speak of. He was a general labourer, doing odd jobs around various farms, basically for room and board and spending money that he used for drinking. Glen mentioned that he now recalled that the fellow had disappeared abruptly, but that no one had questioned his absence. Those who'd noticed, had passed it off assuming he had just moved on.

Now the story came out that he had been afraid someone might have seen him and would identify his truck — or even his face — if he hung around. Since he had killed a woman and injured a kid, he knew he would spend the rest of his life in jail. He headed east and wound up in Winnipeg. He mostly hung out on the streets downtown. His old truck had eventually broken down and he sold it for scrap somewhere in Manitoba. A couple years later, after everything had died down about the accident, he made his way back to Regina and found a home in the streets there, picking up odd jobs as he could find them.

When he saw on the news that some old woman in Weyburn was making noise about having proof of who killed that woman on the highway and injured her kid, he panicked. He couldn't figure out what kind of proof she might have, but he didn't want to take any chances. He had to find out what she was yapping about to the cops and the news people. He didn't want to be remembered by anyone, so he panhandled for the bus fare to Weyburn rather than hitchhike. People always remembered picking up hitchhikers, but nobody paid any attention to who rode the bus. It was easy to find the old lady and he followed her around for a couple of days. Then he found his chance one night when she was walking home from bingo. He started out only by wanting to ask her questions, but she had won some money that night and thought he was trying to rob her. She started to talk loudly about calling the police, and when she started to holler, he grabbed her and wrapped an arm around her face, trying to shut her up. She fought back by hitting him with her purse, and they struggled. He dragged her into the alley and tried once again to get her to tell him what she had on him, and to give it to him. She bit him and he hit her in the face. She struggled more so he kicked her and punched her until she was still. When he realized she was dead, he took her purse and ran off. He found her meagre bingo winnings in an envelope and stuffed them in his pocket, but he couldn't find anything that looked like proof he had killed anybody. He looked for her house key, but she must have kept it in her coat pocket. He didn't want to go back to where he had left her, but he had to know what she had, so he hung around town until the next day. When he saw the police and everybody come to her house, he knew he'd have to skedaddle in case someone spotted him. He had the old lady's purse and was going to toss it, but he saw Glen park his truck and recognized him as being from near Estevan. When he had a chance, he sneaked up and stuffed the purse under the front seat in the truck, tucking it in good so that it wouldn't be found right away.

This time, when he got on the bus, he stayed on, kept moving and changing buses all the way to Thunder Bay. He figured he was far enough away that nobody would catch him. He was always careful of the police and tried to stay out of trouble, doing odd jobs here and there. He never did get over being jumpy every time he saw a cop heading toward him. All those years he had lived in tenuous hope that he was safe until he made that one mistake and was picked up for shoplifting. The poor man's guilt had gotten the best of him so he started imagining all kinds of things, even that they'd look into his past and find out somehow about his more-serious crimes. He had thought about all those crime shows he'd seen on TV. The ones where the culprits always got a break if they told the truth and named the real criminal. Well, he had done the crime, but it was all an accident. Mr. Duncan was the one responsible for it all. The old lady would still be alive if that old farmer hadn't given him two hundred bucks to scare that young Mrs. Grayson into getting her husband to sell the farm. So he told his story in the hope of a lighter sentence only to find out that television is not real life. He still ended up with life in prison. He had killed not once, but twice. Unforgivable.

It was many months later that investigation into Mr. Duncan's private affairs showed he had been playing the stock market and had suffered major losses. One loan led to another — at first from the bank, then from a loan company and then from people he didn't know too much about. He had been having difficulty meeting commitments and was desperate to sell the farm. By the time he eventually did, he had sold enough of his assets, borrowed on others, and owed too many people. He was months away from foreclosure. The money from the sale had barely covered his losses.

"So many lives ruined." Maisie was saddened by the loss suffered by so many people, all over one farmer's need for money and one old lady's bitterness for a hard life lived.

"When I think of what Shelley went through trying to keep me from having to sell the farm for her and Billy's safety, I ..."

"The fear she must have been living with. No wonder she was in such a state the last time she came to my office. I'm sure she was terrified you would find out the truth."

"Senseless waste. Her. Billy. Your mother."

"Yes, Mom was a not-so-innocent victim, too, I guess."

"You know, I had so much time for thinking in prison — and in going over everything that happened — I got to wondering why you never asked me where I was the night your mother died. What got me convicted was that I had no alibi. You knew I wasn't home, but you never asked me where I was."

"You said you drove your truck onto the prairie and spent hours contemplating the events of the last few years."

"And you believed me."

"Why would I not? I know you like to be by yourself when things are bothering you."

"Any other wife might have questioned it. Especially the angry mood I was in."

"I'm not any other wife. I'm your wife and I've never known you to lie to me."

"I lied about that."

She didn't reply. She waited.

"I was with Shelley."

She still didn't reply. She didn't move.

"I was so angry with your mother, I almost did go back to Weyburn to talk to her. I was livid that she judged me so badly. I hated that she judged you badly, too. Most of all, I hated that she'd made such a mess out of our lives. You know I don't like confrontation, but I was ready to confront *her* that evening. But when I got into my truck, it seemed to have a mind of its own. It took me in the opposite direction. Next thing I knew, I was crying on Shelley's grave. I cried like I've never cried before. I was mad because your mother had wrongly accused me of cheating on my wife, and yet here I was, thinking my wife must have been cheating on *me*. Who else but an angry boyfriend would bruise her like that? Why would she want to be with a man who would brutalize her like that? Even break her arm? The same way I knew that I couldn't cheat on her, I knew she couldn't cheat on me. I finally stopped crying and started talking. I talked to her about you and me. How it had been between us and how I had never stopped loving you. But I wanted her to know I had never cheated on her. That I cherished the child she had given me. That I was sorry she wasn't there to see the fine son our boy was growing into and that I was making sure he knew what a fine mama she had been and would have continued to be. I told her ... I told her I loved her. And that I still do. I fell asleep. It must have been a couple of hours later when I woke up. I kissed her name engraved on the stone.

"Then I came home and went into the barn and finished one of the birdhouses Billy and I had never completed. I couldn't come upstairs into the bed of the woman I love after just having slept with the other woman I love."

"I'm glad you told me."

"You're not upset?"

"About what? I know you have enough love in your heart for two women. And I believe we both are deserving of it. I hope one day you will tell your son that story. He needs to hear it."

The Graysons had only been in their new house a few weeks when they got word that Bill's grandfather, Will Thompson, was dead. Glen went to Estevan with his son for the funeral. Ethel Thompson shook his hand and accepted his condolences but remained cool. Even though he had been cleared of all the murder charges, there was still the question of his cheating on their daughter.

When the will was probated, Bill learned that he had received his mother's share of his grandfather's estate. It had been divided equally between him and his aunt and uncle with the stipulation that Ethel Thompson was to receive a generous living allowance for as long as she was alive. The amount Bill received was close to a half million dollars. Enough for him to invest in property of his own.

Ruby and Maisie kept in touch and met for lunch a couple times a year. It was at one of their lunches shortly after Mr. Thompson died that Ruby asked about the relationship between Glen and his former in-laws. Maisie explained that her mother's insistence that Glen and Maisie had been having an affair before his wife died, seemed to have been indelibly etched into the minds of Shelley's parents. They had really needed someone to blame for their daughter's death and in their eyes, Glen was the one who wanted her out of the way.

Ruby stared out the window for a few moments. "You know, Maisie, I never really put two and two together before, but now that I'm distanced from it, I can see how your mother might have come to believe that, too."

"Really? I think she was just being vindictive because Glen and I — to use her word — 'disobeyed' her."

"Do you remember my mentioning to you about Tess appearing to eavesdrop on conversations? I used to hate the way she always busied herself near your door when you had clients inside your office. I particularly remember it was around the time that Shelley Grayson came in with that broken arm and Tess had snuck out for a smoke. Mrs. Grayson was quite vocal about Tess not being at her desk. Of course, we didn't know at the time the stress the poor woman was under. I gave Tess a dressing down after that and she was quite angry with me and with Shelley Grayson. When Glen came in a few days later, Tess was hanging about listening to your conversation with him. She heard him ask you to go for dinner and told your mother about it. I know this for a fact because I heard her telling your mother about it in the waiting room after Shelley was killed. I'm sorry. It never occurred to me that this might be what your mother was talking about. As time went on, and Madeline became confused about things, she became more and more determined that you and Glen were having an affair. Maybe that's the proof she was talking about? The gossip that Tess had passed on to her?"

"Well, Ruby, I guess we'll never know for sure. But I have a strong feeling that you're right. I wonder if Tess listened in on telephone conversations, too. I should have listened to you when you warned me. Hindsight." Maisie shrugged and placed her hand over her friend's. "Thanks for telling me now. And for the record, Glen and I did not have an affair while Shelley was alive. Please believe me."

"Maisie, I believe you."

FORTY-SIX
1990

IT WAS MAISIE'S FIFTIETH BIRTHDAY. Glen had celebrated his sixtieth a few months earlier. It was also their eighteenth wedding anniversary.

Maisie was sitting on the back steps of the house, drinking coffee and watching the latest foal romp in the corral nearest them. The screen door slapped behind her.

"She's a real beauty."

"Why, thank you. That's nice to hear on my fiftieth birthday." She turned and smiled coyly.

"You are, too, sweetheart, but I was talking about the foal."

"I knew who you meant and yes, she is a beauty."

He sat one step lower, so they were eye to eye. He kissed her cheek. "It's gonna be a scorcher today." He gestured at the endless expanse of clear blue sky.

"Yes. I'm glad I decided to take the day off. I want to enjoy every minute of it. Bill said he and Michelle would come out this evening for a piece of birthday cake."

"Oh, are you going to heat up the kitchen on this hot day by baking?"

Maisie cuffed him on the shoulder. "No. You are going to the bakery in town and buying me a cake, all decorated with blue icing and two candles: a five and a zero."

"Why blue icing? I thought pink was for girls."

"My birthstone is sapphire."

"I never knew that. Blue it is then."

"I've been sitting here thinking about my fifty years and do you realize that I've known you for more years of my life than not?"

"Really?" He looked surprised. "Yes, I guess that's so."

"I'm almost as old as my mother was when my dad died. That seems so long ago." She leaned her forehead on his shoulder. "I can't imagine being a widow so young."

"I have no intention of making you a widow anytime soon. With Bill being on his own now, and you cutting back hours at the office, we're just starting to live."

She slid down to the step beside him. "I'd like us to do some travelling."

"Me, too. Maybe we could spend some time down south this fall. Before you get into your busy season."

"Why don't we go to Arizona? Or Texas?"

"You want to leave the prairies to go to the desert? I thought you liked spending time on the beach and enjoying the ocean views."

"Yeah, I do. I just thought it might be nice to do some golfing or something."

"Golfing. You don't golf."

"You could teach me."

The screen door squeaked open and slapped shut again.

"Nobody answered the doorbell so we let ourselves in."

Jeremy was standing on the landing behind them.

"What are you doing here?" Maisie was beaming as she climbed the steps to hug her brother. "And what do you mean 'we'?"

"I'm here, too, just grabbing a coffee," Jeanne called from the kitchen.

"This is wonderful. Hey, did you guys come for my birthday?"

"I wouldn't miss celebrating my baby sister's getting old for anything."

She looked at Glen. "Did you know they were coming? And you never said anything?"

"Honey, we came whether Glen invited us or not." Jeanne hugged Maisie. "Since Jeremy sold the clinic, he keeps wanting to hit the highway for any excuse. Your birthday was as good as any. Don't look so panic stricken. We've already decided to book into a hotel in the city."

"You won't do any such thing. You'll stay right here." She turned to Glen. "Whatever you were planning on cooking for me for supper double the order."

Everyone moved to the round table under the vine-covered gazebo on the patio. Before long, the men were in the kitchen preparing a large platter of pancakes while Jeanne and Maisie caught up on the latest activities of their sons.

Scotty had married recently and had become the father of twin daughters. He was into real estate in Swift Current and doing quite well. Bill was almost ready to write his exam to become a chartered accountant and had been seeing Michelle Lacoste since his last year in university. She had been a year behind him and had moved to Regina when she graduated. She was a year older than he, and had considered going into law school, but instead accepted an offer to work in a travel agency — not at all what her parents had expected from her. She had an outgoing personality and loved travelling to distant places so it was a career that suited her. Glen and Maisie had taken an instant liking to the girl and she was most definitely in love with Bill. And he with her.

"This is a real nice spread you have here, Glen." Jeanne, who loved animals but was partial to horses, watched the ones in the paddock. "You look like you've got a nice stock of racers."

Glen, at loose ends after giving up farming and spending all those years in prison, had developed an interest in sulky racing, and after a few years of attending and working at races, decided he would like to go into the breeding of horses used for the sport. He went into it with the intention of keeping his stable small, concentrating on quality rather than quantity.

"As I've said before, you can take the boy out of the country but you can't take the country out of the boy." Maisie smiled and laid her hand on Glen's arm. "I'm so happy he found a new love that keeps him happy but not overworked."

The screen door slapped again and a tall man with the same build as Glen stood on the veranda with his back to them looking at the door. Glen looked up and smiled.

"Neil."

Neil turned and laughed. "You and your screen doors."

Glen went to share a hug with his brother.

Maisie squinted her eyes. A pattern seemed to be forming here. It was too much of a coincidence that both hers and Glen's siblings, who lived hundreds of miles away, would just happen to show up on the same day. Especially when that day happened to be her fiftieth birthday plus their wedding anniversary.

"Neil Grayson." She walked toward her brother-in-law. "You're not going to try and tell me that you just happened to be in the neighbourhood."

"As a matter of fact..." He laughed as he gave her a big kiss on the mouth.

"Glen, what is going on here?"

"Going on? Nothing. Nothing's going on." He was grinning from ear to ear.

Neil slid his arm around Maisie's and slapped his brother on the back. "You bet there's nothing going on. It's just that when I found out my cheap brother wasn't taking you away anywhere special to celebrate your big Five-O, I figured the celebration would have to come to you. So I got in touch with your brother and told my brother to expect company and here we are."

It was later in the afternoon that Bill and Michelle arrived. "Happy birthday, Mom. Happy anniversary Mom and Dad."

FORTY-SEVEN

CLOSER TO SUPPER TIME, A commercial van pulled around back and parked near the lawn. Two men and a woman got out and opened the back doors of the vehicle. Glen went over to them and pointed toward the patio table.

"Sorry, folks. We're going to have to go inside for a while to allow these people to do their thing." He was walking back to everyone seated on the patio.

"What is 'their thing'?" Maisie asked.

"You'll see. Come on. Let's continue our conversation in the living room." He ushered everyone inside.

Maisie wondered what in the world Glen had up his sleeve. Inside the house, he poured drinks for all, and Bill went into the bedroom, coming back with photo albums. The reminiscing went on for a couple of hours before Maisie went into the kitchen to sneak a look out the window. The backyard was being transformed into a fairyland. Strings of small lights had been hung around the yard and the woman was attaching balloons to the clothesline. Wedding bells hung from the wood strips in the gazebo. Happy anniversary signs were mixed with happy birthday streamers. She crossed her arms and watched as one man puttered at a large barbecue and the other set out plates and food on a picnic table they must have brought with them.

She felt Glen's arm slide around her from behind. "Happy birthday, darlin'."

She turned and cried into his shoulder. "You big goof."

The others found their way into the room and Jeanne and Michelle decided to go out and offer their help to set up the patio table with the dishes and cutlery.

When they all stepped out a short time later, Maisie heard the country and western music coming from speakers on corners of the patio. "Good thing we don't live in the city with all this noise going on."

Everyone dug into the steaks and licked their fingers eating corn on the cob. When the birthday cake was brought out, Maisie burst into tears again. The cake was iced in blue with white candles in the centre: a five and a zero. She smacked Glen on the shoulder. "You just let me go on and on, didn't you? I feel like a fool."

Neil and Jeremy disappeared momentarily and returned bearing gifts. Bill whispered to Michelle and she opened her purse and produced a card with a small bow on it.

The candles were lit and everyone sang "Happy Birthday". Maisie blew the candles out and opened her gifts. Jeremy and Jeanne gave her a T-shirt with the words "Aged to Perfection" printed on the front. With it, was a pair of small hoop gold earrings. Neil gave her a bottle of Yves Saint Laurent perfume and a silk scarf. The envelope from Bill and Michelle contained a pair of open-ended tickets to Hawaii.

"What the —?" She looked at the young couple.

"Don't freak out, Mom. Michelle gets a discount. Besides, it's meant for yours and Dad's anniversary as well as your birthday."

Maisie handed them to Glen and gave each of the kids a kiss and a hug. "Thank you both so much. Your dad and I were just talking about where we might go for a vacation this fall."

Glen smiled at Maisie. "It's not the desert, but I understand there are some nice golf courses on the islands."

He then reached into his pocket and pulled out a small gift-wrapped box. She opened it to find a ring with a sapphire surrounded by tiny diamonds. He had not only gotten her the blue-iced cake, but a sapphire as well. "You really are a big goof."

"That's the second time you've called me that tonight and I distinctly remember the day we got married you said there would be no goofs or squares in your house."

"You proved me wrong. I love you, you big goof." She kissed him through her tears.

"Bill, did you bring that item I asked you to pick up for your father?"

"Yep. It's in my van. Uncle Neil, will you help me get it?"

The two of them went around the side of the house and returned rolling a large package covered with a big green garbage bag.

Neil placed it in front of Glen who immediately lifted the covering. His mouth fell open when he saw a leather golf bag on a beautiful chrome cart. There was an iron, a putter and a driver sitting inside.

"They're only token clubs because you have to choose the ones you're comfortable with. Happy anniversary, dear."

Someone popped the cork off a champagne bottle. Bill was grinning with the foaming bottle in his hand. "Not meaning to rain on your parade, Mom and Dad, but if you remember, it was eighteen years ago this September that we celebrated with ginger ale the evening you guys became engaged."

"Yes, that's right." Maisie smiled at the memory. "It was outside by a picnic table also, as I recall."

"Well, I'm a big boy now and can drink champagne. So ... Michelle and I decided it might be a good night to announce *our* engagement."

Before anyone responded, Michelle raised her hand to show the diamond ring on her finger. She was sitting on a patio chair beside

Bill's wheelchair and leaned closer to him so she could put her arm around his shoulder. He smiled and took her hand in his and kissed it. "I'll let Michelle give you our other news."

She looked around the group nervously then her eyes settled on Glen and Maisie. "We also want to let you know, Mr. & Mrs. Grayson, that in seven months, you are going to be grandparents. I hope that doesn't upset you. I don't want it to throw a damper on our engagement announcement." She looked afraid and one step away from crying.

Glen and Maisie looked at each other. Then Glen went over to the young couple to kiss his future daughter-in-law on the forehead before turning to his son and shaking his hand. "Son, you have just made all my dreams come true."

"In spite of my not becoming a farmer like you and your father and his father before him?" He looked at Glen with apprehension.

"Because you *didn't* become a farmer. You are your own man, son. You formed your own mould and I couldn't be more proud." He crouched and wrapped the couple in a group hug.

"Maisie, get over here. We're going to be grandparents!" They enjoyed a four-way hug this time.

Neil shouted, "Dammit, I'm going to be a great-uncle. Where's that champagne?"

The champagne was poured into all the glasses but one. When the newly engaged twosome were toasted, Michelle drank her glass of ginger ale with a huge smile on her face and a hand resting protectively on her tummy.

1995

MAISIE WATCHED HER HUSBAND PROD the young roan into a slow gait. Their four-year-old granddaughter sat astride the horse, grinning at all who watched. Michelle, who was six months pregnant with their second child, knew their daughter was safe with her grandfather in control. Glenna Michelle Grayson had no fear around the horses or even the few sheep that were kept in a separate field.

"She seems happiest when she's out here with her grandpa and the animals." Bill had brought his family out to show his parents his new motorized wheelchair.

Michelle was sitting next to Maisie. "I don't think you know how much I enjoy coming out here. The country air is so fresh."

They looked up when the little girl giggled loudly at something her grandfather had said. "Glenna really does have a good time out here. She's always begging us to bring her out. I think my parents get jealous when she tells them how much fun she has here."

"It's nice that she has the opportunity to enjoy the best of both worlds. She can come here to the country whenever she wants, and yet she has the opportunity to grow up in the city." Maisie smiled at her daughter-in-law.

Michelle smiled, too, watching the relationship between the old man and his granddaughter.

"That's true. Although, I know she much prefers it out here. And she lives for her grandpa. Don't you think it would be nice if when she grows up, she marries a farmer?"

Author's Note

I have attempted to keep the settings in southern Saskatchewan as close to actual as possible. However, in the need to have a town strategically placed between Regina and Weyburn, I created the fictitious town of Centreville. It is not elaborated upon in the story but the location was a necessary geographical addition. I apologize for creating a town that exists only in my imagination.

About the Author

A prairie-born girl, Phyllis Bohonis listened often to her parents' tales of farm life in the dirty thirties and hungry forties on the prairies of Saskatchewan. Her mother was happy to become a city dweller post WWII while her dad never lost his longing for the farm. They settled for a large garden in the city and road trips back to the prairies.

Born in Estevan, Saskatchewan, Phyllis was brought to Ontario as a toddler and grew up on the beautiful shores of Lake Superior. Now living in Ottawa, she has become well-known for weaving gripping tales of romance and mystery set in places she has either lived or visited. All of her novels are set in Canada and most feature fascinating characters who are fifty plus.

Never Marry a Farmer is Phyllis's seventh novel.

ACKNOWLEDGEMENTS

My eternal thanks to Sherrill Wark without whom my books would never be published.

To my nephew, photographer extraordinaire, Larry Kuzminski a.k.a. KuzPhotography, whose talent with a camera never ceases to amaze me. He did it again this time in picking up on the tension in the novel by capturing the broken fence for the cover.

To my parents Carl and Rosa Young for their never-ending stories of the west and instilling in me a pride of who I am.